Multi-Tier Application Programming with PHP

Practical Guide for Architects and Programmers

The Morgan Kaufmann Practical Guides Series
Series Editor: Michael J. Donahoo

For further information on these books and for a list of forthcoming titles, please visit our website at http://www.mkp.com/practical

Multi-Tier Application Programming with PHP

Practical Guide for Architects
and Programmers

David Wall

AMSTERDAM • BOSTON • HEIDELBERG • LONDON
NEW YORK • OXFORD • PARIS • SAN DIEGO
SAN FRANCISCO • SINGAPORE • SYDNEY • TOKYO
Morgan Kaufmann Publishers is an imprint of Elsevier

Senior Editor:	Rick Adams
Publishing Services Manager:	Andre Cuello
Associate Editor:	Karyn Johnson
Project Manager:	Kristin Macek
Design, illustration, and composition:	Cepha Imaging Private Limited
Cover Design:	Yvo Riezebos Design
Cover Image:	Cargo containers being stacked at terminal. © Sandra Baker/The Image Bank
Copyeditor:	Graphic World Publishing Services
Proofreader:	Graphic World Publishing Services
Printer:	The Maple-Vail Book Manufacturing Group

Morgan Kaufmann Publishers is an Imprint of Elsevier.
500 Sansome Street, Suite 400, San Francisco, CA 94111

This book is printed on acid-free paper.

Library of Congress Cataloging-in-Publication Data

Application Submitted

ISBN: 0-12-732350-3

For information on all Morgan Kaufmann publications,
visit our website at www.mkp.com

Printed in the United States of America
08 07 06 05 04   5 4 3 2 1

Pour ma chère Catou. Tu es ma lumière.

Contents

Preface

This book aspires to replace trust in commercial products with reliance on open-source software and your own ingenuity.

We've all been in a situation in which a customer wants to solve some complicated information-services problem without spending much money. Maybe the project is a one-off demonstration that's unlikely to lead to much of a sale. Maybe it's a proof-of-concept project that may never get real funding. Maybe, and this isn't uncommon at all, the customer is just cheap and wants a real, highly capable, production solution for the absolute least amount of money possible. The application typically is feature rich, with a substantial data model backing it up. It may be something like a travel reservation system, a catalog, a data warehouse full of scientific of business data, or, as is modeled in several chapters of this book, an accounting system.

These are the sorts of applications for which Microsoft touts the .NET Framework and Sun Microsystems sells Enterprise Java. Those are extraordinarily capable development environments. They are also more or less proprietary, and dependent on expensive software licenses.

The environment that seems to be emerging in many companies is one in which the first budget line item to fall is the one for software licenses. That means open-source software fits the budget, and often its capabilities stack up quite favorably against its commercially licensed competitors. But if the motto of the open-source community is "do it yourself," there's bound to be some professional services time required to make the software do what's needed.

Multi-Tier Application Programming with PHP: Practical Guide for Architects and Programmers is meant for people who find themselves—or would like to find themselves—in the position of having to provide those professional services.

Goals and Audience of this Book

The aim of this book is to show you how to solve complicated information-systems problems with little more than software you can download freely from the Web, namely PHP and an open-source database server, such as MySQL or PostgreSQL. To solve such complicated problems, you'll want to use multi-tier application architecture, specifically a strategy called the model-view-controller (MVC) pattern.

Goals

Before you start designing applications, you'll need to understand what multi-tier design is all about, and how to implement it with PHP and related technologies. You'll also need some design guidance as to when it's appropriate to try to structure your applications as multi-tier entities under PHP, when it's better to go for a full-blown solution under an application server (as with Enterprise Java), and when a more traditional PHP solution is best.

The essence of multi-tier (usually, it boils down to three-tier) application design is the separation of the logical functions of an application into several layers:

- The accessor layer (the model) manages interaction with a database management system (DBMS). Its job is to query the database as efficiently as possible, making optimum use of the available database connections and sharing database access across multiple lower-level activities where possible. It exposes methods that represent abstractions of what's in the database.

- The business-logic layer (the controller) decides what sort of data to extract from the database under various conditions. Further, it can process that data to yield meaningful information. For example, the business-logic layer might be set up to request revenue and expenditure data from the persistence layer, then process those pieces of information and expose a method that returns a profit figure.

- The presentation layer (the view) is concerned with providing an interface to the user. It presents a user interface (in hypertext markup language [HTML], typically) that the user can manipulate, and it formats the results of the business-logic layer's work in an attractive way.

The advantage of designing applications this way is ease of maintenance and modification, as well as better performance under load.

PHP has met tremendous success in the space between static Web pages (simple, not very flexible, and hard to maintain) and three- or four-tier enterprise applications under an application server like WebSphere or WebLogic (which are hard to learn, complicated, expensive, and not worth the trouble for any but the largest projects). For the bulk of network applications—which require database connectivity, interaction with a user via forms, an ability to output HTML, and some mechanism for maintaining state in the inherently stateless environment of hypertext transport protocol (HTTP)—PHP and MySQL do everything required. Solutions built around these technologies are fun to design, easy to create, low in cost, and equal or greater in performance to similar applications written with the Microsoft .NET Framework or Enterprise Java.

The subject of this book is taking PHP a step further by separating the presentation layer from the business-logic layer. The book aims to teach programmers how to do this, and why such a layered design is superior to more traditional approaches in many situations.

Readers should come away from *Multi-Tier Application Programming with PHP: Practical Guide for Architects and Programmers* different in several ways:

- They should be familiar with the principles of multi-tier software architecture.

- They should be more skilled with the PHP language, and particularly with those elements that are part of PEAR DB or new in PHP 5.

- They should tend to think about PHP in association with large software projects for which they might have discounted it before.

This book does not aspire to teach you PHP. Lots of excellent tutorial and reference books exist, and there's a great deal of PHP educational material online. This book shows how PHP can be used in a new way—as a tool for creating multi-tier frameworks into which useful applications can be built. You can enjoy the benefits of multi-tier software design under PHP with a much smaller investment in learning than would be required by other languages.

This book deals with programming—actual code samples and commentaries on them—primarily in the areas that are unique to multi-tier design. A chapter deals with object orientation in PHP as it applies to the architecture, whereas other chapters have to do with HTTP and simple object access protocol (SOAP), the two communication protocols most useful in tying together multiple layers. There's also coverage of database design and query construction, and some information about tricks you can use in generating user interfaces.

Audience

The intended audience of *Multi-Tier Application Programming with PHP: Practical Guide for Architects and Programmers* includes people with an interest in PHP beyond its applications as a quick and cheap way to solve server-side programming problems in the course of building Web sites. They're not so much interested in PHP as an alternative to ASP and Perl, but in PHP as a language that can deliver excellent results when placed in direct competition with Microsoft .NET and Enterprise Java.

The people who will appreciate this book most are those who have a working knowledge of HTML and JavaScript, and familiarity with at least one full-fledged programming language, such as C, Java, or Visual Basic. They probably also will know how to program in PHP, ASP, or Perl for the purpose of doing server-side scripting work, including how to connect to and use database servers (possibly under the relatively new PEAR DB system). For that reason, they'll know the essentials of structured query language (SQL) as well.

The people who read and learn from this book will be able do something (implement a multi-tier architecture) for nearly nothing (PHP is free, many of its associated database servers are free or nearly so, and PHP is a lot easier to learn than Microsoft .NET and Enterprise Java).

The Road Ahead

Here's a quick introduction to the structure of this book, chapter by chapter.

1. Introduction. This chapter explains the theory of multi-tier design and why you'd want to use one. It also gets into the question of when you'd want to consider PHP and an open-source database server for implementing a multi-tier design, and when a commercial solution might prove superior.

2. Principles of Object Orientation in PHP. This chapter shows you how PHP, particularly its newer versions, implement the principles of object orientation.

3. HTTP in PHP. Key to any online application is HTTP. PHP has a particular way of interacting with HTTP, and this chapter explains it to you.

4. SOAP under PHP. As you'll see in Chapter 4, SOAP is a very flexible way of communicating between tiers, even if there's a firewall or other security mechanism in the way (that's because SOAP rides on top of HTTP or simple mail transport protocol [SMTP], two protocols to which that firewalls usually allow free passage). Techniques for implementing SOAP with the NuSOAP libraries are explained in this chapter.

5. Designing and Implementing a Multi-Tier Application in PHP: A Succinct Example. This chapter deals with design principles, including the question of how to establish communications among layers if everything is separated by a network. You'll find a complete multi-tier application (a simple Great Circle navigation calculator) described here, enabling you to work through a full project with relative speed.

6. The Persistence Layer. In Chapter 6, we begin the elaborate example that concerns us throughout much of this book: Currawong Accounting. Named for an Australian bird, Currawong Accounting is a multicurrency bookkeeping application. In this chapter, we design a data model (a database schema) for Currawong and implement it in MySQL, using the dependency features of InnoDB tables.

7. The Accessor Layer. With our database in place, we set about writing the PHP programs that execute SQL queries. This chapter is very much concerned with the PEAR DB way of interfacing with a database, as well as with establishing SOAP servers with the help of the NuSOAP library.

8. Business Logic. The logic layer is where calculations take place, and in Currawong Accounting it's where we do our report creation. Further, the logic layer in Currawong is interesting because it receives HTTP POST input and makes request of the accessor layer as a SOAP client.

9. The Presentation Layer. Concerned with providing an interface (a human interface in the form of Web pages, in the Currawong case), the presentation layer involves HTML markup. It also involves HTML forms, some direct calls the accessor layer for the purpose of showing database table contents, and interactions with the logic layer.

10. The Elsewhere Layer. Because Currawong Accounting is meant to run on a Web server, it will have access to all sorts of resources on the public Internet. Among these: Web services that give information on currency exchange rates. The elsewhere layer of Currawong Accounting queries one of these services in order to discover the relative values of the currencies the application tracks.

Setting Up Your Development Environment

In learning any programming language or design strategy, it's vitally important that you actually do the work—go hands on with the code and try to solve some problems. The main point of doing this is not so much the solving of the problems as the making of mistakes, because it is through mistakes that we learn. Software work, in which little things like the sequence of arguments or the placement of a brace can have far-reaching effects, is particularly well suited to mistake making.

The key thing is to be able to figure out your mistakes quickly, learn from them, and move on to the next thing. Battering away at one problem, for hours because you're SURE you've done everything right and it JUST WON'T WORK, ranks among life's most frustrating experiences. It's particularly unamusing when the error turns out to be trivial.

Similarly not fun is troubleshooting your infrastructure. The programs in this book make use of the very reliable and field-proven PHP interpreter and the MySQL database engine, but those pieces of software, in and of themselves, are not why you should be reading this book. It's what you can do with them that we're interested in here. So get them installed right and don't worry about them.

The point: Get your working environment built right and get on with the learning. Then, you'll be ready to get on with the production coding, as well. Your development environment is your factory production floor. The rest of this section offers some tips on doing so.

On the Arrangement of Machines

The whole point of multi-tier software architecture is the possibility of separating software components so they run on different machines, thus improving reliability, scalability, and, under some conditions, performance (you'll read all about the advantages and disadvantages of multi-tier design in Chapter 1). In a development environment, however, it's not as critical that you distribute pieces of your applications across multiple machines. That's because the advantages of distributing the tiers become most evident when the application is experiencing heavy load—in other words, in production.

On the other hand, it's nice to be able to carry your entire development project around on a single notebook computer. One possible solution to the problem of network simulation involves virtual machines. VMWare (http://www.vmware.com) makes a number of products that allow you to run multiple virtual machines within your "real" operating system (VMWare Workstation is the simplest of the lot, and fits the purposes of this book). The software is pretty clever; it walls off a section of your machine's memory and hard disk and allows you to treat those protected resources as a separate machine. You have to install an operating system (which may or may not be the same as your "host" operating system) on the protected area and everything. VMWare manages the work of sharing the CPU among your host system and your virtual machines (you need a lot of RAM if you want to have more than one virtual machine running at once, though). The machines share the network card, too, so both can get separate DHCP addresses from the same router and communicate with each other over the local area network (LAN).

Server Software

Programs written in PHP will run on any machine for which there is a PHP interpreter. At the moment, compiled interpreters exist for about 10 operating systems, including IBM OS/2 and AmigaOS, and you can port the freely downloadable source code to a new one if you want. Regardless, the chief PHP environments are Microsoft Windows and the various kinds of Linux, and those are the ones we focus on here.

Linux

You'll want to configure a Linux system as a LAMP server (Linux, Apache, MySQL, PHP) for the purposes of this book. In other words, you'll want to install these pieces of software:

- Linux (http://www.linux.org). Choose your favorite distribution. Anything based on the 2.4.x kernel will certainly work, as will significantly older versions.

- Apache (http://www.apache.org). Install the Apache HTTP server on top of Linux. The easiest way to do this is by installing the package that fits your Linux distribution (an RPM file for Red Hat Linux, for example), but you can compile the source if you prefer.

- MySQL (http://www.mysql.com). Next comes the MySQL database server. Again, use your distribution's package-management solution if you can, or build it yourself.

- PHP (http://www.php.net). Install PHP last. You can compile the source, or install the package that fits your distribution.

Microsoft Windows

Under Microsoft Windows, you have a choice of two major Web servers:

- Microsoft Internet Information Services (IIS). Windows' native HTTP server, IIS can be installed from the Windows distribution CD-ROM.

- Apache (http://www.apache.org). Download and install the Microsoft Windows binary files.

Once you have an HTTP server in place, you can install the rest of the critical server software:

- MySQL (http://www.mysql.com). You'll want to download the Windows binary from the MySQL site. It installs automatically, with practically no decisions for you to make.

- PHP (http://www.php.net). As with Linux, install the PHP binary last. If you chose the IIS Web server, configuration is automatic. If you opted for Apache under Windows, you have to do some manual configuration that's documented in a file that comes with the PHP binary kit.

The Client Side

My client computer is a notebook running Microsoft Windows 2000 (it happens to the be the Server variety of Windows 2000, but that's not because of anything related to PHP). I sincerely would like to use Linux outside of the server environment (read about the new file system rumored to be part of Longhorn—that's project name for the next version of Microsoft Windows—and you'll see why), but I have not yet made the leap with my working notebook.

On the client side, you'll be doing two things most of the time: writing code and testing it.

Writing code in PHP, HTML, JavaScript, and SQL—the four languages you'll use in following this book—is best handled by your text editor of choice, which for me is a product called NoteTab Pro from a company called Fookes Software. Read all about it, and download a trial version, from http://www.notetab.com. I write all my code and prose—every last word of this book, as a matter of fact—in NoteTab Pro. It has a tabbed interface with which you can have many documents open at once, its search-and-replace function supports regular expressions, and its macro language is intelligent. Writing in plain text removes formatting surprises from my life, and formatting surprises are surprises I don't need. About the only thing I really wish NoteTab had is syntax highlighting for various programming languages, mainly PHP. Editor wars being what they are, though, I will leave my discussion of the subject at that.

To test your PHP programs, you'll need a Web browser. It's true that not all PHP programs are meant to be rendered in browser-interpretable markup languages, and in fact the accessor- and logic-layer programs described in this book do not generate HTML output. To test these, though, we'll use a special HTML document that makes the required calls and displays debugging output, all within a browser window (you'll see how to create that tester later). In writing this book, I did my development and testing with Microsoft Internet Explorer 6.0. You can get your own copy of that browser from http://www.microsoft.com/windows/ie. The HTML and JavaScript in these pages aren't too fancy, though, and should work well in any semimodern Web browser.

You'll want to do testing of your SQL statements independent of PHP and HTML. That means you'll need a client for whatever database server you choose to use. If you're going to use MySQL—and that's what appears in this book's examples—you'll very likely be happy with MySQL Control Center. It's available at http://www.mysql.com/products/mysqlcc. Its capabilities are covered more fully in Chapters 6 and 7.

Other software tools I keep in my PHP programming toolkit include:

- Effetech HTTP Sniffer (http://www.effetech.com). A monitoring program that keeps track of HTTP calls among network nodes. When all else fails, you can use this to make absolutely sure that your Web services are returning the results you are expecting them to return.

- Search and Replace Funduc Software (http://www.funduc.com/srshareware.htm). A simple, elegant program that will look through many files to find (and, if you like, replace) a specified string or regular expression. It's handy for work like changing a machine name or IP address globally.

- CASE Studio (http://www.casestudio.com). A database entity modeler (schema-generation tool), CASE studio will connect to a database server (any of several kinds, including all the popular open-source ones) and figure out the table relationships in a specified existing database.

I have not outfitted my development environment with any of the Zend Studio software (http://www.zend.com) yet, mainly because I haven't felt like giving up the money (the version of Zend Studio with the handiest features costs $195, U.S. dollars). I've worked a bit with their time-limited demo version, though, and I think it's great. The ability to step through programs as they execute is extraordinarily useful, and the environment's variable-monitoring capability eliminates the need to insert thousands of echo statements during debugging work. Code completion and the on-screen function reference speed development, too. I'll probably go to Zend Studio before long.

Shortcut: Setting Up the Example Applications

Setting up the example applications is easy. Essentially, once you have the proper server infrastructure set up, you can just copy the application directories into the server's Web root and begin using them right away. Here's a step-by-step procedure, assuming you have nothing but a Linux or Microsoft Windows server to begin. This section is designed to help you get the example applications up and running quickly; there is some overlap with the more deliberate steps described in the preceding section.

1. Install and test the Web server of your choice. Apache Web Server (http://www. apache.org) is the best option for Linux, whereas both Apache and Microsoft Internet Information Services are good alternatives for Windows. Use Apache 1.3.x or 2.0.x—either branch of the Apache product line is acceptable.

2. Install and test MySQL (http://www.mysql.com) for your machine. It's important that you use MySQL 4.0.1x, or a newer version, because it's only in these that the InnoDB table type (used to provide enforced relationships among tables) is available. If you want to use a database other than MySQL, you'll have to edit the code in the accessor layer—a small but important task—to modify the way in which the programs connect to the database.

3. Install and test PHP (http://www.php.net) for your machine, making sure that it interprets a simple "Hello, World" script as expected. Use PHP version 4.3.x or newer. PHP 5.x is acceptable.

4. Locate the Web root directory on your machine. On an Apache server, it's usually called htdocs; on an IIS machine, it's usually called wwwroot.

5. Into that folder, copy the entire contents (including subdirectories) of the acct and greatCircle directories that you downloaded from the book's support site.

6. Copy the contents of the Required Libraries folder—graph, nusoap-0.6, and PEARDB—into a directory that's specified in the include_path line of your server's php.ini file. Usually, one of these is /php/includes.

7. Before the applications will work properly, you'll have to run their database-preparation scripts.

   ■ For the Great Circle navigation program, run cities.sql and citiesPopulator.sql, in that order.

   ■ For Currawong Accounting, run /DBSetup/currawongTables.sql and /DBSetup/populator.sql, in that order.

You should then be able to run the Great Circle program by navigating to this URL: http://<servername>/greatCircle/calcGreatCircle.php. You should be able to run Currawong Accounting by opening this URL: http://<servername>/acct/app.html.

Other Resources

Most of the nonsoftware resources you'll use in your PHP development work have to do with information. PHP isn't quite as vast as, say, Java, but it's not trivial, and you will almost certainly want to refer to a reference often. References take the form of Web sites, books, discussion groups, and—heaven forfend!—human beings.

Books

Books most definitely have a place on the desks of the software architect and programmer. Very often, it's easier to go to a book for an answer than to a reference site, even for quick-reference questions. Books really come in handy when the question is more complicated than, "What are the keys in the associative array returned by the localtime() function?" Very often, authors have solved problems like yours and have published their strategies. The books that I referred to most often during this project were:

- *Programming PHP* by Rasmus Lerdorf and Kevin Tatroe (Sebastopol, CA, O'Reilly, 2002). The standard text for getting things done in PHP 4.1, it's the one I turn to when I've been working with some other language and need information about how the standard problems are solved in PHP.

- *MySQL Cookbook* by Paul DuBois (Sebastopol, CA, O'Reilly, 2003). More than a reference for MySQL, this book shows you how to solve problems—it's extraordinarily practical.

- *Web Database Applications with PHP & MySQL* by Hugh Williams and David Lane (Sebastopol, CA, O'Reilly, 2002). A fair collection of PHP solutions to elaborate problems.

- *JavaScript Bible* by Danny Goodman (IDG Books, Boston, 1998). A combination tutorial/reference to JavaScript (and the tricky parts of HTML, as well), this book has the right combination of solutions to problems and straight object-reference material. Full disclosure: I did some of the technical editing work on this book.

- *Linux: Rute User's Tutorial and Exposition* by Paul Sheer (Prentice Hall PTR, 2002). An excellent guide to the Linux operating system, well suited to someone who wants to configure a server to run reliably in the background.

- *Database Design for Mere Mortals* by Michael Hernandez (Addison-Wesley, 2003). Database design is a really specialized field, but Hernandez does a good job of teaching it. Because getting your database design right is the greater part of getting your multi-tier application right, it pays to learn design well.

Web Sites

The Internet makes heaps of information available easily and quickly, and usually free of charge in the case of PHP and its related technologies. Here are some of the sites you'll find handy as you do development work:

- PHP.net (http://www.php.net). The authoritative PHP site contains the official documentation, and lots of user comments that will usually help you solve your own problems.

- MySQL.com (http://www.mysql.com). The official MySQL site includes complete documentation of the MySQL variant of the SQL language, as well as links to many MySQL utilities.

- Sourceforge (http://www.sourceforge.net). Have a look here for software projects in progress, PHP-related or otherwise. Because source code is always available (and licensing usually liberal), you can often adapt resources here to fit your needs.

- PHPBuilder (http://www.phpbuilder.net). Another code library site, this one PHP specific, PHPBuilder often will show you how someone else has already solved your problem, or one similar.

- Safari (http://safari.oreilly.com). This commercial site (which offers a free two-week demo) enables you to access the full text of hundreds of technical books from several big publishers. It's a great place to look for recipes, code snippets, and quick answers, but it is designed to make reading or printing long passages inconvenient (that's how they sell paper books).

Discussion Groups

Discussion groups, facilitated by the Internet, are a great way to get answers to development-related questions. It can take some time to phrase your question in a useful way, and you'll run into smartypants replies more often that would be ideal, but generally these groups are great resources:

- comp.lang.php

- php.general

- php.db

- Various mailing lists (http://www.php.net/mailing-lists.php)

Human Beings

There's a significant PHP community developing, and lots of people—training companies, consultancies, product vendors, and others—have an interest in encouraging its growth. As a result, you'll find it fairly easy to find a PHP event to attend. The PHP home page (http://www.php.net) includes a calendar of events, which in turn links to the pages of local PHP users groups that host activities. Most major cities have at least one PHP get-together at a local bar or restaurant every month.

Good luck implementing multi-tier architectures under PHP. Please share your experiences with me, as well as your comments on this book and your ideas for future editions. Visit my Web site at http://www.davidwall.com, and reach me by electronic mail at david@davidwall.com.

Acknowledgments

A book, particularly a technical one, is a collaborative effort. Not only does an author have to consult with other people in his effort to fill the gaps in his knowledge, he must build atop the tangible prior efforts of others. This is particularly true when the author is working with open-source software, which derives from a community. I have benefited from the assistance, direct and indirect, of dozens of people in the course of writing this book.

Thanks to Karyn Johnson and the rest of the editorial team at Morgan Kaufmann. I would also like to thank the project manager, Kristin Macek, the design manager, Cate Barr, and the production editor, Dan Fitzgerald. They all work hard to deliver quality books.

Thanks to James Connor, Matt Wade, Guillermo Francia, and Peter Gale, who reviewed the code and text and contributed a great deal to them. Their comments were invaluable.

Thanks to Herman Veluwenkamp, whose spectacular Graph class features prominently in Chapter 8.

Kudos to the PHP community, which delivers better software and far better support than most commercial enterprises.

Thanks to Bruce and Connie Wilkinson, Adam and Nikki Bergman, Philippe and Lydie Vacher, Greg and Wen Smith, Bryan and Suzanne Pfaffenberger, Derek and Gwen Tom, Jacqueline Vacher, Gary Chin, Geoff May, Diana Yap, Ken Lau, Nicole Pritchard, Daniel Sjuc, Jo Wong, Paul Comrie-Thomson, Alessandro Lima, and Jairson Vitorino. They are friends and colleagues I am lucky to know.

Thanks to my family as always.

David Wall
Paris
January 2004

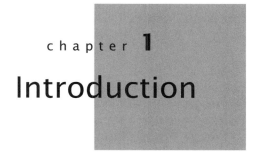

chapter **1**

Introduction

Multi-tier software enables you to spread computing resources, which is to say, software components, across a network. By designing your software applications in such a way that their constituent parts exist on multiple machines, you can achieve greater reliability, better performance, easier management, and cost savings. In other words, multi-tier architecture gives you a head start in achieving what are usually the most important goals of software design.

This chapter explains the theory of multi-tier design and lays down a bit of background, conceptually and lexicographically. It also gets into the question of when you'd want to consider PHP and an open-source database server for implementing a multi-tier design, and when a commercial solution might prove superior.

1.1 Defining Multi-Tier Software Design

The basic idea of a multi-tier design is that all of the logical functions of the application are (or at least have the potential to be) separated on multiple computers interconnected by a network. Each logical function, usually referred to as a layer or tier, receives input from and provides output to other layers. The functional layers are:

- Persistence. The database or other storage mechanism that keeps data in an organized way.

- Accessor. The programs that pass queries to the persistence layer (in other words, the programs in which structured query language (SQL) statements are hard-coded). These programs expose "get" and "set" functions.

- Logic. The programs that process user input and stored data and come up with a useful result.

- Presentation. The programs that format the results of the logic layer as hypertext markup language (HTML), extensible markup language (XML), or whatever else the user requires.

- Requester/consumer. The Web browser, XML parser, or other client that makes requests of the application and receives its output.

- Elsewhere. The external Web services, HTML pages, and other resources to which applications make reference. The elsewhere layer may provide information of public interest, such as information on currency exchange rates or the weather. In other cases, the elsewhere layer may have to do with providing information that is external but still private, such as price lists from a vendor. The part of the elsewhere layer that actually provides the data is generally not under the direct control of the architect or programmer, but the software concerned with accessing it is.

This inventory of the tiers that make up a multi-tier application should be broadly familiar to anyone who has studied application architecture. This description, though, differs from standard in three respects:

1. It explicitly states that the persistence layer (the database and its database management system) and the accessor layer, which feeds SQL queries to the persistence layer, are separate.

2. It explicitly lists the requester/consumer layer as part of the application, even though the software running there is usually not under the control of the developer building the rest of the application (in the case of a browser, it's from the Mozilla team or Microsoft or whomever).

3. It acknowledges that remote resources (the elsewhere layer) can be an integral part of a multi-tier application.

Overall, the design looks like what is shown in Figure 1.1.

1.2   Advantages of a Multi-Tier System

Multi-tier software applications earn their keep because they offer certain advantages over monolithic or simple client-server applications. Organizations thinking about implementing such a system should make sure that their requirements match with the strong points of multi-tier design, and that the weaknesses of the approach (discussed in the next section) do not overshadow the strengths.

Simply put, multi-tier systems, in comparison with monolithic or client-server systems, offer greater return on investment over time because of their greater adaptability and ease of maintenance (at least from a programmer's perspective). Depending on specific

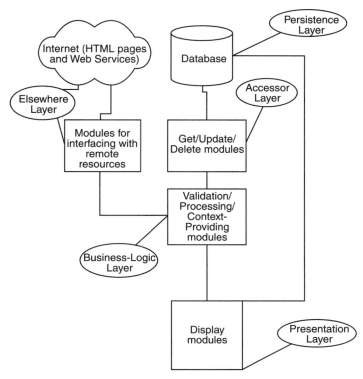

Figure 1.1: Multi-tier software design under PHP makes it possible to spread computing resources across a network

conditions, multi-tier applications may or may not offer advantages in terms of absolute performance as well.

This section provides a run down of the chief selling points, from a commercial point of view, of multi-tier software systems. It shows you why multi-tier software architecture under PHP will help your organization become more efficient and profitable.

1.2.1   Software Modularity

The functional elements of a multi-tier software application are broken up into auto-nomous units. Those units may be classes or procedural programs; it does not matter. The important thing is that a given element expects a certain input, provides a certain output, and does so via known protocols (like straight hypertext transport protocol [HTTP], or sim-ple object access protocol [SOAP] over HTTP, or SOAP over simple mail transport protocol [SMTP]). As long as these characteristics are documented, it's possible for sets of modules to interact in different ways, so as to adapt better to various business requirements.

Modularity and abstraction breed adaptability, and they also allow additional flexibility. Though all software modules in this book's illustrative software systems are implemented in PHP (mostly as procedural programs), it would be easy to migrate them to an object-oriented implementation gradually, testing throughout. It would also be possible to fit classes or programs written in languages other than PHP into the software designs described in this book. If we were software design consultants, and we had a customer with a set of SOAP-aware accessor-layer classes implemented in Java, would we implement redundant software in PHP in order to provide a new service to a user? We would not. A new PHP-based layer of software on the business logic layer would speak to the Java classes.

1.2.2   Reliability

With modularity also comes reliability. It's a basic tenet of software engineering that incremental development is generally good. You get the basic framework going, then add and test one feature at a time. You test recursively to verify that newly added features haven't broken old ones. A multi-tier software system in which separate programs on each layer handle specific tasks is inherently compliant with this principle. When you add a class, you can (and should) test it, to make sure that it doesn't break what was working before.

1.2.3   Division of Responsibility and Ease of Management

When software is broken into functionally distinct layers, it's easier to divide human responsibility for the layers among multiple teams. You might choose to make one group of programmers responsible for designing and maintaining the accessor layer, for example, telling them only what functions would need to be exposed and what values should be returned. Let them figure out the most efficient way to meet those requirements without worrying about other aspects of the system. The scaling limitations that usually impinge upon a project of intellectual creation (which is what a software project is—these limitations of scaling are described by Frederick P. Brooks in *The Mythical Man-Month* [Addison-Wesley, Boston, 1995]) don't apply as strongly because the lines of delineation between layers are so distinct.

1.2.4   Ease of Documentation

To an extent, multi-tier software applications are self-documenting, in that it should be clear that a program on the presentation layer (which will certainly be denoted by a unique directory, if not a unique server or two) has to do with delivering information in a form that's meaningful to some client (whether that client is a person using a Web browser or a remote software application consuming XML, or something else). Programmers can easily give their programs descriptive filenames and comments. Required support files, Web services description language (WSDL) files, for example, provide further documentation. There's quite a lot of information available in a multi-tier software system even before the first line of human-language documentation is written.

1.2.5 Security

Multi-tier software, by its very design, incorporates what could be called encapsulation or compartmentalization. This advantage is particularly evident with respect to the schema of the database on the back end. Because no classes or programs other than those on the accessor layer contain any SQL, only people with access to the accessor layer code will have an idea of what the table structure looks like. Because the general public should have access only to the presentation layer, even the most grievous error should not result in error messages that reveal table names or other sensitive information. A multi-tier design is like putting layers of insulation between potentially sensitive code and the people most likely to want to do bad things with such code.

Even internally, division of responsibility, covered earlier in this section, leads to increased security. Fewer developers need access to the details of the database in order to design, build, and test accessor-layer programs.

1.2.6 Performance and Scalability

A multi-tier design enables you to distribute some or all of an application's functional layers onto their own machines. By dedicating a particular class (on a particular server) to handling database queries of a specific kind, you can use it to service all sorts of business operations. In Currawong Accounting, the large example application covered in Chapters 6 through 10 of this book, a single program determines the balance of a given account on a given date. It's used by everything from the program that depicts the check register on the presentation layer to a program that generates a graph of the balance over time.

Performance can vary under different circumstances, and any design work you do will have to be tailored to allow for the quantity and nature (database accesses, graphics requests, graphics generation activities, etc.) of accesses to the application you're setting up. There's usually a requirement for a bit of testing and optimization as well. The basic advantages of scalability remain, though: Multiple machines do the same work faster than a single machine, and with greater reliability.

Multi-tier software applications tend to be particularly good at scaling, which is to say they are adept at handling increasing amounts of activity. As you do the exercises described in this book, such as Currawong Accounting and the great-circle navigation example, you'll probably put everything on a single server. That makes sense when it's just you playing around with the system. If you were to take it live, though, and expect it to handle many transactions each hour, it would make sense to distribute at least some of the layers onto their own machines. That way, to cite one possible configuration, you could have a processor (and hard disk and other resources) dedicated to database queries, and another dedicated to HTTP service and business logic. Splitting the layers up is no big deal, because they're designed to communicate with each other (via HTTP, SOAP, and the various database-connectivity protocols) across a network.

1.3   Disadvantages of a Multi-Tier System

Multi-tier software architecture has some weak points and is not appropriate for every situation. A system of many machines connected by a network is, inherently, more complicated than a single machine. Parts of a complex application depend on the proper behavior and prompt response of other parts.

That said, it's up to you to determine whether a multi-tier design in PHP suits a particular application, based on the details of the problem to be solved and the environment in which the solution is to be implemented. This section details some of the problems to consider.

1.3.1   Execution Speed

The code in a PHP class or procedural program that exists as part of a multi-tier application executes at the same speed as any other PHP code on the same machine. Reductions in execution speed begin to appear for the program as a whole, though. This is due to a number of factors, many of them related.

- Process spawning. Every time one class or program makes reference to another, an additional process starts up. This involves overhead, both in terms of the start-up time and because of the overall greater load on the processor (assuming the second process is local to the first).

- Communications overhead. Aside from network delays (covered next), programs that communicate with one another have to spend time preparing information for transmission and then sending it. At the other end, the data must be received and unpacked. This all takes time.

- Poor process management. One of the chief selling points of heavy-duty object servers like BEA WebLogic and IBM WebSphere is that they manage the lifecycles of processes with an eye on the big picture. If an instance of a class that performs a particular kind of database query comes into existence as a result of a particular business activity, the server will keep that process (an object, usually) alive as long as there's a reasonable likelihood another business activity will need it soon. This doesn't happen in PHP, and it leads to some inefficiencies.

1.3.2   Network Latency

When you start to separate layers onto multiple machines, the speed with which interserver communication takes place becomes an issue. That's because, in order for an HTTP request or SOAP message to go from one machine to another, it must pass all the way down the network protocol stack, transit the network, and climb back up the network protocol stack at the other end. Most likely, a return message will have to do the same thing. This adds significantly to the overall execution time of the application taken as a whole.

That said, network delays can be reduced to acceptable levels. If all machines in the system are on a common local area network (LAN), you can expect acceptably low latency from an ordinary 100-BaseT Ethernet. Because there are only a few machines involved in most cases, it's easy to outfit them all with interfaces (cards) for a private data network, as well, guaranteeing that their traffic need not compete with less time-sensitive traffic on the carrier medium. Even if multiple local networks and some routers are involved, straightforward strategies can be used to implement class-of-service (CoS) rules that help guarantee priority to critical application packets.

1.3.3 Security

As pointed out earlier, there are security advantages and disadvantages inherent in a multi-tier architecture. Chief among the disadvantages is that in a multiple-machine solution, several computers (rather than just one) are necessarily connected to a network and are therefore open to attack via that network. It's been said that the most secure computer is one that's not connected to anything, but it's also true that such computers aren't remarkably useful. You can minimize the risk of interconnecting the machines that make up a multi-tier application by doing so on a private Class C (192.168.x.x) network that isn't connected to the world outside the machine room at all.

Nonetheless, data network security is a universal problem about which there exists an enormous amount of expertise. People know how to secure computers against attack across a data network. That, combined with the fact that only the presentation layer needs to be outside the inner organizational firewall, helps reduce the risk of attack.

It is also true that the communications links among layers are extraordinarily slender. All connections between layers (except for the link between the accessor layer and the database management system) take place over HTTP, a simple protocol that requires only one Transmission Control Protocol (TCP) port (perhaps two, if some communications will be over an encrypted version of the protocol). The link between the accessor layer and the database management system, which should be well behind the firewall anyway, takes place via SQL, through a TCP port determined by the database server manufacturer (and usually changeable, if you like).

That, further combined with the fact that everything described in this book will run on a stripped-down Linux server with very few services running, minimizes the security risks associated with multi-tier software architecture.

1.4 Questions and Exercises

1. What metrics would you use, in other words, what would you measure, to determine when a multi-tier software system that was hosted on a single machine should be spread out across several computers?

2. How might you design the data network that would host a multi-tier application? Consider network latency, security, and ease-of-access requirements.

3. If demands on its database were such that an organization wanted to spread the database management services across multiple machines, what are different ways of doing that? Which would best suit open-source database management systems, such as PostgresSQL and MySQL? Which would work better for commercial products, such as Oracle and Microsoft SQL Server?

4. Say you wanted to use a faster language, like C or Java, on the business logic layer and PHP everywhere else. What advantages and disadvantages would this introduce into your application and its management?

chapter 2

Principles of Object Orientation in PHP

This book concerns itself with architecture, which means it's about attractive and efficient design on the macro scale. It's also, to a certain extent, about clever design on lower levels. That means you need to be aware of all design possibilities available to you in PHP, which means (particularly since the release of PHP 5) that you need to understand the language's way of handling object-oriented design and programming. Object-oriented code can be more attractive and more flexible than procedural code, and sometimes it's worth using PHP's object-orientation features even if they are not as extensive as those of Java, C++, and other languages that were designed to be object oriented from the beginning.

Though PHP is most widely reputed as a scripting language, it has considerable object-orientation capabilities. It's a good idea to use object-oriented design and implementation wherever possible. Such design makes your code more self-documenting and easier to trace. This chapter provides a quick summary of the principles and rules of syntax that govern object orientation under PHP.

PHP's object-oriented characteristics underwent a great transformation between version 4.3 and version 5. As of PHP 5, the language has practically all features of "real" object-oriented languages, and developers have, practically speaking, a choice of writing procedural programs, object-oriented classes, or a combination of the two. The applications in this book are primarily procedural, but they make some use of object orientation (for example, in Chapter 8, in making reference to the Graph class) and it makes sense to have some background in the subject. This chapter aims to provide the required knowledge.

This chapter provides you with a look at how object orientation works in PHP, shows you the syntax for defining and instantiating classes and for referring to variables and functions within them, explains how to save yourself some work through the judicious use of inheritance, and shows how an instance of a class can modify its own values.

2.1 Creating Classes

A class, conceptually, is a container that holds variables and functions. Multiple independent instances of a given class can exist in memory at one point in time. This is, in fact, the point of having classes, as it's often advantageous to have a group of objects (as the instances are called) that have similar characteristics but are in fact different.

To cite an example from outside of software, my bicycle and your bicycle are both bicycles. They both have two wheels, no motor, and pedals that drive the rear wheel by means of a chain. My bike, though, is red and has a design meant for efficient long-distance travel on paved surfaces. Your bike is blue and is meant to withstand off-road use. They're distinct instances of the same kind of thing. Despite all their differences, both vehicles can be characterized (or, if one needs the metaphor spelled out, can be classed) as bicycles.

Before we can have individual instances, we must define generic groups, or classes.

2.1.1 Declaring a Class

To declare a class named Foo, use the keyword class, like this:

```
class Foo {

// Class contents go here.

}
```

It is customary, for clarity, to begin class names with capital letters; hence class Foo.

That definition is altogether excellent, but when the PHP interpreter tries to create an instance of a class (more about how to make it do that appears later in this chapter) it looks for a special function within the class called a constructor.

2.1.2 Adding a Constructor

As of PHP 5, all constructor functions are called __construct(). Prior to PHP 5, a class's constructor had the same name as the class in which it was defined. The PHP interpreter runs the constructor function any time a new instance of the class is created. Our Foo class needs a constructor:

```
class Foo {

function __construct() {
   // Statements here run every time an instance of the class is created.
   }

}
```

Most of the time, we'll want to do something in the constructor function. We might, for example, initialize variables or instantiate other classes that support the local one.

As is possible with any function, constructors can take arguments. Just specify them as parameters in the function (constructor) definition as usual. We can easily modify our class to take a value as an argument for its constructor:

```
class Foo {

function __construct($incomingValue) {
   // Statements here run every time an instance of the class is created.
   }

}
```

Many languages allow you to have multiple constructors in a class, each with a different number or type of parameters. That's not possible in PHP. You can have only one function of a given name, even if that name is also the name of a class.

2.1.3 Adding Methods and Properties (a.k.a. Functions and Variables)

The functions that exist within a class are called either functions (as in the rest of PHP) or methods (in line with object-oriented programming convention). Variables defined within a class can be called variables, instance variables, or properties. Be prepared to see any of these in documentation. Adding variables and functions to a class is easy; the procedure is exactly the same as in non–object-oriented PHP.

```
class Foo {

$name = "";
$colorOfSky = "blue";

function __construct($incomingValue) {
   $name = $incomingValue;
   }

function bar() {
   echo "The color of the sky is $colorOfSky.";
   }

}
```

The class now has two member variables, $name and $colorOfSky, and one member function other than its constructor, bar().

If you want, you can limit the scope in which a method or property can be accessed. This is the function of the keywords private and protected, which are discussed with examples later in this chapter.

2.2   Using a Class

Having defined a class, we may create instances of that class in our code. Once we have done that, we can use the functions and variables that exist in those instances.

2.2.1   Instantiating a Class

The process of creating an individual instance of a class is called instantiation. To create an instance of a class, we use the new keyword and assign the results to a variable, like this:

```
$fooInstance1 = new Foo("Gary");
```

As a result of the execution of that line of code, we have an instance of class Foo accessible through variable $fooInstance1.

2.2.2   Accessing Variables in a Class Instance

The syntax PHP uses for accessing the variables and functions that are members of a class instance are somewhat unusual. PHP does not use the traditional dot-hierarchy notation that C++, Java, and other languages use.

Suppose you wanted to assign a value to the $colorOfSky variable that's a member of $fooInstance1. You'd mention the variable that contains the instance of the object you want to work with, then the variable within that instance you want to set, and then the new value for the variable. The syntax looks like this:

```
$fooInstance1->colorOfSky = "green";
```

Notice that even though the variable in class Foo is called $colorOfSky, the name of the variable is not preceded by a dollar sign character ($) in this context.

2.2.3   Accessing Methods in a Class Instance

The syntax with which you invoke the functions that make up a class is similar to that with which you manipulate variables. The arrow notation appears again.

To call function bar() within the instance of class Foo that is contained in $fooInstance1, you'd use this line:

```
$fooInstance1->bar();
```

2.3 More Advanced Aspects of PHP Object Orientation

A programmer can accomplish a great deal with the aspects of object orientation covered in this chapter up to this point. There are a couple of features of object orientation in PHP, though, that can save you some trouble if you know how to use them. These are inheritance, when a class takes on the characteristics of another class, and the use of the this keyword, with which a class can modify its own characteristics.

2.3.1 Getting a Class to Refer to Itself

Many times, the functions of a class will need to modify variables that exist within the same class. PHP provides programmers with a special variable, $this, to mean the current class, or the class in which execution is presently taking place.

One popular application of $this is in getter and setter functions. Consider the following class:

```
class Demo {

$A = "";

function getA() {
   return $this->A;
   }

function setA($newValue) {
   $this->processValue($newValue);
   $this->A = $newValue;
   }
function processValue($value) {
   // Do something with $value and return
   }

function __construct() {
   // Function code here.
   }

}
```

In that class, the variable $A is read and written by a couple of lines of code that make reference to $this. Again, it just means "in the current class." Take special note of the fact that when you refer to $A as a subsidiary of $this (as $this->A), you don't use the dollar sign.

2.3.2   Inheritance

Suppose you have a very simple class, with two functions and two variables. Its code looks like this:

```php
class alpha {

$a1 = "";
$a2 = "";

function alphaOne() {
   // Function code here.
   }

function alphaTwo() {
   // Function code here.
   }

function __construct() {
   // Function code here.
   }


}
```

Then, you realize that the program you're writing would benefit by having a second class that does everything class alpha does, plus a couple of other things. Rather than create a near-copy of class alpha, you can create a second class that inherits its characteristics, like this:

```php
class Bravo extends Alpha {

$b1 = "";

function bravoOne() {
   // Function code here.
   }

function __construct() {
   // Function code here.
   }


}
```

With both of those classes declared, you can then instantiate an instance of class bravo

```php
$bravoInstance = new Bravo();
```

and expect the following to work without fault:

```
$bravoInstance->b1 = 42;
$bravoInstance->a1 = 88;
$resultOne    = $bravoInstance->bravoOne();
$resultTwo    = $bravoInstance->alphaOne();
$resultThree = $bravoInstance->alphaTwo();
```

All instances of class bravo have the functions and variables of class alpha, because class bravo extends class alpha, and therefore inherits its members.

2.3.3   Public, Private, and Protected Members

In PHP 5, some new options are available with respect to inheritance and the degree to which a class's members are available to objects that extend it. By endowing the PHP language with public, private, and protected keywords, PHP's object-orientation model is brought more into line with fully object-oriented languages like Smalltalk and Java.

Consider the ways in which a member of a class can be accessed:

- From within the class itself,
- From within a class that extends the class itself, and
- Externally, from any code that can operate on an instance of the class.

These conditions correspond to private, protected, and public access, respectively. Consider these example classes:

```
class Alpha {

$a1 = "a1";
protected $a2 = "a2";
private $a3 = "a3";

function alphaOne() {

    $this->a1 = "a1a"; // Legal.
    $this->a2 = "a2a"; // Legal; a2 is protected, but in the same class.
    $this->a3 = "a3a"; // Legal; a3 is private, but in the same class.

    $this->alphaTwo(); // Legal; alphaTwo is protected, but in the same class.
    $this->alphaThree(); // Legal; alphaThree is private, but in the same class.

    }

protected function alphaTwo() {
    // Function code here.
```

```
      }

   private function alphaThree() {
      // Function code here.
      }

   function __construct() {
      // Function code here.
      }

   }
```

Then, consider this class that extends Alpha:

```
   class Bravo extends Alpha {

   $b1 = "b1";

   function bravoOne() {

      $this->b1 = "b1b"; // Legal; $b1 is local to class Bravo.

      $this->alphaOne(); // Legal; alphaOne() is in the parent class, but it is
                            public.

      $this->alphaTwo(); // Legal; alphaTwo() is in the parent class, but it is
                            protected and so accessible here.

      $this->alphaThree(); // ILLEGAL; alphaThree() is in the parent class, but
                              it is private and so not usable here.

      }

   function __construct() {
      // Function code here.
      }

   }
```

Furthermore, consider the availability of members of Alpha and Bravo in code that instantiates them. This is just an excerpt, not a working program:

```
   $localA = new Alpha();
```

```
$localB = new Bravo();

$localB->bravoOne() // Legal; bravoOne() is public.
$localA->alphaOne() // Legal; alphaOne() is public.

$localA->alphaTwo() // ILLEGAL; alphaTwo is protected.
$localB->alphaTwo() // ILLEGAL; alphaTwo is protected; it is accessible only
                           within class Bravo.
$localA->alphaThree() // ILLEGAL; alphaTwo is private.
```

The points to remember are these:

■ Members of a class that are public (either explicitly declared public, or just not specified private or protected) are accessible locally, in instances of child classes, and externally.

■ Members of a class that are protected are accessible locally and within instances that extend the class in which they are contained.

■ Members of a class that are private are accessible only within the class in which they are contained.

2.3.4 Overriding Class Methods

One advantage of inheritance is that it allows you to selectively override member definitions in child classes. For example, if class Alpha defines method alphaOne() and class Bravo extends class Alpha, class Bravo can "overwrite" the inherited version of alphaOne() with its own definition (while, most likely, leaving other inherited members unmodified). This could be handy in a multi-tier design if, for example, you wanted two classes that were functionally identical except for the structured query language (SQL) statement they passed to the database server.

The following excerpts show how it can work. Here is the definition of class Alpha:

```
class Alpha {

function alphaOne() {

    echo "Function alphaOne in class Alpha";

    }


function alphaTwo() {

    echo "Function alphaTwo in class Alpha";
```

```
    }

function __construct() {
    // Function code here.
    }

}
```

Then, consider this class that expands upon Alpha:

```
class Bravo extends Alpha {

function alphaOne() {

    echo "Function alphaOne in class Bravo";

    }

function bravoOne() {

    echo "Function bravoOne in class Bravo";

    }

function __construct() {
    // Function code here.
    }

}
```

With those two classes in place, it is possible to instantiate class Bravo

```
$localBravo = new Bravo();
```

and then invoke some methods:

```
$localBravo->bravoOne(); // Yields "Function bravoOne in class Bravo"
$localBravo->alphaOne(); // Yields "Function alphaOne in class Bravo"
```

In other words, the definition of alphaOne() in the child (inheriting) class (Bravo in this case) overrides the definition of alphaOne() in the parent (inherited) class (Alpha).

You can prevent this kind of method overriding from happening (as of PHP 5) by declaring your methods with the keyword final. By defining a method as final, you allow it to be inherited, but not overridden. Here's an example:

```
class Alpha {

final function alphaOne() {
```

```
    echo "Function alphaOne in class Alpha";

    }

function __construct() {
    // Function code here.
    }

}

class Bravo extends Alpha {

function alphaOne() { // ILLEGAL; alphaOne is final in class Alpha.

    echo "Function alphaOne in class Bravo";

    }

function bravoOne() {

    echo "Function bravoOne in class Bravo";

    }

function __construct() {
    // Function code here.
    }

}
```

2.4 **Questions and Exercises**

1. Under what conditions might object-oriented programming technique be well rewarded? Under what conditions might it be more trouble than it's worth?
2. What might be some problems with intermingling object-oriented and procedural techniques within a single PHP program?
3. A key principle of multi-tier software design is the isolation of functional units on autonomous layers. How is that different from object orientation?
4. Why would you choose to encapsulate members within classes? In other words, why would you make use of private and protected members? Isn't it better to have access to all members from all instances?

chapter **3**

HTTP in PHP

The hypertext transport protocol (HTTP) defines a simple series of procedures by which a client computer may make a request of a server computer, and the server computer may reply. The protocol is central to the everyday operation of the World Wide Web, in which it is used to request and provide files to browsers in response to URL entries and clicks on hyperlinks.

Bear in mind that in some cases, notably those involved in a multi-tier software application, the concepts of "client" and "server" can be somewhat muddled. Even if both machines involved in an HTTP transaction are in a data center and would be referred to in conversation as "servers," the one making a request is the HTTP client and the one responding to that request is the HTTP server.

Because much of the work that PHP does has to do with Web browsers, the language has evolved a number of structures and mechanisms having to do with HTTP. As a PHP programmer, you should have a good understanding of these elements of the language. They are all the more important because other protocols, chiefly simple object access protocol (SOAP), covered in Chapter 5, ride (or can ride) on top of HTTP.

This chapter introduces you to the HTTP protocol as it pertains to PHP. It provides an overview of how the protocol works in the context of a simple page request, then builds on that foundation to show how it can be used to supply input values, arguments, effectively, to a server-side software program. From there, we'll see how the PHP language can be used to grab, examine, and manipulate values communicated by HTTP. There's also coverage of how to access cookies, which are small pieces of data stored on the client side, persistently if you like, through PHP.

You can approach HTTP on a couple of levels. You can treat it as a "black box" concept if you want, using well-documented procedures (for retrieving data from a form, saving cookies, etc.) without really knowing what goes on behind the metaphorical curtain.

Alternately, you can dig deeper into HTTP and really know what the protocol does in response to commands you issue in your PHP software. This chapter assumes you're interested in the details, and provides the recipes along the way.

> The best way to learn about the real-life operation of HTTP is to install a network-monitoring program of the sort commonly called a sniffer. Sniffers can provide far more information than you need to learn about HTTP, though, and can also be quite costly. I recommend a specialized HTTP-monitoring program called HttpDetect, from Effetech. HttpDetect sits in the background, watching the network traffic for HTTP activity. When it spots some, it records the traffic to a table. You get a convenient view of the full HTTP request and response headers, as well as the data that was sent or received as part of the request. The HttpDetect product works equally well on clients and servers.

Effetech asks a reasonable registration fee for its excellent software; the fee is slightly higher if you plan to use HttpDetect commercially. If you're planning to do any sort of network programming that involves HTTP (which is to say, any but the simplest PHP work and certainly anything involving SOAP—the sorts of things this book deals with) you'll benefit tremendously by having HttpDetect in your toolkit. You can't troubleshoot what you can't examine, and HttpDetect exposes HTTP traffic clearly.

Effetech's Web site is http://effetech.com.

3.1   Understanding HTTP

HTTP has to do with making requests for documents, and receiving documents in response. The documents may be static, or may be custom generated in response to each request. HTTP requests can carry variable values, which enables the protocol to carry user-entered information from client to server. This information can then be employed by the server-side programs invoked by the requests.

The full HTTP 1.1 specification is defined by RFC 2616, which is available here: ftp://ftp.rfc-editor.org/in-notes/rfc2616.txt.

3.1.1   A Simple Page Request and Response

The oldest and simplest use of HTTP is as a means of requesting a static document—one that is not generated specifically because of any particular HTTP request. Though this situation is usually not relevant to multi-tier PHP applications (except for such uses as splash screens and navigation menus), it's worth examining because the simple cases make it easier to see what's happening in the more elaborate situations.

Request

An HTTP transaction begins with a uniform resource locator (URL). The user of a browser enters a URL into the appropriate part of his or her browser window, or clicks a link (for which a URL is embedded in the hypertext markup language [HTML]). The browser (otherwise known, in the jargon of the HTTP specification, as the user agent) submits the URL to the server (which is itself specified in the URL) and waits for a response.

To expand on the concept of a request somewhat, let's consider an "ordinary" URL:

```
http://www.davidwall.com/
```

When appearing in the "Location" box (or "Address" box, or "URL" box, or whatever your browser calls it—if it's graphical and has a box at all), that URL is used in a GET request. There are two main HTTP methods (GET and POST) for requesting pages; GET is the more widely used one.

Examined fully, a browser's request for that URL looks like this:

```
GET /HTTP/1.1
Accept: image/gif, image/x-xbitmap, image/jpeg, image/pjpeg,
application/vnd.ms-powerpoint, application/vnd.ms-excel, application/msword,
application/x-shockwave-flash, */*
Accept-Language: en-us
Accept-Encoding: gzip, deflate
User-Agent: Mozilla/4.0 (compatible; MSIE 6.0; Windows NT 5.0; APC)
Host: www.davidwall.com
Connection: Keep-Alive
```

That request was generated by Microsoft Internet Explorer 6.0, running under Windows 2000 Server.

Notice that the first line specifies the method of the request, GET, and the version of the protocol specification: HTTP 1.1. The slash (/) that follows GET specifies the file that is being requested, relative to the host's Web service root. The slash is actually a special case; it means the request is for the default document in the root directory. The default document is determined by the configuration of the Web server, and is usually index.html or something similar.

Other lines (called headers) in the request denote Multimedia Internet Mail Extension (MIME) types and language encodings that the browser can handle, and provide the server with some information about the client (the Web browser) with which this request originated. TCP/IP (together with Domain Name Service [DNS], or other internetworking protocols) uses the Host header to route the rest of the request to the right server.

There's a blank line at the end of an HTTP GET request.

Response

In answer to an HTTP request (a GET request in this case) comes an HTTP response. As is true of a request, a response is a series of special lines of text (the headers). Unlike a request, though, a response (other than a response indicating an error condition) is followed by further data, the requested document.

The response to the HTTP GET request examined in the last section looks like this:

```
HTTP/1.1 200 OK
Date: Mon, 24 Nov 2003 04:03:21 GMT
Server: Apache/1.3.27
Last-Modified: Thu, 13 Nov 2003 00:21:26 GMT
ETag: "9b05b-3b60-3fb2ce86"
Accept-Ranges: bytes
Content-Length: 15200
Keep-Alive: timeout=5, max=100
Connection: Keep-Alive
Content-Type: text/html
<...page data omitted...>
```

The most important part of that response is the first line, which indicates success—the request can be fulfilled. Success is indicated by the "200 OK" code. See the sidebar for other possible HTTP response codes, good and bad.

It's also important to note the Content-Type header, which is a MIME type specification indicating that the data that follows the response header is an HTML document. There are scores of MIME types, covering everything from plain text, to extensible markup language (XML), to streaming audio-visual media in various formats.

HTTP Response Codes The list of legal HTTP response codes is defined by RFC 2616 (available at ftp://ftp.rfc-editor.org/in-notes/rfc2616.txt), but in general you'll find it useful to know the general pattern they employ. Each series of response codes corresponds to a particular class of conditions:

- 200-series codes indicate success.
- 300-series codes indicate a redirection to a new URL.
- 400-series codes indicate a client-side error (like a request for a nonexistent document—the famous "404 Not Found" error).
- 500-series codes indicate a server-side error.

3.1.2   A More Complex GET Request

Ordinary document retrievals, as accomplished by typing a URL into a browser window, are the simplest application of the HTTP GET method. A slightly more complex technique allows programmers much greater flexibility in allowing interaction between server-side programs and end users on the client side.

Consider this URL, taken from the presentation layer of the Currawong Accounting application discussed in Chapters 6 through 10:

```
http://192.168.1.201/acct/presentation/editAccount.php?id=6
```

That's a GET request to a particular PHP program that provides a single name/value pair. The name/value pair can be referred to within the called program, and for that reason this technique allows variable information to move from the client to the server. It is a characteristic of a GET request that name/value pairs are communicated as part of the URL in that way.

The request, viewed in an HTTP monitor like HttpDetect, looks largely the same as a simple GET request:

```
GET /acct/presentation/editAccount.php?id=6 HTTP/1.1
Accept: */*
Accept-Language: en-us
Accept-Encoding: gzip, deflate
User-Agent: Mozilla/4.0 (compatible; MSIE 6.0; Windows NT 5.0; APC)
Host: 192.168.1.201
Connection: Keep-Alive
```

The only difference is in the document requested:

```
/acct/presentation/editAccount.php?id=6.
```

That line calls a program called editAccount.php, which is stored in the /acct/presentation/ directory relative to the Web document root of the machine with IP address 192.168.1.201.

The response looks unremarkable, as well, at least from an HTTP perspective. Here is the response header:

```
HTTP/1.1 200 OK
Date: Mon, 24 Nov 2003 05:34:21 GMT
Server: Apache/1.3.26 (Win32) mod_perl/1.25 mod_ssl/2.8.10
OpenSSL/0.9.6c DAV/1.0.3 AuthNuSphere/1.0.0
X-Powered-By: PHP/4.3.3
Keep-Alive: timeout=15, max=100
Connection: Keep-Alive
Transfer-Encoding: chunked
Content-Type: text/html

<...page data omitted...>
```

There's nothing in the header to indicate a special response to the "id=6" name/value pair that appeared in the corresponding GET request, but because editAccount.php is designed to access the name/value pair and process the value, the page data differs depending on the value of id. You'll see how to access name/value pairs in GET requests later in this chapter.

3.1.3   A POST Request

Slightly more complicated than HTTP GET requests, HTTP POST requests most often result from the submission of HTML forms. Consider an HTML document that contains an opening FORM tag that looks like this:

```
<FORM ACTION="http://db2/test/post/postTest.php" METHOD="POST">
```

That opening FORM tag indicates that, when submitted, the contents of the form will go to the program postTest.php at the specified location, and that the HTTP POST method will be used to convey the form values to the server. Assuming that there is a single element in the form (disregarding the submit button itself), the HTTP POST request would resemble this:

```
POST /test/post/postTest.php HTTP/1.1
Accept: image/gif, image/x-xbitmap, image/jpeg, image/pjpeg,
application/vnd.ms-powerpoint, application/vnd.ms-excel, application/msword,
application/x-shockwave-flash, */*
Referer: http://db2/test/post/postTestClientSimple.html
Accept-Language: en-us
Content-Type: application/x-www-form-urlencoded
Accept-Encoding: gzip, deflate
User-Agent: Mozilla/4.0 (compatible; MSIE 6.0; Windows NT 5.0; APC)
Host: db2
Content-Length: 16
Connection: Keep-Alive
Cache-Control: no-cache

textBox=Tribbles
```

The primary difference between an HTTP POST request and an HTTP GET request is that in a POST request, the name/value pairs are embedded in the body of the message, rather than being visible in the URL. It's not too hard to generate HTTP POST requests to order, but it's harder than just editing a URL, which is all that's required to generate a custom HTTP GET request. For that reason, POST requests are slightly more secure than GET requests.

3.2   Working with HTTP in PHP

HTTP in terms of its specification is interesting, but as PHP programmers planning to use the protocol as one of our tools in creating multi-tier software applications, we want to know how PHP interacts with HTTP. It's important to know how to receive and make use of GET and POST requests in a program, and make use of HTTP's other features.

3.2.1   Accessing GET Variables

In making reference to GET variables from within PHP programs, it makes sense to make sure that you really have some (this is especially relevant if you're designing a program that's meant to take input from both GET and POST requests—you'd never have both at the same time). PHP provides the $_SERVER array to, among other things, help you determine if you're working with an HTTP GET request or an HTTP POST request.

The $_SERVER array contains a number of named elements, each defining a characteristic of the server under which the PHP program is running. The $_SERVER array contains such information as the type of HTTP server that invoked the program, the path and filename of the PHP program itself, and, most interesting to us right now, the HTTP request method used to invoke the program. The $_SERVER['REQUEST_METHOD'] element can be checked for "GET" and "POST" to see which method was used to call the program.

The code looks like this:

```
if ($_SERVER['REQUEST_METHOD'] == 'GET') {
    // React to GET request
    }
```

Nothing to it, really. You just check $_SERVER['REQUEST_METHOD'] for the string literal "GET" and react if you find it. Usually, that means you'll want to evaluate another automatically created global array, this one called $_GET, for elements named after the arguments sent in the GET request. To put it another way, the $_GET array has named elements for each of the name/value pairs included in the invoking URL. Note that another array, $HTTP_GET_VARS, exists in PHP for purposes of backward compatibility but has been deprecated in favor for $_GET.

The $_GET associative array is the key to accessing variables communicated to the server side via an HTTP GET request. When you send a series of name/value pairs to a PHP program as part of an HTTP GET request, the names become keys in the $_GET array and the values become the values that correspond to those keys. For example, if you sent this URL to a PHP program

```
http://192.168.1.201/test/getTest.php?alpha=a&beta=b&gamma=c
```

then you'd be able to make reference to any of these values in getTest.php:

```
$_GET['alpha']
$_GET['beta']
$_GET['gamma']
```

The $_GET array is "superglobal," meaning it's available in all contexts (including within function definitions) in getTest.php. There is never a need to declare a superglobal array such as $_GET.

3.2.2 Accessing POST Variables

As is the case with HTTP GET requests, it's good practice to make sure you're working with an HTTP POST request before you start querying the superglobal array that's supposed to hold the POST values.

The technique is identical: You examine the REQUEST_METHOD element of the $_SERVER array, checking in this case to see if it's equal to "POST". If it is, you proceed to pick named values out of the $_POST array, looking for them under names that correspond to those in your name/value pairs. In a POST request, the names correspond to the NAME attributes of the elements of the form that was submitted in generating the request. Again, note that another array, $HTTP_POST_VARS, exists in PHP for purposes of backward compatibility but has been deprecated in favor for $_POST. Here is typical code:

```
if ($_SERVER['REQUEST_METHOD'] == 'POST') {
// React to POST request
}
```

Like the $_GET array, the $_POST array is a superglobal associative array accessible from any point in a PHP program without the need for declaration within functions. It contains the name/value pairs that arrived as part of an HTTP POST request, with the names as keys and the values as values.

Consider this simple HTML page, which contains a short HTML form:

postTestClientSimple.html

```
<HTML>
<HEAD>

<TITLE>POST Tester</TITLE>

</HEAD>

<BODY>

<H1>Simple POST Submission Test Client</H1>

<FORM ACTION="http://db2/test/postTest.php" METHOD="POST">

<P>
<INPUT TYPE="TEXT" SIZE=15 NAME="textBox1" VALUE="Latrodectus">

<P>
<INPUT TYPE="TEXT" SIZE=15 NAME="textBox2" VALUE="Hasseltii">

<P>
<INPUT TYPE="SUBMIT" VALUE="Submit">

</FORM>

</BODY>
</HTML>
```

When the Submit button is clicked, an HTTP POST request is sent to http://db2/test/postTest.php. The request looks something like this:

```
POST /test/postTest.php HTTP/1.1
Accept: image/gif, image/x-xbitmap, image/jpeg, image/pjpeg,
application/vnd.ms-powerpoint, application/vnd.ms-excel, application/msword,
application/x-shockwave-flash, */*
Referer: http://db2/test/postTestClientSimple.html
Accept-Language: en-us
Content-Type: application/x-www-form-urlencoded
Accept-Encoding: gzip, deflate
User-Agent: Mozilla/4.0 (compatible; MSIE 6.0; Windows NT 5.0; APC)
Host: db2
Content-Length: 16
Connection: Keep-Alive
Cache-Control: no-cache

textBox=Tribbles
```

The request is accepted by postTest.php, whose code is as follows:

```
postTest.php

function demoFunction()
{
echo "<P>Look Ma, no declarations!";
echo "<P>In the function:";
echo "<BR>";
print_r($_POST);
}
print_r($_POST);

demoFunction();
```

Note that the print_r() function (a native PHP function that can meaningfully print out several different datatypes, including objects, and is therefore especially useful in debugging situations) is called twice. The first time is in the main body of the program, so it's not so surprising that $_POST is available for access. The second reference is inside demoFunction(), though, and there's no special global line to declare $_POST within the function scope. Nonetheless, $_POST is perfectly accessible.

Figure 3.1 shows the form submitted to postTest.php and its results.

3.2.3 Accessing Various HTML Form Elements

Much of the work you will do in PHP will center on accessing the entries users have made into HTML form elements of various kinds. This section documents strategies for interacting with selection lists (single and multiple selection), checkboxes, and radio buttons

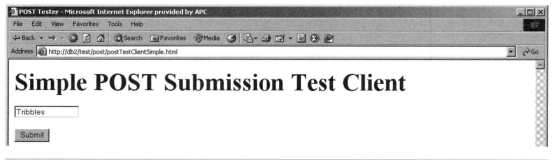

Figure 3.1: The submitted contents of an HTML form are accessed via the $_POST array.

whose user-specified contents are submitted by HTTP POST requests. The preceding section dealt with simple text boxes.

Simple Selection Lists

A simple selection list allows the user to choose one element from a series of values. When sent to the server in an HTTP POST request, the VALUE attribute of the selected element (which need not be the same as the visible label) is available as...

```
$_POST['elementName']
```

...where elementName is the NAME attribute of the selection list in the originating HTML document. Here is an example:

```
selectClientSimple.php

<HTML>
<HEAD>

<TITLE>POST Tester</TITLE>

</HEAD>
```

```
<BODY>

<H1>Test Client</H1>

<FORM ACTION="http://db2/test/post/selectSimple.php" METHOD="POST">

<P>
<SELECT NAME="stateName">
<OPTION VALUE="Alabama">Alabama</OPTION>
<OPTION VALUE="Alaska">Alaska</OPTION>
<OPTION VALUE="Arizona">Arizona</OPTION>
<OPTION VALUE="Arkansas">Arkansas</OPTION>
<OPTION VALUE="California">California</OPTION>
<OPTION VALUE="Colorado">Colorado</OPTION>
</SELECT>

<P>
<INPUT TYPE="SUBMIT" VALUE="Submit">

</FORM>

</BODY>
</HTML>
```

That form submits to this PHP program, which shows the selected state:

```
selectSimple.php

echo "The selected element is...";

echo $_POST['stateName'];
```

Figure 3.2 illustrates the appearance of the two files as rendered in a Web browser.

Multiple-Selection Selection Lists

In HTML, selection lists that allow multiple simultaneous selections are nearly identical to their single-selection cousins (the addition of the single attribute MULTIPLE changes their behavior). In PHP, though, this

```
$_POST['elementName']
```

where elementName is again the NAME attribute of the selection list in the originating HTML document, contains a subarray. The elements of the subarray are the HTML VALUE attributes of the selected elements.

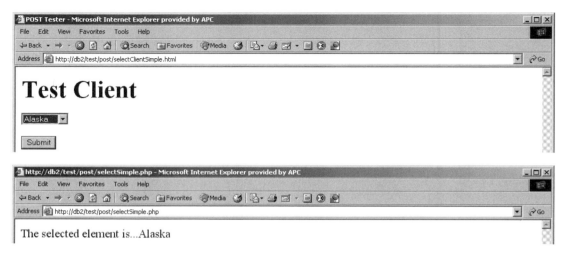

Figure 3.2: A simple selection list is easy to reference through the $_POST array.

This HTML document includes a multiple-selection selection list:

selectClientMultiple.html

```
<HTML>
<HEAD>

<TITLE>POST Tester</TITLE>

</HEAD>

<BODY>

<H1>Test Client</H1>
<FORM ACTION="http://db2/test/post/selectMultiple.php" METHOD="POST">

<P>
<SELECT NAME="stateName[]" MULTIPLE>
<OPTION VALUE="Alabama">Alabama</OPTION>
<OPTION VALUE="Alaska">Alaska</OPTION>
<OPTION VALUE="Arizona">Arizona</OPTION>
<OPTION VALUE="Arkansas">Arkansas</OPTION>
<OPTION VALUE="California">California</OPTION>
<OPTION VALUE="Colorado">Colorado</OPTION>
</SELECT>
```

```
<P>
<INPUT TYPE="SUBMIT" VALUE="Submit">

</FORM>

</BODY>
</HTML>
```

That form submits to this program:

```
selectMultiple.php

echo "The value of \$_POST['stateName'] is...<BR>";

echo $_POST['stateName'];

echo "<P>";

echo "The selected elements are... <BR>";

foreach ($_POST['stateName'] as $key => $value)
    {
    echo $value;
    echo "<BR>";
    }
```

In that program, the foreach loop goes through each element in the $_POST['statename'] array, echoing the value of each element. Figure 3.3 shows how this looks in practice.

Checkboxes

The key procedure in determining which of a series of checkboxes is checked is to see which keys evaluate to true. The keys of checked checkboxes evaluate to true; the keys of unchecked checkboxes evaluate to false.

This example shows how to access checkbox values through $_POST.

```
checkboxClient.html

<HTML>
<HEAD>

<TITLE>POST Tester</TITLE>

</HEAD>

<BODY>
```

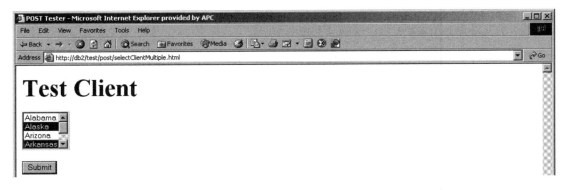

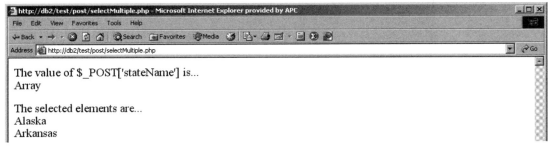

Figure 3.3: Accessing a multiple-selection selection list is a little more complicated, but not hard.

```
<H1>Test Client</H1>

<FORM ACTION="http://db2/test/post/checkbox.php" METHOD="POST">

<P>
<INPUT TYPE="CHECKBOX" NAME="agree">   I agree.
<INPUT TYPE="CHECKBOX" NAME="donateMoney">   I would like to donate money.
<!- Note that   indicates a non-breaking space character -->

<P>
<INPUT TYPE="SUBMIT" VALUE="Submit">

</FORM>

</BODY>
</HTML>
```

That form sends the contents of its form to this server-side program:

```
checkbox.php
```

```
echo "The contents of $_POST are...<BR>";
print_r($_POST);

echo "<P>The value of \$_POST['agree'] is...<BR>";
echo $_POST['agree'];

echo "<P>The value of \$_POST['donateMoney'] is...<BR>";
echo $_POST['donateMoney'];

echo "<P>";

echo "The selected box(es) is/are...<BR>";

// Convert $_POST array to $parameters for clarity.

foreach ($_POST as $key => $value)
    {
    if ($key)
        {
        echo $key;
        echo "<BR>";
        }
    }
```

Simply put, the HTML VALUE attributes of checkboxes that are checked show up in the $_POST array, whereas the VALUE attributes of those that are not checked do not appear in the $_POST array. Figure 3.4 shows how this works in practice.

Radio Buttons

In HTML, radio buttons are very similar to checkboxes, with the key difference that all radio buttons in a set have the same HTML NAME attribute. Because they are radio buttons, only one of the radio buttons in a set can be active at one time.

Figuring out which radio button the user chose can be easily determined from the $_POST array. If you examine the following element,

```
$_POST['elementName']
```

it will be equal to the HTML VALUE attribute of the selected radio button. This program shows an example of this strategy:

```
radioClient.php

<HTML>
<HEAD>
```

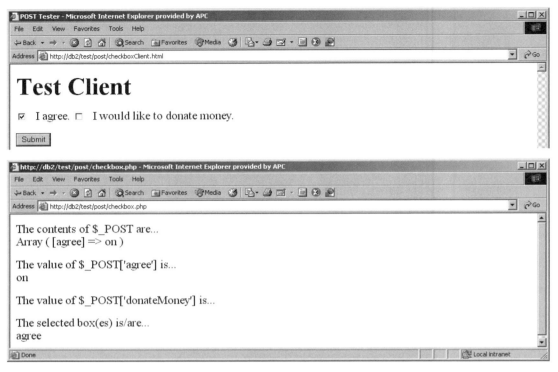

Figure 3.4: Each checkbox has a unique NAME attribute, with respect to HTTP POST.

```
<TITLE>POST Tester</TITLE>

</HEAD>

<BODY>

<H1>Test Client</H1>

<FORM ACTION="http://db2/test/post/radio.php" METHOD="POST">

<P>

<BR> <INPUT TYPE="RADIO" NAME="radioWaves" VALUE="Yes"> Yes.
<BR> <INPUT TYPE="RADIO" NAME="radioWaves" VALUE="Probably"> Probably.
<BR> <INPUT TYPE="RADIO" NAME="radioWaves" VALUE="Probably Not"> Probably Not.
<BR> <INPUT TYPE="RADIO" NAME="radioWaves" VALUE="No"> No.

<P>
```

```
<INPUT TYPE="SUBMIT" VALUE="Submit">

</FORM>

</BODY>
</HTML>
```

The form in that HTML document submits to radio.php:

```
radio.php
```

```
echo "The contents of $_POST are...<BR>";
print_r($_POST);
```

```
echo "<P>The value of \$_POST['radioWaves'] is...<BR>";
echo $_POST['radioWaves'];
echo "<P>";

echo "The selected option is...<BR>";

echo $_POST['radioWaves'];
```

In that program, a simple examination of $_POST['radioWaves'] gives the HTML VALUE attribute of the selected radio button. The behavior of this program is shown in Figure 3.5.

3.3 Cookies

A key provision of the HTTP protocol is the ability of the server to store and retrieve small pieces of data on the client. These little pieces of data are called cookies, and they help compensate for a strategic limitation of HTTP: its statelessness.

HTTP is said to be stateless because, by default, there is no way to correlate two sequential request/response transactions involving the same client and same server. If Server A gets a request from Client B and responds to it as required, then a few seconds later gets another request from Client B, there's no way to know that the second request almost certainly came from the same user and perhaps should be dealt with accordingly. If the two pages were parts of a game, for example, it might be helpful to track users as they progressed from one page to the next, perhaps incorporating their cumulative score in each subsequent page.

Fortunately, HTTP provides for cookies. There are several ways to set and retrieve cookies. JavaScript and other client-side scripting languages can do it, as can Perl, Active Server Pages (ASP), and pretty much every other server-side scripting language. The next section shows how to do it in PHP.

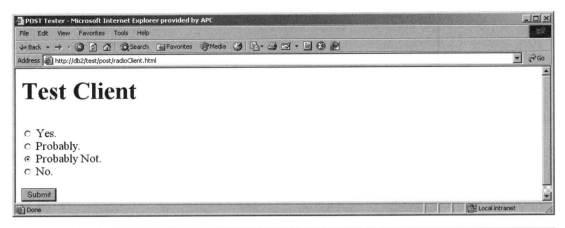

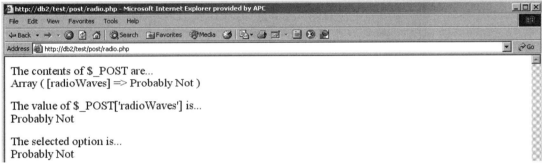

Figure 3.5: Radio buttons all have the same HTML NAME attribute, accessible through the $_POST array.

3.3.1 Setting Cookies

To set a cookie with PHP, use the setcookie function. It's easy to use:

```
setcookie('username', 'derektom');
```

That single line of code is the simplest way to define a cookie and give it a value—it's the logical equivalent of establishing a variable and assigning a value to it. The setcookie function sets up a cookie called username and gives it the value derektom.

Because that cookie-creating function call lacks an expiration specification, though, the cookie called username will be stored only in volatile memory and will live only as long as the client, the browser, typically, remains running. When the client program closes, the cookie is not written to persistent storage and therefore ceases to exist. It is not available the next time the client starts up.

In order to make a cookie persist beyond the time the client is shut down (or, for that matter, to make it expire before the client shuts down), you need to supplement the setcookie call with an expiration specification. It should take the form of a number representing a quantity of milliseconds after midnight on 1 January 1970. You can get the current timestamp like this:

```
$now = time();
```

That means you can calculate a number representing the "time to live" that you want and end up with the needed expiration timestamp.

```
$now = time();
$expirationDate = $now + 259200000; // 259200000 is 1000 * 60 * 60 * 24 * 3,
or the number of milliseconds in three days.
setcookie('username', 'derektom', $expirationDate);
```

If you want to do so, you can put restrictions on the pages that can retrieve the cookie setcookie sets. If you do this,

```
setcookie('username', 'derektom', $expirationDate, '/game/');
```

then only code contained in files whose URLs include /game/ will be able to retrieve the value of username (or even detect that username exists). A similar restriction takes effect when you qualify setcookie like this:

```
setcookie('username','derektom',$expirationDate, $path, 'mmrpg.davidwall.com');
```

By using the fifth argument of setcookie, we ensure that only pages whose domain paths end in mmrpg.davidwall.com will be able to retrieve the cookie. Note that specifying 'mmrpg.davidwall.com' allows domains like a.mmrpg.davidwall.com and b.mmrpg.davidwall.com to access the cookie. If the setcookie call had specified '.mmrpg.davidwall.com' (with a leading dot), then only pages served from mmrpg.davidwall.com itself (not from any subsidiary domains) would be able to read the cookie.

The sixth setcookie argument can be set to 1. When it is set to 1, the cookie may be accessed only over a secure connection. When the sixth argument is set to 0, or not specified at all, the cookie may be accessed over a clear connection.

Note that you may have to use null arguments as placeholders. If you wanted to restrict the domain that could access a cookie but not specify an expiration date or path restriction, you would have to use this technique:

```
setcookie('username', 'derektom', ", ",'mmrpg.davidwall.com');
```

The empty quotation marks act as placeholders.

3.3.2 Retrieving Cookies

Retrieving a cookie in PHP is even easier than setting one. The key procedure is to examine the $_COOKIE global array, which is an associative array with keys that correspond to cookie names. Say you'd established a cookie called username, as was done in Section 3.3.1. You could retrieve it like this:

```
echo "The value of the username cookie is $_COOKIE['username']";
```

If you were not sure whether the username cookie existed, you could use function isset to find out:

```
if (isset($_COOKIE['username'])
{
echo "The value of the username cookie is $_COOKIE['username']";
}
```

Furthermore, because $_COOKIE is an associative array, it can be traversed like any other associative array. If you didn't know the names of all the cookies that had been set, this would find them all for you:

```
foreach ($_COOKIE as $name => $value)
{
echo "New cookie/value pair: $name = $value";
}
```

3.3.3 Deleting Cookies

The procedure for getting rid of a cookie that's already been set is similar to the procedure for creating a new cookie. The trick is, you set the expiration timestamp for a point in the past, which effectively expires the cookie right away.

If there were a cookie in $_COOKIE called username, and you no longer required its services, you could call setcookie() like this:

```
$now = time();
$expirationDate = $now - 100000; // Minus an arbitrary number of milliseconds
setcookie('username', 'derektom', $expirationDate);
```

By subtracting a number (the exact number doesn't matter) from the value that results from the time function, we get a time in the past. The username cookie is therefore past its expiration point, and disappears from $_COOKIE.

3.4 Sessions

If you wanted to, you could manually adapt the cookie-management capabilities of HTTP and PHP to track a user throughout a session. That is, your PHP code could be set up so that every page requested by the user included a check for a cookie of a certain name, which, if it existed, would contain a unique value. If it didn't exist, it could be created and assigned a unique value. The unique value would serve to identify the user and would remain constant across multiple transactions.

Sessions are important because they allow you to provide continuity to the user. Once someone has logged in, he or she can remain logged in throughout the session. Preferences can be maintained, and data accumulated. Cookies are the difference between a simple-minded application that forgets its users after each interaction and an apparently more intelligent application that can keep track of them for extended periods.

Generating and keeping track of those unique values would be a major hassle, though. Because session tracking, otherwise known as state maintenance, is such a common requirement of browser-based software applications, PHP has some built-in mechanisms for the purpose that are easy to use.

3.4.1 Preparing the PHP Server for Session Tracking

Depending on how you configure your PHP server, it either will or will not automatically issue a unique identifier to every new site visitor it serves. That is, you can determine whether the PHP interpreter (the PHP executable that runs .php files) tracks sessions by default.

A setting in php.ini determines the behavior. If this line

```
session.auto_start=1
```

appears in php.ini, the server will automatically issue session identifiers to every new client it encounters. If the same value is set equal to 0

```
session.auto_start=0
```

then there is no automatic session tracking and, if it is needed, session tracking must be started manually, as covered in the next section.

3.4.2 Establishing a Session

If the php.ini file of a particular PHP server does not include activation of the session. auto_start variable, session tracking must be initiated manually. It is not a complicated process, requiring only a single line of code.

If you wish to initiate session tracking on a client, include this line in a PHP page served to that client:

```
session_start();
```

The effect is the same as if session.auto_start had been enabled. All subsequent session-related techniques may be used in exactly the same way.

When a session is established (either automatically or explicitly), a session identifier springs into existence. A session identifier is a random sequence of letters and numbers. It is stored in two places: on the client in an element of the $_COOKIE array, and on the server in a file. Further data associated with the session (more on how to create that data appears in the next section) is stored on the server only, but the identifier is stored on both sides of the connection.

Because the identifier is stored on the client side as an element in the $_COOKIE associative array, we can retrieve it in much the same way we'd retrieve any other value out of that array. You have to get the key of the identifier element in a special way, though. Here's the code:

```
$sessionKey = session_name();
```

Then, we can use $sessionKey to get the right value out of the $_COOKIE array:

```
$identifier = $_COOKIE[$sessionKey];
```

After that runs, $identifier will contain a long string of letters and numerals, and may be manipulated like any other string. There's usually no reason to do this, though, other than to inform yourself of how session tracking works on the client side.

What happens if the client is set up to reject cookies? PHP works around the limitation. The PHP interpreter will, for example, automatically modify HTML links to include session identifier values in HTTP GET form (that is, incorporated into the URL). The ACTION attributes of PHP-generated HTML forms are modified to include the session identifier, too.

3.4.3   Setting a Session Variable

Session variables are similar to cookies in that session variables, like cookies, are stored in a global array. The difference is that most session data (all except the single reference to the session identifier, as covered in the previous section) is stored on the server side, whereas all cookie data reside on the client.

To establish a session variable, simply establish a new element in the $_SESSION associative array:

```
$_SESSION['username'] = 'derektom';
```

3.4.4   Retrieving a Session Variable

The element identified by the username key can be retrieved at any time in the future, as long as the session is active, which is to say, until the client, the browser, is closed. This kind of retrieval is routine:

```
echo $_SESSION['username'];
```

And, as is the case with any associative array, code like this is valid with $_SESSION:

```
foreach ($_SESSION as $name => $value)
{
echo "New cookie/value pair: $name = $value";
}
```

3.5 Questions and Exercises

1. What are the relative advantages and disadvantages of HTTP GET and POST requests?

2. What are some of the risks associated with using an HTML HIDDEN field in conjunction with HTTP POST requests?

3. How can HTTP GET and POST compensate for cookies being disabled in browser settings?

4. What problems with session maintenance would you anticipate if an application were spread across multiple servers whose activities were regulated by a load balancer? How might you get around these problems?

chapter 4

Simple Object Access Protocol Under PHP

When implementing multi-tier software applications, you need to be able to make calls from programs running on Machine A to programs running on Machine B. For example, you might have a module on the business-logic layer that calculates the profit or loss of a certain business unit during a certain time period. In order to make that calculation, the logic module needs to make requests of one or more programs on the accessor layer. Assuming the accessor layer exists on another physical host, a mechanism needs to be devised to facilitate the passing of requests and responses between the two layers.

Various solutions for this problem exist, but none are as simple or as versatile as simple object access protocol (SOAP). SOAP allows the creation of Web services, which are standardized computing resources that take input from across a network and respond in an advertised way. Web services may or may not be significant to the future of the software industry at large—lots of software companies would like them to become so—but they certainly are convenient to the creation of multi-tier software applications.

SOAP is a specification for extensible markup language (XML) messages that travel between endpoints. It is a way for software programs to invoke other software programs (or parts of them) over the network. Just as you can make calls to locally defined functions from within an ordinary PHP program and expect to receive values in return, you can use SOAP to call functions that are defined in other programs, and in fact on completely separate machines. Just as is possible with calls to local functions, you can use SOAP to send one or more parameters along with a function invocation.

In terms of networking, SOAP messages travel on top of hypertext transport protocol (HTTP) or simple mail transport protocol (SMTP). That is, you must establish an HTTP or SMTP link to a remote resource before attempting to send SOAP messages there. In this book, we'll use HTTP exclusively as a means of carrying SOAP messages. SMTP support is a newer addition to the SOAP specification, and it's generally easier to get HTTP traffic through firewalls and other network obstructions than SMTP traffic. Therefore, HTTP is usually the better choice, unless some specific condition requires that an application use SMTP to carry its SOAP messages.

A function can be exposed through a SOAP server, meaning it can accept SOAP messages from elsewhere on the network and return results in response. A single SOAP server object can expose lots of functions. These functions, when exposed, become Web services—computing resources that may be accessed over the network via Web protocols.

This chapter explains SOAP and Web services technologies, and gives you some idea of why you'd want to use them in your software architecture work. It also shows you the state of the art in SOAP packages for PHP, and demonstrates their use by means of some simple message-sending example applications.

> SOAP is a large and complicated subject, with many related specifications and technologies. *Programming Web Services with SOAP* by James Snell, Doug Tidwell, and Pavel Kulchenko (O'Reilly, Sebastopol, CA, 2001) will help you understand the basics. *Understanding Web Services: XML, WSDL, SOAP, and UDDI* by Eric Newcomer (Addison-Wesley, Boston, 2002) is worthwhile as well. The World Wide Web Consortium hosts the definitive documents on the SOAP and WSDL specifications here: http://www.w3c.org/2002/ws/. Uniform Description, Discovery, and Integration (UDDI), on the other hand, is under the control of Organization for the Advancement of Structured Information Standards (OASIS). The UDDI specification appears here: http://www.oasis-open.org/committees/uddi-spec/doc/tcspecs.htm.

4.1   Understanding SOAP

At the end of the day, Web pages are defined by hypertext markup language (HTML) documents, which are in turn a particular kind of text document. When we surf the Web, we're retrieving particular text files—streams of characters, if you prefer—which cause our browsers to behave in a certain way. Specifically, the streams of characters tell our browsers to display text, links, headers, and to retrieve other files (such as images), and to display them in particular locations.

The transport of the HTML text streams is accomplished by means of HTTP, which was covered in greater length in Chapter 3. One interesting aspect of HTTP is that it is both widely required and generally harmless, which means that routers are firewalls that are configured so that it's easier to get an HTTP request/response pair to pass between two given computers than any other kind of message exchange. Even if the two computers are separated by great distance and are connected only by the public Internet, it's usually possible for them to trade HTTP messages.

Therein lies a solution to the problem of interprocess communication. If the character streams provided by the HTTP request and response could be made to carry function calls rather than HTML pages meant for display, then the problem would be solved.

XML is a general-purpose markup language. It's far less specialized than HTML and can be used for many different purposes. One of its applications is in formatting the messages that processes send back and forth as calls to remote methods and functions are made.

Because the messages are in XML, it's not strictly necessary that the programs generating them all be written in the same language. As long as they all generate SOAP messages, it's perfectly acceptable for a PHP program to make a request of, and receive a response from, a Web service written in C#, Java, or Perl. In fact, there's an example of a PHP program making a call to a Web service implemented in Java in Chapter 10.

4.1.1 A SOAP Request

Suppose we have a program on the business-logic layer of a multi-tier application. It's called updateCurrencies.php, and one of its functions needs to access a remote Web service (on a public-resource site called XMethods.net) to get the exchange rates of various currencies. The module in the business-logic layer can send out the names of two countries, and expects in return a real number (a float) that indicates the ratio of the value of the first country's currency to the value of the second country's currency.

In this situation, the Web service on XMethods.net would have to have a SOAP server active, and updateCurrencies.php would have to instantiate an instance of a SOAP client object. The SOAP client object would then send request messages, possibly with supplementary parameters, to the SOAP server, which would respond. Overall, the operation is very much like a call to a function in which a function name is invoked (and parameters possibly sent), and the function does some processing and returns a result. The only difference is in the amount of overhead (both locally and on the remote system) and in the intervening data network.

It is useful to look at the HTTP messages that pass between the machine running updateCurrencies.php and the Web service on XMethods.net (SOAP messages, again, ride on top of HTTP messages). The request from the business-logic layer to the remote resource looks like this:

```
POST /soap HTTP/1.0
User-Agent: NuSOAP v0.6
Host: services.xmethods.net
Content-Type: text/xml
Content-Length: 635
SOAPAction: ""

<?xml version="1.0"?>
<SOAP-ENV:Envelope
```

```
SOAP-ENV:encodingStyle="http://schemas.xmlsoap.org/soap/encoding/"
xmlns:SOAP-ENV="http://schemas.xmlsoap.org/soap/envelope/"
xmlns:xsd="http://www.w3.org/2001/XMLSchema"
xmlns:xsi="http://www.w3.org/2001/XMLSchema-instance"
xmlns:SOAP-ENC="http://schemas.xmlsoap.org/soap/encoding/"
xmlns:si="http://soapinterop.org/xsd"
xmlns:galactivism="urn:xmethods-CurrencyExchange">


<SOAP-ENV:Body>
<galactivism:getRate>
<country1 xsi:type="xsd:string">Australia</country1>
<country2 xsi:type="xsd:string">United States</country2>
</galactivism:getRate>
</SOAP-ENV:Body>


</SOAP-ENV:Envelope>
```

Some whitespace has been inserted into this excerpt for clarity, but the structure of the request is evident. First of all, this is an HTTP POST request, precisely the same as the HTTP POST requests covered in Chapter 3. It complies with the HTTP 1.0 specification in every way. The only unusual piece of this request is that it carries a payload. That payload is in the form of an XML document, which contains a call to a Web service called getRate() and two parameters (country1 and country2) for that Web service to process.

The next section examines the response that the XMethods.net Web service sends back.

4.1.2   A SOAP Response

The response, from XMethods.net to the business-logic layer, looks like this:

```
HTTP/1.1 200 OK
Date: Tue, 25 Nov 2003 07:38:56 GMT
Server: Electric/1.0
Content-Type: text/xml
Content-Length: 492
X-Cache: MISS from www.xmethods.net
Connection: close


<?xml version='1.0' encoding='UTF-8'?>


<soap:Envelope
xmlns:soap='http://schemas.xmlsoap.org/soap/envelope/'
```

```
xmlns:xsi='http://www.w3.org/2001/XMLSchema-instance'
xmlns:xsd='http://www.w3.org/2001/XMLSchema'
xmlns:soapenc='http://schemas.xmlsoap.org/soap/encoding/'
soap:encodingStyle='http://schemas.xmlsoap.org/soap/encoding/'>


<soap:Body>
<n:getRateResponse xmlns:n='urn:xmethods-CurrencyExchange'>
<Result xsi:type='xsd:float'>0.7206</Result>
</n:getRateResponse>
</soap:Body>


</soap:Envelope>
```

Again, some whitespace has been inserted to make things a bit easier to understand. This is a garden-variety HTTP response, similar to those discussed in Chapter 3. Here, the body is another XML document, a somewhat shorter one, that contains a Result element. This is the single value that was returned by the call to getRate(). It is a float value: 0.7206, which is the ratio of one U.S. dollar to one Australian dollar at the time of the call to the Web service.

All of these traces were done with Ethereal (http://www.ethereal.com/), a free and open-source network analyzer. Figure 4.1 shows Ethereal in action.

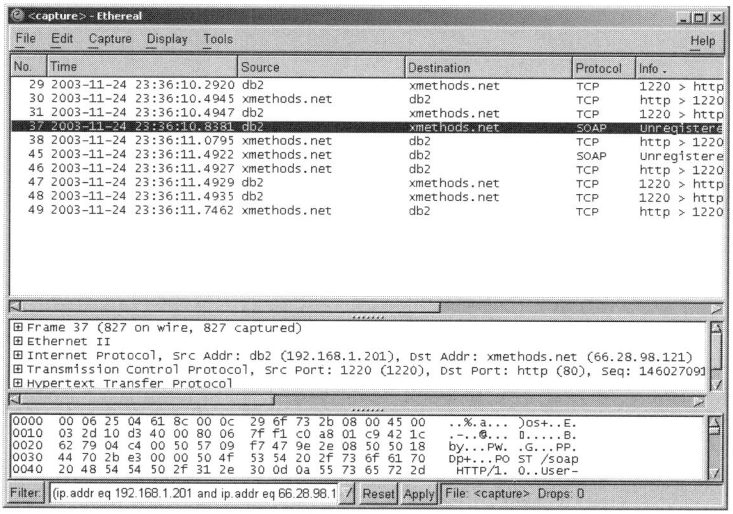

Figure 4.1: Ethereal makes it easy to monitor SOAP activity.

4.2   Implementing SOAP in PHP

Three cheers for Dietrich Ayala, who has done the PHP community a favor by creating NuSOAP. NuSOAP is a PHP library—a series of PHP files you can easily import into your own programs by means of a require or require_once statement—that supports the creation of SOAP clients and servers. It's available at http://dietrich.ganx4.com/nusoap/index.php.

It's blisteringly easy to create a SOAP server object with NuSOAP, then register your own functions with it. It's that easy to convert your functions to Web services. Invoking them is similarly simple. In essence, there are four steps involved in exposing a function as a Web service with NuSOAP:

1. Import the NuSOAP library,
2. Instantiate a soap_server object,
3. Register a function with the soap_server object using the register() function, and
4. Direct the incoming HTTP data to the soap_server object using the service() function.

Section 4.2.1 shows you how to carry out the four steps in more detail.

> There are a couple of other SOAP implementations in progress, and in various stages of readiness. Among them are the PHP-SOAP, in alpha testing at the time of this writing (http://phpsoaptoolkit.sourceforge.net/phpsoap/) and the SOAP module in PHP Extension and Application Repository (PEAR), in beta (http://pear.php.net/package/SOAP).

4.2.1   A Simple Application of NuSOAP

Let's have a look at a simple application of NuSOAP.

Setting Up a SOAP Server

To establish a SOAP server with NuSOAP, you must first have a function you wish to expose as a Web service. Any function is suitable for the purpose. In this example, we'll use this one:

```
function hello($name) {
return "hello $name!";
}
```

That's a very simple function that does nothing but take a string as a parameter, insert that string into a larger string, and return the result. Notice that there's nothing unusual about this function, which is going to be exposed as a Web service.

To expose the function as a Web service, we must first import the NuSOAP library:

```
require_once('nusoap-0.6/nusoap.php');
```

Then, we must create a soap_server object (soap_server objects are defined in nusoap.php)

```
$s = new soap_server;
```

and register our function with the soap_server object:

```
$s->register('hello');
```

This last line is interesting. It invokes the register() method of the object known as $s, which in this case is the soap_server object. The parameter passed to register() is the name of the function we wish to expose as a Web service, namely hello(), but without the customary parentheses.

The only other characteristic the server program needs is a line of code that refers incoming HTTP POST requests to the NuSOAP library for evaluation. Again, the solution is to invoke a method of $s, the soap_server object:

```
$s->service($HTTP_RAW_POST_DATA);
```

It's a black box, after all. Incoming HTTP POST requests get sent to the soap_server object, where they're passed on to one of the registered functions as appropriate. By the way, $HTTP_RAW_POST_DATA is a special variable that the PHP interpreter makes available to programs whenever the incoming data is of a Multimedia Internet Mail Extension (MIME) type other than application/x-www.form-urlencoded, which is the MIME type that's usually associated with a form. In the case of a SOAP request, the MIME type is application/soap+xml, so the contents of the HTTP POST request are accessed through $HTTP_RAW_POST_DATA.

What, then, sends the HTTP POST request? The SOAP client does.

Setting Up a SOAP Client

There's no point in having a Web service, otherwise known as a SOAP server, if there isn't also something to call it. NuSOAP makes SOAP clients even easier to create than SOAP servers.

NuSOAP called its SOAP client object a soapclient (in contrast to soap_server), so be careful with your underscore characters. When you create a soapclient object, you have to associate it with the server to which it will refer. This reference takes the form of a full HTTP uniform resource locator (URL). The URL specifies the location of the PHP containing the Web services (functions and soap_server object) that the client will access.

To create the soapclient object, you must first invoke the NuSOAP library, just as was required on the server

```
require_once('nusoap-0.6/nusoap.php');
```

then instantiate a soapclient object with the full URL of the server file as a parameter:

```
$client = new soapclient('http://davidwall.com/php/server.php');
```

With the client object in place, it is possible to invoke a remote function through the call() function of the soapclient object. The call() function takes the name of the remote function and an array containing the parameters to be sent to that remote function, so the first step is to populate the array of parameter. The names for the elements in the array correspond to the name of the arguments specified in the functions that are exposed as Web services:

```
$parameters = array('name'=>'David');
```

With that array established, we can invoke the call() function of the soapclient object, known in this case by the handle $client:

```
echo $client->call('hello',$parameters);
```

That line sends the $parameters array to the hello() function on the SOAP server associated with $client, and the result is written to output.

One could not reasonably ask for a simpler means of making SOAP calls across an HTTP link. NuSOAP enables us to import a library, then expose PHP functions as Web services with just a couple of lines of code. Referring to those services as a client is even easier.

4.2.2   A More Complex Application of NuSOAP

Here, we'll put together a simple program that makes the call to the XMethods.net getRate() Web service that was documented in the beginning of this chapter. It's a simple program that requires only a special file written in Web services description language (WSDL) to send the required call to the remote resource.

Here's a full listing of the program that makes the call.

```
demoSOAP.php


require_once('nusoap-0.6/nusoap.php'); // Import NuSOAP library.


$country1 = $_GET['country1']; // Get user input from HTML form.
$country2 = $_GET['country2']; // Get user input from HTML form.


$parameters = array(
'country1' => $country1,
'country2' => $country2
);
```

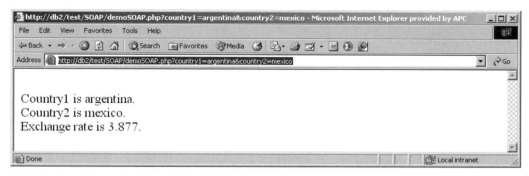

Figure 4.2: Even a very simple PHP program can make reference to a Web service on the Internet.

```
$soapclient = new soapclient('Currency.wsdl','wsdl');// Create client object
$xRate = $soapclient->call('getRate',$parameters); // Make remote function
                                                       call

echo "<BR>Country1 is $country1.";
echo "<BR>Country2 is $country2.";

echo "<BR>Exchange rate is $xRate.";
```

Based on what you read in Chapter 3, you should recognize that this application takes input from the $_GET array, which means that we can adjust its input by sending it different URLs formatted like this one:

```
http://db2/test/SOAP/demoSOAP.php?country1=argentina&country2=mexico
```

The documentation for the getRate() service on XMethods.net (accessible from the http://www.xmethods.net home page) includes the fact that it takes only spelled-out country names. It also includes a reference to the WSDL file that explains how the service works—Currency.wsdl. Because the getRate service on XMethods is made use of in Currawong Accounting, this file is listed and explained in detail in Chapter 10.

Figure 4.2 shows the results of a run of demoSOAP.php, including its URL.

4.3 Questions and Exercises

1. Consider the security implications of using SOAP. To what extent can SOAP be made secure by using Secure Sockets Layer (SSL) encryption to carry HTTP—HTTP Secure (HTTPS)—instead of plain HTTP? How about by running SOAP on ordinary HTTP, but over a virtual private network?

2. Write a simple application that, instead of responding with a simple datatype, sends back an associative array. Can you do one that sends back an object?

3. What are some reasonable applications for Web services on the public Internet? What are some applications that might not work well for technical reasons?

4. Do some research into standards documents and explain the relationship between SOAP and XML-Remote Procedure Call (XML-RPC) in terms of Web services.

chapter 5

Designing and Implementing a Multi-Tier Application in PHP: A Succinct Example

This chapter gets straight to the essence of multi-tier design under PHP by walking through the design and implementation of a complete application. Though the application is simple in some ways—its database consists of a single table, for example, and there is no elsewhere layer—it illustrates some important points. The idea is that you'll get a taste of these key concepts here, and explore them more fully in later chapters.

5.1 Examining the Problem

The requirement we aim to solve in this chapter is one of navigation. Our customer, an airline, wants us to provide an application that calculates the distance between various world cities. For example, a pilot should be able to open up our application—delivered via one or more Web pages, naturally—and specify an origin city and a destination city. The application should then return a value, in kilometers, that represents the shortest possible air route between the two cities. This value will be used for fuel calculations and other planning purposes.

The Earth, as you may have heard, is roughly spherical. The shortest distance between two points on the surface of a sphere is along a circle whose edge includes the two points, and whose center, furthermore, is the center of the Earth. Such a route is called a Great Circle route. The Great Circle route between two nearby points is nearly indistinguishable from a straight line, but a Great Circle path between two widely spaced points can seem odd to people accustomed to thinking in terms of flat surfaces. This is why the shortest path between New York and Hong Kong, for example, goes nearly over the North Pole. Federal Express has a freight hub in Anchorage, Alaska, for a reason: That city is roughly equidistant from Tokyo, New York, and London.

In any case, the customer wants us to develop an application that takes latitude and longitude values for a given city from a database and uses them to calculate the Great Circle distance between the two places. The solution to the problem, as well as the interface that allows the user to specify the two cities of interest, should be one or more browser-renderable pages.

5.1.1 Sketching Out the Layers

Not surprisingly, the customer's requirement represents an excellent opportunity to use multi-tier software architecture.

- The database. The customer wants latitude and longitude information about various cities to be stored in a database. They don't specify a particular kind of database, but we know that the odds are good that at some point in the life of our application the airline will migrate from one database platform to another. At the very least, we want the ability to do our development and testing under one kind of database before connecting our application to the airline's database server. It seems like a good idea to treat our database and its server as a discrete unit—the database layer.

- The accessors. With a database layer that's distinct from everything else, we need a collection of software elements that act as interfaces between the database and the software that relies on its data. Structured query language (SQL) is the specific go-between, but we want to abstract the SQL statements a bit. This is the function of the objects in the accessor layer. The accessor layer should be easily reconfigured to connect to a new kind of database server, as well. For that reason, it will make use of the PEAR DB classes, which will be discussed further later in this chapter, and in Chapter 7 on database access.

- The business logic. The customer provided us with a statement of the business logic for this application. The application is to calculate Great Circle distances. How? Based on the latitudes and longitudes of the two endpoint cities. If we can find a mathematical formula that takes such input and provides the required output, and can encode that algorithm into the PHP language, we have a business logic layer.

- The presentation mechanism. The user interface shouldn't be too complicated, and it may even be possible to fit it all into one piece of software. The presentation layer has to first present the user with lists of possible origin and destination cities and allow him or her to select one of each. Upon submission of those values, the user interface should present the calculated Great Circle distance, and make it easy for the user to do another calculation with a different pair of cities.

It's all modular, and it'll be easier to build, maintain, and modify because of that characteristic. Multi-tier design seems like the right design choice for this application. Figure 5.1 shows the proposed architecture for our solution.

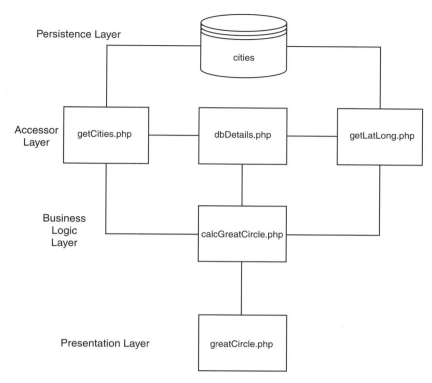

Figure 5.1: The Great Circle application in schematic form.

5.1.2 Communication Between the Layers

How, though, will the layers communicate with one another? Communication requires a protocol, either a custom-designed and -implemented one or a standard one that's adopted. What characteristics will our interlayer communication protocol need? Here's a list:

- Support for intermachine communications. It's possible that the various layers of this application will reside on different hardware platforms. It's safe to assume that they'll be connected by a TCP/IP network, and that standard protocols, such as domain name service (DNS), hypertext transport protocol (HTTP), and simple mail transport protocol (SMTP), will exist on the network.

- Support for the exchange of simple and complex data types. Considering the problem to be solved here, it seems likely that we'll need to move complex data structures, such as indexed and associative arrays, between layers. Our job will be much simpler if the communications protocol lets us move such structures without drama.

- Ease of implementation. We want to spend our time as designers and, to a lesser extent, implementors of a software solution. The application we create should be notable as one that solves its assigned problem efficiently, not as one that uses a particular interlayer communications protocol.

Later chapters deal with the question of why, but the quick answer to the question of which interlayer communication protocol to use is: simple object access protocol (SOAP). SOAP satisfies all of our performance requirements, and it's easy to implement because (as is often the case in PHP) there's a freely available library that will do the heavy lifting for us. We just whack a reference to the library into our software and start using SOAP communication.

5.2   The Database Layer

The persistence layer (assuming that it's a database, anyhow) speaks SQL. It receives SQL queries in, and replies with SQL result sets (or messages that indicate success or failure). In the larger scheme of multi-tier architecture, the persistence layer receives incoming SQL queries from the PHP programs in the accessor layer. As a matter of principle, nothing but programs on the accessor layer should read from or write to the database. That's a very important idea in multi-tier application architecture.

5.2.1   Creating the Table

Our application has a very simple back end that comprises only one table, which has only four columns. There are no real issues of database design to be worked through in this case—no foreign keys, dependencies, or relationships to be established and verified.

The table, to be called cities, needs only to hold the name of each city to which the airline flies and the latitude and longitude of each. Because it's good form—something you should always include in your tables—there will be an automatically incremented id column, as well, just in case there is ever a need to establish relationships with this table.

Here's the SQL code that establishes the table we need in the MySQL database server:

```
cities.sql

DROP TABLE IF EXISTS cities;

CREATE TABLE 'cities' (
    'id' int(11) NOT NULL auto_increment,
    'cityName' varchar(30) NOT NULL default ",
    'latitude' double NOT NULL default '-9999',
    'longitude' double NOT NULL default '-9999',
    PRIMARY KEY ('id')
)
TYPE=MyISAM;
```

Note that the default values given for the latitude and longitude columns are obviously invalid. If we'd used 0 instead, we'd have run the risk of confusion because 0,0 is a real location off the west coast of Africa.

To run that code on a typical MySQL server (assuming you had not created a database to contain the cities table), you'd use a sequence of commands beginning with these:

```
mysql
mysql>create database cities;
Query OK, 1 row affected (0.05 seconds)
mysql>quit
Bye.
```

Those lines logged you in, created a database called cities (the database and the table will have the same name), and logged you out. Then, at the operating system's command line, you'd enter this:

```
mysql cities < cities.sql
```

That runs the SQL statements in cities.sql against the database called cities.

Continuing, there are some rules about the data that is to be stored in the cities table:

- The latitude column contains a decimal representation of degrees latitude, with 0 being the equator, positive numbers being north latitudes, and negative numbers being south latitudes.

- The longitude column contains a decimal representation of degrees longitude, with 0 being the prime meridian through Greenwich, positive numbers being west longitudes, and negative numbers being east longitudes.

Both latitude and longitude values are therefore between −180 and 180.

5.2.2 Populating the Table

To make our table useful, we need to populate it with some city names, latitudes, and longitudes. These SQL statements fill the cities table with data (note that the id column is populated automatically):

```
citiesPopulator.sql

INSERT INTO cities (cityName, latitude, longitude)
values('Sydney', -33.87, -151.22);

INSERT INTO cities (cityName, latitude, longitude)
values('Darwin', -12.47, -130.83);

INSERT INTO cities (cityName, latitude, longitude)
values('Hong Kong', 22.28, -114.15);
```

```
INSERT INTO cities (cityName, latitude, longitude)
values('Mumbai', 19, -72.8);

INSERT INTO cities (cityName, latitude, longitude)
values('Shanghai', 31.23, -121.47);

INSERT INTO cities (cityName, latitude, longitude)
values('Seoul', 37.55, -126.97);

INSERT INTO cities (cityName, latitude, longitude)
values('Copenhagen', 55.67, -12.58);

INSERT INTO cities (cityName, latitude, longitude)
values('Paris', 42.87, -2.33);

INSERT INTO cities (cityName, latitude, longitude)
values('Cairo', 30.05, -31.25);

INSERT INTO cities (cityName, latitude, longitude)
values('Cape Town', -33.92, -18.22);

INSERT INTO cities (cityName, latitude, longitude)
values('Washington', 38.9, 77.03);

INSERT INTO cities (cityName, latitude, longitude)
values('San Francisco', 37.78, 122.42);

INSERT INTO cities (cityName, latitude, longitude)
values('Santiago', -33.45, 70.67);

INSERT INTO cities (cityName, latitude, longitude)
values('Recife', -8.05, 34.87);
```

To run that code, use the same syntax as before at the operating system's command line:

```
mysql cities < citiesPopulator.sql
```

You can see the effects of the populator script by entering the SQL query,

```
SELECT * from cities
```

which should yield results like this:

id	cityName	latitude	longitude
1	Sydney	-33.87	-151.22
2	Darwin	-12.47	-130.83

3	Hong Kong	22.28	-114.15
4	Mumbai	19	-72.8
5	Shanghai	31.23	-121.47
6	Seoul	37.55	-126.97
7	Copenhagen	55.67	-12.58
8	Paris	42.87	-2.33
9	Cairo	30.05	-31.25
10	Cape Town	-33.92	-18.22
11	Washington	38.9	77.03
12	San Francisco	37.78	122.42
13	Santiago	-33.45	70.67
14	Recife	-8.05	34.87

5.3 The Accessor Layer

The accessor layer is the first layer at which we find software written in the PHP language. Essentially, the accessor layer exists to keep SQL statements out of the business logic layer. That's done for reasons of security and improved reliability.

Functions in the accessor layer typically are accessor and mutator functions (otherwise called "getter" and "setter" functions), which retrieve and modify values in the database, respectively. With such functions in place, software lower in the application—in the logic layer, specifically—can (indeed, should) refer to the getter and setter functions and not include a single line of SQL.

The purpose of the accessor layer in this application is to provide two sets of data, each under a different condition. First, when the application is generating the user interface, the accessor layer needs to provide a list, in other words, an array, of the cities whose details are included in the database. Second, the accessor layer needs to be able to take a city name as input and, in response, return an array containing that city's latitude and longitude values. The accessor layer is going to include two significant functions.

5.3.1 Isolating the Database Details

Because the accessor layer is the interface between the database and the software that makes use of it, much of the code in the accessor layer is concerned with connecting to the database server. Furthermore, because there's only one table supporting this simple application, all PHP programs in the accessor layer will connect to it.

This program will use the PEAR DB class for database connectivity, largely because PEAR DB makes it easy to change database server types (say, from MySQL to Oracle) if the need arises. PEAR DB requires certain information when it establishes a connection, including the hostname of the machine on which the database runs, the username and password to be used in establishing a connection, and the name of the table to be queried.

Furthermore, PEAR DB requires a specific string that identifies the type of database server being connected to the application. A list of various servers' key strings appears in the PEAR DB documentation and in Chapter 7, but for now just know that the identifying string that corresponds to a MySQL server is mysql.

Each program in the accessor layer will need all of these details. Because it's possible that they'll change—that the server will move to a different machine, or that the username and password will change—it makes sense to isolate all of the details in a single file. The file can then be imported (using a require_once() statement, typically) into any piece of software that will access the database.

Here is a listing of the most important lines from dbDetails.php:

```
$phptype = 'mysql';     // Type of database server (PEAR-DB standard name string).
$hostspec = 'db2';      // Hostname of database server (or IP address).
$database = 'cities';   // Database name.
$username = 'access';   // Database username.
$password = 'php';      // Database password.
```

The configuration details are all there and commented, ready for modification.

5.3.2 Getting City Names from the Database

The first requirement of this application's accessor layer is that it provide an array containing all the cities whose geographic details appear in the cities table. This is a straightforward matter of an SQL statement based on the SELECT command, but there's a fair bit of PHP packaging that has to go on around it.

The application uses getCities.php to satisfy the city-listing requirement. That file, like all files discussed in this book, is available on the Internet site. It's also listed fully here, but interspersed with explanatory text to clarify what's going on.

```
require_once('nusoap-0.6/nusoap.php');
require_once('dbDetails.php');
```

The first order of business is to import some libraries. The first line imports Dietrich Ayala's NuSOAP library and the second brings in the simple declarations of database details that we moved to a separate file for ease of maintenance.

```
// Establish NuSOAP soap_server object
//and register function as Web Service...

$s = new soap_server;
$s->register('getCities');
$s->service($HTTP_RAW_POST_DATA);
```

These lines refer to NuSOAP classes and establish a SOAP server to which other layers can connect. The SOAP server is set up to catch HTTP requests, and the getCities() function, to be declared momentarily, is made available for external access.

```
function getCities() {
```

```
// Make globals from dbDetails.php available within function scope.

global $phptype;  // Type of database server.
global $hostspec; // Hostname of database server.
global $database; // Database name.
global $username; // Database username.
global $password; // Database password.

// Assemble Data Source Name (DSN) and connect, allowing for errors...

$dsn = "$phptype://$username:$password@$hostspec/$database";

$db = DB::connect($dsn);

if (DB::isError($db)) {
   die ($db->getMessage());
     }
```

The first part of the getCities() function concerns itself with connecting to the database whose details are defined by the variables in dbDetails.php. The variables have to be made available inside the function (that's what the five lines beginning with global are for). Then, they can be used to assemble a datasource name (DSN), which is a uniform resource locator (URL)-like string that PEAR DB uses to establish a connection to a database. An attempt to connect is made; the attempt results in an object that has to be examined to see if it's an error, in which case everything is off.

```
// Assemble and send SQL statement, allowing for errors...

$sql = "SELECT cityName FROM cities ORDER BY cityName";

$result = $db->query($sql);

if (DB::isError($result))
   {
   $errorMessage = $result->getMessage();
   die ($errorMessage);
   }
```

With the connection to the database established, the function proceeds to set a variable equal to an SQL query string (the decision to put the ORDER BY instruction here, rather than in the presentation layer, certainly is debatable). The query then gets sent to the database, which results in an object. That object has to be checked to see if it's an error. If it's not an error, it's an object representing the results of the query.

```
// Extract rows from query results, fitting pieces of data into
```

```
// $returnArray (an associative array) for returning.

while ($row = $result->fetchRow())
   {
   $returnArray[$i]=$row[0];
   ++$i;
   }
```

This loop exists to use MySQL's fetchRow() function against every row in the result object, thus extracting it. Because we know the result set has only one column (the SQL statement requested only cityName), we can take the first element of every row array ($row[0]—the only element) and put it into another array, $returnArray.

```
// Disconnect from database and return $returnArray...

$db->disconnect();

return $returnArray;

}
```

Having extracted all returned rows, the function terminates the database connection and returns $returnArray. Because this function is exposed as a SOAP service, $returnArray could be sent out across the network via the SOAP protocol. It's not a problem; SOAP handles the transmission of arrays without any hassle.

5.3.3   Getting Latitudes and Longitudes from the Database

The other function of the Great Circle application's accessor layer is to get latitude and longitude of a specified city from the database. This piece of accessor software has to take a city name as a parameter and use it in extracting coordinate data from the cities table.

This functionality appears in getLatLong.php, which is listed and commented upon here:

```
require_once('nusoap-0.6/nusoap.php');
require_once('dbDetails.php');

// Establish NuSOAP soap_server object
// and register function as Web Service...

$s = new soap_server;
$s->register('getLatLong');
$s->service($HTTP_RAW_POST_DATA);
```

The program opens much like getCities.php, but with the getLatLong() function being exposed this time.

```
function getLatLong($city) {

// Make globals from dbDetails.php available within function scope.

global $phptype;  // Type of database server.
global $hostspec; // Hostname of database server.
global $database; // Database name.
global $username; // Database username.
global $password; // Database password.

// Assemble Data Source Name (DSN) and connect, allowing for errors...

$dsn = "$phptype://$username:$password@$hostspec/$database";

$db = DB::connect($dsn);

if (DB::isError($db)) {
   die ($db->getMessage());
    }
```

Again, the sole function uses PEAR DB to hook up to a database, assembling a DSN out of the pieces defined in the dbDetails.php file.

```
// Assemble and send SQL statement, allowing for errors...

$sql = "SELECT latitude,longitude FROM cities WHERE cityName='$city'";
```

The SQL query includes $city (note the quotation marks around the variable reference), which came into the function as a parameter.

```
$result = $db->query($sql);

if (DB::isError($result)) {
   $errorMessage = $result->getMessage();
   die ($errorMessage);
    }
```

Then, the function sends the SQL query to the database, and makes sure the result is something other than an error.

```
// Extract rows from query results, fitting pieces of data into
// $returnArray (an associative array) for returning.

while ($row = $result->fetchRow()) {
```

```
$latitude = $row[0];
$longitude = $row[1];

$returnArray['city'] = $city;
$returnArray['latitude'] = $latitude;
$returnArray['longitude'] = $longitude;
}
```

This function differs from getCities() in that it uses the query results, which comprise three columns, to create an associative array. The code inside the while loop relies on the fact that the sequence of the columns in the result set is known—a situation that results from the explicit listing of column names in the SELECT statement.

```
// Disconnect from database and return $returnArray...

$db->disconnect();

return $returnArray;

}
```

When the work of querying the database and transferring the results to an associative array is done, the function shuts down the database connection and returns the associative array containing coordinate information.

5.4   The Business Logic Layer

The business logic layer is where you tackle the problems your program was created to solve. In the logic layer, classes decide what information they need in order to solve their assigned problems, request that information from the accessor layer, manipulate that information as required, and return the ultimate results to the presentation layer for formatting.

The business logic layer in this application does the spherical geometry—the Great Circle calculation itself. The calculation program, calcGreatCircle.php, uses an algorithm that assumes the Earth is perfectly spherical, which it isn't. The calculation is not the point here, so if you're thinking about using this application as a serious navigation tool, think again.

In terms of software requirements, calcGreatCircle.php is interesting because it has to be both a SOAP server and a SOAP client. As a SOAP server, it takes city name pairs from the presentation layer. As a SOAP client, it forwards those city names to the accessor layer, getLatLong.php, specifically, in order to retrieve the latitude and longitude of each.

Here are the contents of calcGreatCircle.php, the sole element of the Great Circle application's business logic layer:

```
require_once('nusoap-0.6/nusoap.php');

// Establish NuSOAP soap_server object
//and register function as Web Service...

$s = new soap_server;
$s->register('calculateGreatCircle');
$s->service($HTTP_RAW_POST_DATA);
```

Only the NuSOAP library is imported; there's no need for the database stuff here. The calculateGreatCircle() function is exposed as a SOAP service.

```
function toRad($degrees) {

// Converts $degrees to equivalent value in radians.

$radians = $degrees * (pi()/180);
return $radians;

}
```

The function toRad() is a utility function that calculateGreatCircle() makes use of. It converts a value expressed in degrees into an equivalent value expressed in radians. This function is not exposed as a SOAP service; it's accessed only by calculateGreatCircle().

```
function calculateGreatCircle($city1, $city2) {

// Calculates Great Circle distance (in km) between $city1 and $city2
// Establish $parameters array and call Web Service to get latitude and
    longitude for $city1...

$parameters = array('city'=>$city1);
$soapclient = new soapclient('http://db2/greatCircle/getLatLong.php');
$returnedArray = $soapclient->call('getLatLong',$parameters);

// Populate simple variables for clarity...

$lat1 = $returnedArray[latitude];
$long1 = $returnedArray[longitude];


// Establish $parameters array and call Web Service to get latitude and
    longitude for $city2...

$parameters = array('city'=>$city2);
```

```php
$soapclient = new soapclient('http://db2/greatCircle/getLatLong.php');
$returnedArray = $soapclient->call('getLatLong',$parameters);

// Populate simple variables for clarity...

$lat2 = $returnedArray[latitude];
$long2 = $returnedArray[longitude];

// Convert degrees to radians

$lat1 = toRad($lat1);
$long1 = toRad($long1);
$lat2 = toRad($lat2);
$long2 = toRad($long2);

// Calculate distance...

$theta = $long2 - $long1;
$distance = acos((sin($lat1) * sin($lat2)) + (cos($lat1) * cos($lat2) *
            cos($theta)));

if ($distance < 0) {
   $distance = $distance + pi();
   }

// Multiply by constant to get kilometers...

$distance = $distance * 6371.2;

return $distance;

}
```

The rest of calcGreatCircle.php has to do with the Great Circle calculation itself, which isn't remarkable except for its extensive use of PHP's trigonometry functions.

5.5 The Presentation Layer

The presentation layer exists for the purpose of providing a user interface, whether the user is a machine or a human being. If the user is a human being, the user interface will likely take the form of an hypertext markup language (HTML) document. They will likely include text boxes, buttons, and selection lists—all the usual elements we see when we use our computers. The details of user interface design (how to arrange your program's interface elements, how your commands should behave, what sort of feedback your users should get, and so on) make up an elaborate field of programming specialty. They're largely beyond the scope of this book, so we'll deal only with the characteristics of the user interface that have to do with communicating with the rest of the application.

If the user is a machine, another software application of some kind, our program should probably generate an extensible markup language (XML) document as output. The beauty of the multi-tier architecture comes through when you consider that it would be just as easy to provide XML, rather than HTML, documents at the presentation layer. With XML results being generated, the application becomes, broadly speaking, more of a Web service (to be used by other machines rather than by people) than a business application. That means someone else could use your whole application as a module in his or her project.

The presentation layer of the Great Circle application comprises a single page, which perhaps not ideally, contains a combination of PHP and HTML code. Its "life cycle" has two parts. First, it displays lists of candidate origin and destination cities, each with a corresponding radio button, and a master Submit button at the bottom of the page. That's shown in Figure 5.2.

When the user chooses cities and clicks the Submit button, the page changes to include the calculated distance between the two previously selected cities, as depicted in Figure 5.3.

Here's a commentary on the presentation layer program, greatCircle.php (the name, which makes no mention of the presentation layer, was chosen because the user may have to type this filename as part of a URL):

```
require_once('nusoap-0.6/nusoap.php');

// Extract from $_POST array to allow for register_globals being off

$city1 = $_POST['origin'];
$city2 = $_POST['destination'];
```

Variables $_POST['origin'] and $_POST[destination] correspond to the name attributes of the two sets of radio buttons in the HTML that appear later in greatCircle.php. When a form is submitted to this program (it's submitted to itself, a process that's explained later in this section), the value attribute of the selected radio button from each group is the value of $_POST['origin'] and $_POST[destination]. Note that it's no longer good practice to refer to $origin and $destination directly, as was reasonable with the older versions of PHP that shipped with the register_globals option (in php.ini) on bydefault. Modern versions of PHP have register_globals off, so we must approach form contents via the superglobal $_POST (or $_GET) array. See Chapter 4 for more information on HTTP POST and HTTP GET operations.

```
// Establish $parameters array and call Web Service to get distance

$parameters = array('city1'=>$city1, 'city2'=>$city2);
$soapclient = new soapclient('http://db2/greatCircle/calcGreatCircle.php');
```

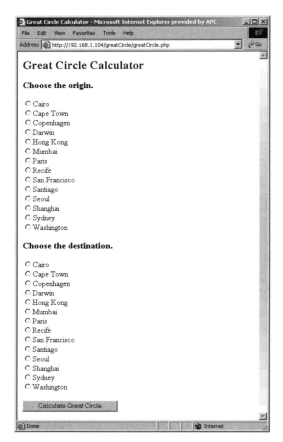

Figure 5.2: The Great Circle presentation layer, before submission of a city pair.

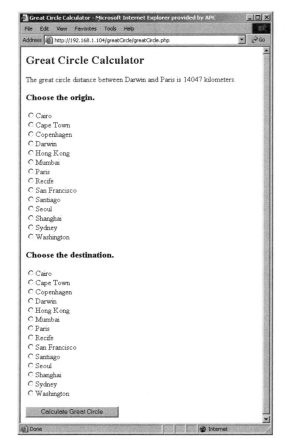

Figure 5.3: The Great Circle presentation layer, after submission of a city pair and ready for another challenge.

```
$distance = $soapclient->call('calculateGreatCircle',$parameters);
$distance = round($distance);
```

The function makes a call to the business logic layer, sending the two city names as parameters for calcGreatCircle to process. The round() function strips the fractional portion from the result, because the algorithm used isn't accurate enough to merit such precision.

```
// Establish $parameters array and call Web Service to get list of cities...

$parameters = array();
```

```
$soapclient = new soapclient('http://db2/greatCircle/getCities.php');
$cities = $soapclient->call('getCities',$parameters);
```

Another SOAP call, this time directly to the accessor layer, secures an array of city names. This array is used twice in generating the HTML interface.

```
<html>

<head>
<title>Great Circle Calculator</title>
</head>

<body>

<H2>Great Circle Calculator</H2>


if ($city1 != "" AND $city2 != "") {
echo "The great circle distance between $city1 and $city2 is $distance
   kilometers.";
}
```

This conditional statement ensures that the calculated Great Circle distance is displayed only if such a calculated distance exists. The result isn't shown the first time the page is loaded, in other words.

```
<form action="<?php $PHP_SELF; ?>" method="post">

<H3>Choose the origin.</H3>


foreach ($cities as $city) {
   echo "<input type='RADIO' name='origin'
value='$city'>$city <br>\n";
}
```

A simple PHP loop goes through the $cities array and generates the HTML radio buttons representing origin cities.

```
<H3>Choose the destination.</H3>


foreach ($cities as $city) {
   echo "<input type='RADIO' name='destination' value='$city'>$city <br>\n";
}
```

A nearly identical loop, also operating on the `$cities` array, generates the HTML radio buttons representing destination cities.

```
<P>

<input type="SUBMIT" name="submitButton" value="Calculate Great Circle">

</form>

</body>

</html>
```

The remainder of the program is simple HTML code.

5.6 Questions and Exercises

Here are some questions and exercises meant to further your thinking about the material contained in this chapter.

1. This chapter didn't implement the elsewhere layer, which was introduced at the beginning of the chapter. How might an elsewhere layer be put to advantageous use in the Great Circle application?

2. If you were to expand the scope of the Great Circle application to enable the user to specify a city name manually, rather than choosing one from a list, what problems might this introduce? How could you deal with them?

3. If you didn't want to use SOAP for interlayer communication, what other strategies could you use?

4. See if you can redesign the presentation layer of the Great Circle application so that the PHP code is completely separated from the HTML code.

chapter **6**

The Persistence Layer

Careful design and construction of your multi-tier application's back end is vital to the success of the application as a whole. If you carefully design the database that persistently stores your application's information, you'll have an easier time building the rest of its software modules. This chapter aims to show you how to design and set up your application's back end.

6.1 Choosing a Persistent Storage Mechanism

Technically, your database can be any mechanism capable of storing data when the power goes off. You can use files for this purpose, but lacking a compelling reason to use them, you'll want to use a Relational Database Management System (RDBMS). RDBMSs, we'll just call them database servers, because that's what everyone calls them in real life, have lots of advantages over file-based storage, including:

- Easy storage and retrieval of data. All significant database servers support standard structured query language (SQL), as well as (usually) a number of proprietary and semiproprietary extensions to the basic language.

- Optimization. Through a variety of generally opaque magic, database servers do their best to speed the process of data storage and retrieval.

- The ability to recover from design and implementation errors. Most database servers have a journaling feature that allows you to "turn back the clock" on a database, undoing all changes that occurred since a particular time. This is handy when you make an error in the software that communicates with the database, and it makes unwanted changes to the stored data. They also support the concept of transactions,

73

which are sets of related changes. For example, in a bank, a transfer transaction comprises a reduction in the value of one account and an increase in the value of another. You can't have one without the other, without having a real problem.

■ Security. Database servers manage user access rights, either by examining users' rights on an operating system or by keeping track of their own user lists and rights assignments.

■ Survivability. Database servers have support for data redundancy and backup operations that help guarantee that important data can survive disasters.

For those reasons, the persistent storage in a multi-tier software system is usually handled by a database management server.

6.1.1   Choosing a Database Server

Because we're going to write our accessor layer, the layer of PHP software that directly interacts with the database server, around the PEAR DB library, we're limited (unless we want to write a custom PEAR DB extension) to the servers with which PEAR DB interfaces. Fortunately, the list is long, and includes all the major open-source and commercial database servers:

■ MySQL (http://www.mysql.com)

■ PostgreSQL (http://www.postgresql.com)

■ InterBase (http://www.borland.com/interbase)

■ Mini SQL (mSQL) (http://www.hughes.com.au)

■ Microsoft SQL Server (http://www.microsoft.com/sql)

■ Oracle 7/8/8i (http://www.oracle.com)

■ Open Database Connectivity (ODBC) (http://msdn.microsoft.com)

■ SyBase (http://www.sybase.com)

■ Informix (http://www-3.ibm.com/software/data/informix)

■ FrontBase (http://www.frontbase.com)

The only major database server that's missing is IBM DB2, and non-PEAR libraries exist to allow connectivity to that server. Further, note that ODBC gives us a way to access other databases for which there is an ODBC driver. ODBC adds yet another layer of abstraction (and hence some processing overhead), and it's only relevant in the Microsoft Windows environment, but it's an option.

In this book, we'll use MySQL 4.01. It's free for our purposes, and, with the InnoDB table type that's discussed in the next section, it provides all the features we require. Its performance is good, too—far more than adequate for anything we need here. MySQL is available for download from MySQL AB of Germany.

6.1.2 Selecting Development Tools

Although it's almost always possible to manipulate your database server using only the tools with which it ships, MySQL, for example, has an extensive command-line interface. you'll often benefit by having other tools on hand. These tend to be specialized in purpose, and so make specific parts of the design and implementation process faster and easier. In the case of MySQL, a whole range of excellent tools has sprung up. Many of them are open source and free to use under most circumstances; others are commercial but available in a trial version that has limited capabilities or stops working after a specified time.

On the other hand, you should remember that MySQL has its own command-line interface (documented at http://www.mysql.com). Pretty much every MySQL task can be done with the command-line interface, albeit often with a lot of hassle.

MySQL Control Center

MySQL AB, the same company that puts out MySQL itself, publishes MySQL Control Center (MySQLCC). It's a client that connects to MySQL database servers and the databases that run on them. Though it's still early in its release cycle, not yet at version 1.0 as of publication, and once in a while exhibits some odd behavior (like not telling you there's a problem when you ask it to make an InnODB table, and the server won't let it) it's still hugely useful. It's at http://www.mysql.com.

CASE Studio

A product of Charonware, CASE studio is a database design and documentation tool. Basically, it runs under Windows and hooks up to a database—it supports several database servers—over an ODBC connection. Over that connection, it can reverse engineer an existing database, effectively figuring out all of its table relationships for purposes of documentation or design validation. If you register your copy of CASE Studio, you can work the other way and have the software build a database based on your schematic diagram. You'll find CASE Studio at http://www.casestudio.com.

VMWare

When designing a multi-tier software application, it's not really possible to test the network performance of a system unless you have a number of machines connected on a local area network (LAN). Plus, you'll sometimes want to try different client/server combinations, such as connecting to a Linux-based MySQL server with a copy of MySQL Control Center that's running under Windows. The most economical way to do this is with VMWare, a product that allows you to run several completely independent virtual machines on the same physical hardware. You need a pretty hefty allotment of memory and processor grunt if you want to run more than a couple of virtual machines, but the flexibility of virtual machines is fantastic. Networking among them is easy, and it's easy to start over if you trash a configuration. VMWare can be had in a 30-day demo version at http://www.vmware.com.

6.2   Designing the Database

6.2.1   General Database Design Principles

Take time in designing your database. It is the foundation of your entire application, and time spent doing it right will pay dividends as you design and implement other layers (notably the accessor layer, which refers directly to the database). If your project (or budget) isn't big enough to farm the whole database design and implementation process off to a specialist, then allow yourself to study the problem and try a couple of alternate solutions on your own. As Frederick P. Brooks writes in *The Mythical Man-Month* (Addison-Wesley, Boston, 1991), software projects very often require an extensive false start and then a fresh beginning in order to get things right.

A number of excellent database design books exist. One of those that's most accessible is *Database Design for Mere Mortals* (Addison-Wesley, Boston, 2003), by Michael Hernandez.

The database is for data storage. Period. That principle means that the database should be a structure in which data is stored, and nothing more. No processing should take place in the database layer. Stored procedures are most definitely out. Only the storage of the data, and processes independent of the business problem (such as optimization algorithms and security-management operations) should take place in the database.

6.2.2   Specific Design Requirements

The first step in building a database is to clearly state what the database is meant to do. Consider the scope of the application your persistence layer will serve.

The design of our database has to do with the application that will be built throughout the course of this book. The nature of an application to be built would normally be established through some sort of interview process and requirements-gathering procedure (it would if you were lucky, anyway, and enjoyed the luxury of some time for gathering requirements). Here, the mission statement is just going to appear out of the void, ex nihilo, because this is a book. Here it is.

The Mission Statement

Our customer is an individual who provides technical consulting services to a number of customers around the world. As a result of his work, he bills his customers in a number of currencies, and maintains bank accounts in a number of financial institutions in various countries. He receives payments into and makes disbursements out of each of these accounts (though without great transaction volume), and makes transfers among them.

Our customer requires a software solution that, broadly speaking, has capabilities parallel to those of an ordinary personal-finance program, such as Quicken or Microsoft Money. The customer needs to be able to see transaction histories for each of his accounts, record new transactions, and see reports on, for example, the amount paid to a particular vendor during a specified period. He should be able to add new accounts (including accounts at new institutions, possibly denominated in currencies previously unused in his accounting).

Unlike Quicken and Microsoft Money, though, our customer requires that his solution be able to distinguish among a large number of currencies, and be able to present reports that summarize activities across all accounts in terms of any selected currency. All currency conversions should be performed automatically, with information taken from public resources on the Internet.

Furthermore, the customer wants a single, central data store, to be run on the secure and carefully managed servers of a hosting service. Because the hosting service can most easily provide MySQL servers, that software will likely be the best choice for use on the back end. The rest of the application software should run on the hosting service's computers, as well. The customer should be able to access, via a once-per-session login procedure, all features of the application from any modern Internet browser.

Analyzing the Mission Statement

From the mission statement, we can derive a statement of what our database has to do. Let's begin with a broad statement:

The database for this application will centrally store data related to bank accounts, currencies, and transactions as specified and recorded by our customer (Figure 6.1).

Thinking about that for a second, it becomes clear that a concept such as "bank account" is complicated and potentially depends on a lot of information, like the institution that manages the account. It's important to use care as you go about setting up related tables to store application data.

6.3 Understanding Table Relationships and Normalization

Normalization is an important database concept, and one that we hear a lot about as we explore database design. Essentially, normalization is the application of principles, mostly common-sense ones, and mostly ones you're already aware of, that make relational databases more efficient.

There are six degrees of normalization, referred to as first through fifth normal form and Boyce-Codd Normal Form. First normal form can be abbreviated 1NF, second normal form as 2NF, and so on; Boyce-Codd Normal Form is shortened to BCNF.

Higher normal forms are supersets of lower ones, by definition. A database in 2NF is also in 1NF, and a database in 3NF is also in 2NF and 1NF. Normalization of a database, or examination of a database to determine its degree of normalization, is therefore an iterative process that begins with 1NF and moves up from there. Unless you're dealing with very complicated databases with elaborate relationships among tables, you can safely ignore all but 1NF.

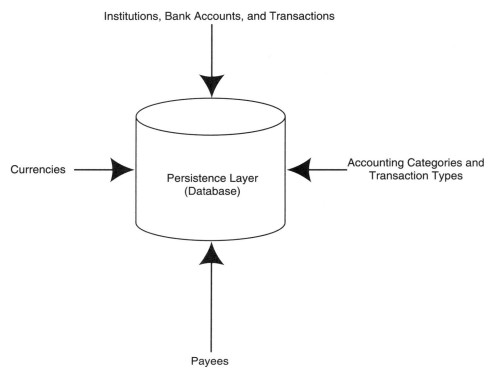

Figure 6.1: The back end of our new application stores data that defines financial records.

6.3.1   First Normal Form

A table in 1NF meets two requirements.

First, it has columns that contain only atomic values, meaning values that cannot be divided meaningfully. This is why we usually split a person's name into two or three columns (firstName, surname, etc.). A single name column, which might contain something like "Benjamin Franklin," would prove a problem if we wanted to sort rows by family name (even more so if the table also contained names in which the family name came first). There are debatable points here. Is a local telephone number meaningful without its area code? Without its country code? It's up to the architect to decide whether a piece of data is atomic or requires further division.

The second requirement of a table in 1NF is that it have no repeating groups. A repeating group is any collection of two or more columns that are logically related to one another. Repeating groups often crop up when you have one-to-many and many-to-many relationships between tables. For example, if we had a company table that included three columns representing links to the contact table, meaning each company could have up to three associated contacts, the table would have a repeating group and the table would not be in 1NF. The following table is not in 1NF.

```
Table: company
name    contact1    contact2    contact3
```

Two of the most obvious problems with this table are that it uses three times as much space as needed for companies with one contact, and there is no neat way to associate more than three contacts with one company. It's a poor design.

The solution to the problem of repeating groups is, as is often the case, more tables. A mapping table establishes many-to-many relationships between the company table and the contact table.

```
Table: company
id    name
1     AlphaCo
2     BoBoCo
3     CapCorp


Table: contact
id    name
1     Alice
2     Bob
3     Camille
4     Dov


Table: companyContactMapping
id    companyID    contactID
1     1            3
2     3            4
3     2            1
4     3            2
5     3            3
```

Note that the mapping table comprises only key values: Its own primary key, plus two foreign key columns—one each for rows in the company table and rows in the contact table. With the addition of the mapping table, the tables are in 1NF. With a bit of studying (via queries that are easily coded into SQL), it becomes clear that Alice works at BoBoCo, Bob and Dov work at CapCorp, and busy Camille holds down jobs at both AlphaCo and CapCorp. The mapping table makes possible a many-to-many relationship.

If the relationship is to be one-to-many instead of many-to-many (if we assume that while a company can have several employees, a person can only work for one company), the table structure is even simpler. We can maintain 1NF by putting a column in the contact table that establishes a link to the company table, like this:

```
Table: company
```

```
id   name
1    AlphaCo
2    BoBoCo
3    CapCorp

Table: contact
id   name         companyID
1    Alice        2
2    Bob          3
3    Camille      1
4    Dov          3
```

Camille no longer has a place at CapCorp, but we have one table fewer and our database still exhibits 1NF.

6.3.2   Further Normal Forms

There is more to database normalization than 1NF, but the higher normal forms become increasingly academic and hard to conceptualize. Practically speaking, if you obey the following rules of 1NF, to wit, you will have an efficient database in all but a few obscure cases.

- Your tables' contents are as atomic as they can be while retaining their usefulness.
- There are no repeating groups in your tables.

For information on the higher normal forms, consult *Database Design for Mere Mortals,* by Michael Hernandez.

6.4   Deciding on a Table Schema

We know that we're going to build a database that serves as a repository of financial data. The database will change over time as checks are written and withdrawals made, and so will be somewhat transaction oriented. It also, though, has a reporting requirement: The user will need to examine the data in the database without making changes to it.

But what, specifically, is in the database? At this point in the design process, we take an initial shot at listing values that will be stored. Here's an initial list for our global bookkeeping application:

- Information about banks,
- Information about accounts,
- Information about transactions (checks, withdrawals, and interaccount transfers), and
- Information about currencies.

In this part of the process, we might think of information such as the net value of all existing accounts and consider storing such information in the database. It is important that such information should not be stored in the database because it's calculated. We should rely on the software elsewhere in our application to come up with such values for us—and indeed we will write a business-logic layer that provides a net value figure.

6.4.1 Initial Table Specifications

Once you have that preliminary list written, you can start to think about converting it to more concrete entities of the kind that can be built into the structure of a database. Specifically, we need to convert our list of information categories into specifications for tables, column headers, and datatypes.

A lot of the time, your general information categories will correspond directly to table names. In this application, for example, we certainly will want to have a table that lists the banks with which our client does business. We'll name that table ACCT_institutions, on the logic that the database server might work with applications other than the global bookkeeping one and, we should have a standard prefix (ACCT_) to distinguish the tables that interest us. Furthermore, it's possible that the customer would want to record accounts at brokerages, mortgage companies, and other financial companies. Hence, ACCT_institutions makes sense as a name.

What data defines a bank? The name, of course. Also the street address, city, state, postal code, country, fax number, and phone number. We should record the name of a contact person at the bank, too. These are our column headers (most of them, anyway, more in a moment). And let's refer to them as "institutions," too, so we can store information about mortgage companies and credit card services as well, and refer to it in an intuitive way. Explicitly stated, the elements that define a financial institution are:

```
institutionName
streetAddress
city
state
postcode
country
contact
```

These will become columns in ACCT_institution, the table that stores data about financial institutions.

Every table should have a primary key, which is a special column header for which all rows have a unique, non-null value. The easiest way to establish a primary key is to establish a column called id, assign it the integer datatype (technically, it's the INT datatype in MySQL), and tell the database server to automatically increment it as rows are added to the table. Don't worry about the details of how to do that right now.

The next step is to decide on datatypes and sizes for all of these column headers. This decision is something of a balancing act, because you never want your table to be unable to accommodate an important piece of data, but neither do you want to waste storage space with columns that are much larger than they need to be.

A complete treatment of MySQL datatypes is outside the scope of this book, and the details of the datatypes available in the database server you choose to use may be different anyway. Refer to your database server's documentation for further information. You'll find some links to documentation for popular servers at the end of this chapter. Be aware, though, that the varchar datatype is a very flexible datatype that essentially holds a character string of some specified maximum length. A column that is to be given the varchar type with a maximum length of 50 characters is defined as varchar(50).

In this table, the revised list of columns, complete with proposed datatypes, looks like this:

```
id: integer
institutionName: varchar(100)
streetAddress: varchar(100)
city: varchar(30)
state: varchar(20)
postcode: varchar(100)
country: varchar(30)
contact: integer
```

Why is the contact column an integer? It would be simple to declare it as another short-ish varchar field, but if you think about the nature of contacts they're people, with their own names, direct phone lines, e-mail addresses, and so on—most of the information that defines them wouldn't really fit into this table. Although we could associate the name Ruth-Anne Krinklemeyer with the institution record itself, that would enable us to ask to speak to only Ruth-Anne when we called the general bank number. It would be far more useful to recognize (and record) Lee-Anne as a separate entity in the database. Specifically, she should be represented by a row in another table, presumably one called ACCT_contacts. This is a relationship between tables, and such relationships are what's special about relational database servers.

The link between a given row in the ACCT_institutions table and the row corresponding to the relevant contact in the ACCT_contacts table is established by an integer. We store an integer in the contact column of the ACCT_institutions table. This integer corresponds to a value in the id column, the primary key, of the ACCT_contacts table. Because the contact column of the ACCT_institutions table is used this way, it's called a foreign key. This is how we establish a relationship, and hence is why we call this sort of database a relational database.

In databases as in life, relationships introduce a whole set of special problems to solve, as well as a way of dealing with other problems. These tradeoffs are addressed in Section 6.3.

Continuing with our specifications for the ACCT_institutions table, it's true that not all countries have states, and not all countries have postal codes. On the other hand, all banks have names, and all banks are located in one country or another. This sort of analysis is required when deciding which fields should be able to be null, and which must have values. It would seem that the state, postcode, faxNumber, phoneNumber, and contact columns could legitimately contain null values, on the logic that it's quite likely that the customer wouldn't know a bank's fax number or that he wouldn't know anyone in particular there. No other column could contain null without compromising the validity of the data in the table.

Figuring out the important data in describing a financial institution is simple enough—you just think about what you'd need if you wanted to contact a particular bank, and add each element to a list. On other jobs, the task of naming columns is more daunting. In those cases, it's often helpful to look at the documents used to describe the entity. Paper checks, purchase orders, engineering change notices, index cards, and lots of other office paperwork can ease the process of identifying key pieces of information.

Better yet, if the customer is replacing an older software system (perhaps even with an existing database), have a look at its design. No doubt business requirements have changed since it was created, but a look at its table structures will help keep you from forgetting about important data.

6.4.2 Further Table Specifications

Our application will require a number of other tables. The details of these tables are discussed in greater detail when we create them using SQL statements, but at this point in the design process it is important to have a solid understanding of the significance of each table in the database, and how each table links to other tables. The best way to do this is with a diagram of the database schema. It's possible to draw such a diagram by hand, but it's easier if you use a documentation and design tool such as CASE Studio (Figure 6.2).

6.5 Translating the Schema into SQL

Eventually, you have to make the leap from theoretical design to practical implementation. When building a database, that means writing some SQL statements that actually create the tables you've been hypothesizing about and establish the required relationships among them. This section explains how to write SQL statements that do what earlier sections of this chapter have discussed.

These statements were written for MySQL 4—they were tested on version 4.01b, to be exact. They, or close approximations of them, should work on pretty much any SQL-compliant database, including all of those in PEAR DB compatibility list. To provide exact

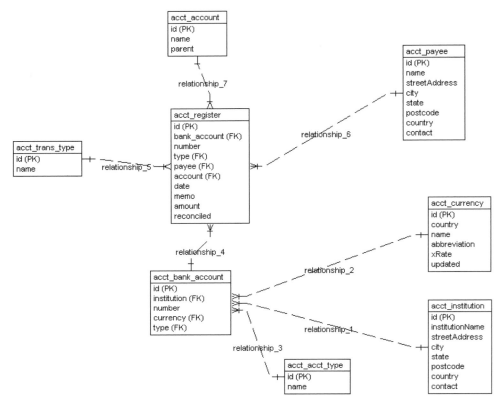

Figure 6.2: The complete database schema for our accounting application shows relationships among tables.

SQL statements for all popular database servers would take a lot of space, so remember that this is the last chapter in which our application is concerned with the peculiarities of any database server. All subsequent chapters will either refer to the database through the accessor layer (the presentation, business logic, and elsewhere layers) or through the PEAR DB classes (the accessor layer itself).

All of the table-creation statements appear together in the file currawongTables.sql. The easiest way to run the statements quickly is from a command line, like this:

```
mysql < currawongTables.sql
```

Alternately, you can open the file in a visual environment, such as MySQLCC, and execute the statements from there.

The contents of currawongTables.sql are dissected in the following sections.

6.5.1 Creating the ACCT_account Table

The ACCT_account table contains facts about categories into which income and expenses are grouped, things like payables, receivables, office rent, and travel expenses. It should not be confused with the ACCT_bank_accounts table, which holds data about accounts at financial institutions that represent assets or debts. Here's the code that creates ACCT_account table, interspersed with comments:

```
DROP TABLE IF EXISTS ACCT_account;
```

The DROP TABLE IF EXISTS statement gets rid of the table if a previous version of it exists. If no such previous version exists, the statement does nothing. DROP statements like this are handy if you expect to be creating your collection of tables several times over, with different characteristics each time—and you probably will, in the course of a typical development job. DROP statements are good practice. On the other hand, they are a kind of delete statement, so you might want to keep backups of your tables and their contents if you're not 100 percent sure of what you're doing.

```
CREATE TABLE 'ACCT_account'
('id' int NOT NULL AUTO_INCREMENT ,
'name' varchar(100) NOT NULL DEFAULT " ,
'parent' int DEFAULT " ,
PRIMARY KEY ('id'))
TYPE=InnoDB;
```

The CREATE TABLE clause sets up a table with an automatically incremented id column, which is later designated the primary key. There are also a couple of other data columns. By setting the table type to InnoDB, we make it possible for other tables, the ones containing the transaction register, for example, to use the id column of this table as a foreign key. A foreign key in an InnoDB table must point to another InnoDB table.

6.5.2 Creating the ACCT_trans_type Table

The ACCT_trans_type table holds information about transaction types, such as cash deposits, checks, electronic transfers, and credit card charges. This table, once populated with standard values, shouldn't change much, though it might get a new row from time to time, particularly as new kinds of accounts are opened.

Here is the code for creating the ACCT_trans_type table:

```
DROP TABLE IF EXISTS ACCT_trans_type;

CREATE TABLE 'ACCT_trans_type'
('id' int NOT NULL AUTO_INCREMENT ,
'name' varchar(25) NOT NULL DEFAULT " ,
PRIMARY KEY ('id')) TYPE=InnoDB;
```

There's nothing complicated to this drop-and-create sequence. The two statements simply get rid of the table if it exists already, then create it afresh as an InnoDB table containing only an auto-incremented primary key column and a text name.

6.5.3   Creating the ACCT_acct-type Table

The ACCT_acct-type table contains a list of categories into which we group financial accounts. This table is meant to contain rows designating varieties of account, such as savings, checking, and mortgage.

Here's the creation code:

```
DROP TABLE IF EXISTS ACCT_acct_type;

CREATE TABLE 'ACCT_acct_type'
('id' int NOT NULL AUTO_INCREMENT ,
'name' varchar(15) NOT NULL DEFAULT " ,
PRIMARY KEY ('id')) TYPE=InnoDB;
```

It's straightforward, simply dropping any extant table of the required name and replacing it with a simple two-column table. The ACCT_acct_type table is of type InnoDB so other tables can use its id column as their foreign keys and expect to have relationships properly enforced.

6.5.4   Creating the ACCT_currency Table

The ACCT_currency table contains the currencies in which transactions take place, as well as their values (exchange rates) relative to the U.S. dollar. Here is the code for setting up the table:

```
DROP TABLE IF EXISTS ACCT_currency;

CREATE TABLE 'ACCT_currency'
('id' int NOT NULL AUTO_INCREMENT ,
'country' varchar(100) NOT NULL DEFAULT " ,
'name' varchar(100) NOT NULL DEFAULT " ,
'abbreviation' varchar(100) NOT NULL DEFAULT " ,
'xRate' real NOT NULL DEFAULT " ,
'updated' timestamp ,
PRIMARY KEY ('id'))
TYPE=InnoDB;
```

The interesting bit in this creation statement is the updated column, which is of datatype timestamp. The timestamp datatype contains, logically enough, information about a date and time, but the great thing about it is that columns of type timestamp are automatically updated to the current date/time value whenever the row containing them is updated.

In this case, the updated column will contain a piece of data that indicates when any column in the row was last changed. Typically, this will correspond to the date and time the exchange rate (contained in the xRate column) was last modified.

6.5.5 Creating the ACCT_payee Table

The ACCT_payee table holds information about people and companies with whom or with which transactions are concluded. Here is how it's set up:

```
DROP TABLE IF EXISTS ACCT_payee;

CREATE TABLE 'ACCT_payee'
('id' int NOT NULL AUTO_INCREMENT ,
'name' varchar(100) NOT NULL DEFAULT " ,
'streetAddress' varchar(100) DEFAULT " ,
'city' varchar(100) DEFAULT " ,
'state' varchar(100) DEFAULT " ,
'postcode' varchar(100) DEFAULT " ,
'country' varchar(100) DEFAULT " ,
'contact' int DEFAULT ",
PRIMARY KEY ('id'))
TYPE=InnoDB;
```

The table is quite unremarkable, other than that it's an InnoDB table so that other tables may use its id column as a foreign key.

6.5.6 Creating the ACCT_institution Table

The ACCT_institution table holds contact information for banks, lenders, brokers, and other financial institutions. It's basically another name-and-address table of the type that has appeared a couple of times in this chapter already. Here's the creation code:

```
DROP TABLE IF EXISTS ACCT_institution;

CREATE TABLE 'ACCT_institution'
('id' int NOT NULL AUTO_INCREMENT ,
'institutionName' varchar(100) NOT NULL DEFAULT " ,
'streetAddress' varchar(100) NOT NULL DEFAULT " ,
'city' varchar(30) NOT NULL DEFAULT " ,
'state' varchar(20) DEFAULT " ,
'postcode' varchar(100) DEFAULT " ,
'country' varchar(30) NOT NULL DEFAULT " ,
'contact' int DEFAULT " ,
PRIMARY KEY ('id'))
TYPE=InnoDB;
```

6.5.7 Creating the ACCT_bank_account Table

The ACCT_bank_account table contains information about accounts at institutions, as distinct from the "accounting accounts" contained in the ACCT_accounts table.

The ACCT_bank_account table is interesting in that it is the first table in this database with foreign keys. A bank account, of course, is associated with a financial institution, a currency, and an account type. Those relationships are reflected in the table definition statement shown here:

```
DROP TABLE IF EXISTS ACCT_bank_account;

CREATE TABLE 'ACCT_bank_account'
('id' int NOT NULL AUTO_INCREMENT ,
'institution' int NOT NULL DEFAULT '',
'number' varchar(100) NOT NULL DEFAULT '' ,
'description' varchar(100) NOT NULL DEFAULT '' ,
'currency' int NOT NULL DEFAULT '',
'type' int NOT NULL DEFAULT '',
PRIMARY KEY ('id'),
INDEX (institution),
FOREIGN KEY (institution)
REFERENCES ACCT_institution(id)
ON UPDATE CASCADE ON DELETE RESTRICT,
INDEX (currency),
FOREIGN KEY (currency)
REFERENCES ACCT_currency(id)
ON UPDATE CASCADE ON DELETE RESTRICT,
INDEX (type),
FOREIGN KEY (type)
REFERENCES ACCT_acct_type(id)
ON UPDATE CASCADE ON DELETE RESTRICT)
TYPE=InnoDB;
```

In defining a foreign key, four operations take place. First, we index the column that is to be defined as a foreign key:

```
INDEX (institution),
```

When a column is indexed, it is ordered for fast searching. Then, we declare explicitly that it is a foreign key:

```
FOREIGN KEY (institution)
```

Then, we establish a connection to a column in a remote table (which, because this is an InnoDB table, must also be of InnoDB type):

```
REFERENCES ACCT_institution(id)
```

Note that the id column of the ACCT_institution table is a primary key, so there can be no ambiguity about which ACCT_institution row is identified by a given value in the

ACCT_bank_account table. Finally, the rules governing the relationship between the two tables are defined:

```
ON UPDATE CASCADE ON DELETE RESTRICT
```

That's actually two distinct rules. The first, ON UPDATE CASCADE, indicates that when the value of the referenced field changes, the value of the referring field should change in the same way. That is, if the id value of the referenced row in the ACCT_currency table changes, the id value of the referring row in the ACCT_bank_account table should change to the same value. By including ON UPDATE CASCADE, we ensure that the reference remains valid even if the referenced table changes.

The second rule, ON DELETE RESTRICT, describes what should happen if someone or something tries to delete the referred-to row. The RESTRICT constraint prevents the deletion from going ahead. To put it another way, an attempt to delete a row that is referred to from a table set up with ON DELETE RESTRICT will encounter an error message.

These kinds of restrictions are new with the InnoDB table type. Other table types, such as the very popular MyISAM type, do not enforce foreign key restrictions.

6.5.8 Creating the ACCT_register Table

The ACCT_register table contains information about transactions that take place among the accounts, such as deposits, checks, transfers, interest payments, and so on. Because it's concerned with describing activities, rather than entities, it stands to reason that ACCT_register would be full of foreign keys. It is:

```
DROP TABLE IF EXISTS ACCT_register;

CREATE TABLE 'ACCT_register'
('id' int NOT NULL AUTO_INCREMENT ,
'bank_account' int NOT NULL DEFAULT '',
'number' int DEFAULT '',
'type' int NOT NULL DEFAULT '',
'payee' int NOT NULL DEFAULT '',
'account' int NOT NULL DEFAULT '',
'date' datetime NOT NULL DEFAULT '' ,
'memo' varchar(100) DEFAULT '' ,
'amount' real NOT NULL DEFAULT '' ,
'reconciled' bool NOT NULL DEFAULT '' ,
PRIMARY KEY ('id'),
INDEX (bank_account),
FOREIGN KEY (bank_account)
REFERENCES ACCT_bank_account(id)
ON UPDATE CASCADE ON DELETE RESTRICT,
INDEX (type),
```

```
FOREIGN KEY (type)
REFERENCES ACCT_trans_type(id)
ON UPDATE CASCADE ON DELETE RESTRICT,
INDEX (payee),
FOREIGN KEY (payee)
REFERENCES ACCT_payee(id)
ON UPDATE CASCADE ON DELETE RESTRICT,
INDEX (account),
FOREIGN KEY (account)
REFERENCES ACCT_account(id)
ON UPDATE CASCADE ON DELETE RESTRICT)
TYPE=InnoDB;
```

Four separate foreign keys are established in this creation statement. Links are made to the ACCT_bank_account, ACCT_trans_type, ACCT_payee, and ACCT_account tables, all of which are central to defining the nature of a financial transaction. In all cases, though, it's the same four-step process to establish a foreign key: INDEX, then FOREIGN KEY, then REFERENCES, then ON UPDATE.

Fundamentals of Relational Databases for N-Tier Applications As this chapter shows, the primary governing principle of a relational database is that everything that is to be recorded appears in exactly one place in the database. Tables exist to group pieces of data into logical collections, enabling us to store, for example, the name and contact details of a particular business contact in one table, while storing the details of his or her company in another table. Our two tables might look like this:

```
Table contact
fname    lname    address    phone


Table company
companyName    address    phone
```

The SQL for creating the contact table would look like this:
```
CREATE TABLE 'contact' ('fname' varchar(30), 'lname' varchar(30),
'address' varchar(100), 'phone' varchar(30)) TYPE=MyISAM;
```

The SQL for creating the company table would look like this:
```
CREATE TABLE 'company' ('companyName' varchar(30), 'address'
varchar(100), 'phone' varchar(30)) TYPE=MyISAM;
```

To continue this example, it is true that the contact (the individual) works for a company, and it is true that we want this relationship to be recorded in our database. If we were to add a column for the company name in the contacts table, even if we left all other company details in the company table, we'd violate the principle of putting everything into the database exactly once. We would have created a maintenance problem, for two reasons:

1. If the company ever changes its name, we'd have to make adjustments not only to the company table, but also potentially to many rows in the contacts table.

2. There would be a risk of the company name value not matching in the two tables, or even in various rows in the contacts table. One contact could be recorded as an employee of "Bergman International;" another might have "Bergman Inc" in the company field. Though logically equivalent to a human being, these two values are not the same when it's time to write a query.

So, we must rely on a different method of establishing relationships between records in the contact table and records in the company table. This is what keys are for.

Recall that when we create a table, we endow it with a special column that's usually defined as an auto-incrementing integer. In populating the table, we never fill this column explicitly, and instead rely on the database server software to populate it automatically as we add columns.

To make a reference between a row in one table and a row in another, the referring row contains a column for a foreign key. A foreign key is a value, stored in one table, that equates to a primary key in another table. In the case of the relationship between contacts and companies, the two tables would look like this:

```
Table contact
id   fname   lname   address   phone   companyID


Table company
id   companyName   address   phone
```

In each table, the id column is designated the primary key.

The companyID column in the contacts table contains a value that appears in the id column of the company table. The companyID column is therefore a foreign key. This relationship is established at table-creation time by means of a FOREIGN KEY... REFERENCES sequence. Here are SQL statements that create the two tables:

```
CREATE TABLE 'company'
('id' int NOT NULL AUTO_INCREMENT ,
'companyName' varchar(30) NOT NULL DEFAULT '',
'address' varchar(50) NOT NULL DEFAULT '' ,
'phone' varchar(20) NOT NULL DEFAULT '',
PRIMARY KEY ('id'))
TYPE=InnoDB
```

```
      CREATE TABLE 'contact'
      ('id' int NOT NULL AUTO_INCREMENT,
      'companyName' varchar(30),
      'address' varchar(100),
      'phone' varchar(30),
      'companyID' int,
      PRIMARY KEY ('id'),
      INDEX (companyID),
      FOREIGN KEY (companyID)
      REFERENCES company(id)
      ON UPDATE CASCADE ON DELETE RESTRICT)
      TYPE=InnoDB
```
The most interesting line in these table-creation statements is this:
```
      'companyID' int NOT NULL REFERENCES company(id),
```
That line establishes the foreign key in contacts, giving it the integer datatype (which is the datatype of the id column in the company table) and using REFERENCES to establish an explicit link to the company table.

6.6   Populating the Tables

This book's supporting files include one called populator.sql, which fills the new tables with standard values that will enable you to use Currawong Accounting right away.

The easiest way to run the populator script is from a command line, like this:

```
mysql < populator.sql
```

There's no point in listing the contents of populator.sql here, because they're very repetitive. The file comprises about a hundred INSERT statements, like this:

```
INSERT INTO ACCT_currency (country, name, abbreviation, xrate)
values('Hong Kong', 'Dollar', 'HKD', 0.13);
```

That statement inserts the specified values into the specified columns of ACCT_currency. Sequence matters. "Hong Kong" goes into the country column because country is first in the columns list, and "Hong Kong" is first in the countries list.

The sequence in which tables are populated by the statements in populator.sql also is important. Have a look at the file and notice that ACCT_bank_account and ACCT_register are among the tables populated last. That's because they depend on making reference to the contents of other tables, such as ACCT_currency. Without an ACCT_currency primary key value to refer to, you could not add a row to ACCT_register.

6.7 Questions and Exercises

1. Briefly state what's required for each of the three most important normal forms (1NF through 3NF). Of the requirements, which would you say is most important to efficiency, and why?

2. What might be a good use for a composite primary key (one that comprises two or more columns)?

3. Why do we usually have a dedicated id column serving as the primary key? What, if anything, is wrong with using a real piece of data?

4. What are the implications of choosing an open-source or GNU Public License (GPL) database server to act as the persistence layer in your application? How does the significance of such a decision change in an academic environment versus a commercial one?

chapter **7**

The Accessor Layer

In a multiple-tier PHP software architecture, only one layer (comprising one set of PHP programs) accesses the persistence layer, which is otherwise known as the database or filesystem. That's the accessor layer.

When, as is usually the case, the persistence layer is a database server, the accessor layer has a lot to do with commands that manipulate the database. In other words, the accessor programs contain lots of structured query language (SQL) statements that add data to the database, remove data from the database, modify data already in the database, and extract particular sets of data from the database.

However, because the accessor layer must deal with the peculiarities of the database server to which it has to connect, it's also concerned with connection protocols. Fortunately, the hard work of establishing a database connection has already been done for you by the PEAR DB in most cases (and, truth be told, it isn't really strenuous even without PEAR). By using PEAR DB, you simply define a datasource name (DSN) in the PHP programs that make up your application's accessor layer, and let PEAR DB make the connection. If you need to change database servers, the job is relatively easy and not too prone to error, because there's little code to change.

This chapter explains the ins and outs of SQL as it pertains to typical software applications. It also shows how to write PHP programs that use the PEAR DB library to access a database, the NuSOAP (simple object access protocol) library to expose functions as Web services, and SQL to manipulate the database that was created in Chapter 6.

7.1 Extracting Data from the Database

A database is useless unless it's possible to extract data from it in a meaningful way. Specifically, we need to be able to tell the database server what data we want it to extract

95

from the database, and how we want it presented. In the simplest case, we might want to see all columns in all rows in a certain table. In slightly more complicated situations, we might want to extract only certain rows, or only certain columns, or only certain columns of certain rows. You get the idea. This section explains how to use SQL SELECT queries effectively.

7.1.1   Using SELECT Queries

You use a SELECT query to get information out of a database. SELECT queries do not make any changes to the tables upon which they operate. To use a SELECT query, you simply specify which records you want to extract, and from which tables.

Extracting All Columns from All Rows

The simplest example of this is the ubiquitous "show all records" query:

```
SELECT * FROM demo;
```

That statement returns all columns and rows from the table named demo:

id	lastName	firstName	yearOfBirth
1	Baldoni	Burt	1956
2	Carey	Casey	1982
3	Delaney	Dave	1977
4	Estacio	Elena	1934
5	Farquhar	Fred	1961
6	Ghiotto	Gail	1966
7	Hertenberger	Hal	1954
8	Imrie	Iggy	1957
9	Jindi	Jerry	1957
10	Karakis	Kelly	1988
11	Loudoun	Laurie	1971
12	McClellan	Midge	1965
13	MacClellan	Mike	1945
14	MacClellan	Mabel	1945
15	McClellan	Marcel	1958
16	Nacelle	Nancy	1962
17	Odd	Otis	1962

In that SQL statement, the star (*) stands for "all columns," and FROM is an SQL keyword that identifies the table against which the query is to run.

Extracting Only Certain Columns from All Rows

A query like the preceding one can easily return an unwieldy quantity of rows. A slightly more complicated syntax enables us to specify that we want to see only certain columns from the demo database:

```
SELECT firstName, lastName FROM demo;
```

In that statement, we limit the data returned in terms of columns. Even if there are many columns in demo in addition to firstName and lastName, only those two columns are returned for each row, like this:

firstName	lastName
Burt	Baldoni
Casey	Carey
Dave	Delaney
Elena	Estacio
Fred	Farquhar
Gail	Ghiotto
Hal	Hertenberger
Iggy	Imrie
Jerry	Jindi
Kelly	Karakis
Laurie	Loudoun
Midge	McClellan
Mike	MacClellan
Mabel	MacClellan
Marcel	McClellan
Nancy	Nacelle
Otis	Odd

That's an important fact to note: The preceding statement and its predecessor return an equal number of rows. They differ only in the number of columns returned. Note also that the second statement, in which column names were specified, displayed the columns in the sequence specified in the query—the opposite of the default sequence.

Extracting Only Rows with Unique Values in Specified Columns

Note that SELECT will happily return duplicate values. This may or may not be what you want. If you require only a list of the distinct values that exist in a particular column, you can do something like this:

```
SELECT DISTINCT lastName FROM demo;
```

That line returns a list of unique lastName values that are represented in the database, like this:

lastName
Baldoni
Carey
Delaney
Estacio
Farquhar
Ghiotto
Hertenberger
Imrie
Jindi
Karakis
Loudoun
MacClellan
McClellan
Nacelle
Odd

Note that McClellan and MacClellan, which appear in the table several times, appears only once in the result set of the statement above.

Extracting Only Certain Rows

In an earlier example, you got an idea of how to return all rows in a table, while limiting the results to certain columns. It's also possible to do the converse: Return all columns, but only certain rows. This is the reason behind adding a WHERE clause to the end of a SELECT clause.

The simplest application of the WHERE clause is in finding strict matches, as with this example:

```
SELECT * FROM demo WHERE lastName='Ghiotto';
```

This returns the following:

lastName	firstName	yearOfBirth
Ghiotto	Gail	1966

Note that the statement causes the return of all columns of rows in which the lastName columns matches "Ghiotto" exactly. In this case, it happens to be just one. Such a match is strictly case sensitive.

=	Equal to
<>	Not equal to
>	Greater than
<	Less than
>=	Greater than or equal to
<=	Less than or equal to
BETWEEN	Greater than or equal to one number, and less than or equal to another
LIKE	Matches a pattern that can include wildcards

Table 7.1: SQL Comparison Operators.

You can describe other kinds of matches with a series of operators that work with the WHERE keyword. These are shown in Table 7.1.

Most of the operators work best (or, at least, most intuitively) with numeric column values. This statement:

```
SELECT firstName, lastName, yearOfBirth FROM demo WHERE yearOfBirth <= 1975;
```

returns specified columns from all rows in which the value in the yearOfBirth column is less than or equal to 1974, effectively generating a list of people born in or before that year:

firstName	lastName	yearOfBirth
Burt	Baldoni	1956
Elena	Estacio	1934
Fred	Farquhar	1961
Gail	Ghiotto	1966
Hal	Hertenberger	1954
Iggy	Imrie	1957
Jerry	Jindi	1957
Laurie	Loudoun	1971
Midge	McClellan	1965
Mike	MacClellan	1945
Mabel	MacClellan	1945
Marcel	McClellan	1958
Nancy	Nacelle	1962
Otis	Odd	1962

The LIKE operator is handiest when you are uncertain about spellings. This statement:

```
SELECT firstName, lastName, yearOfBirth FROM demo WHERE lastName LIKE
'M%cClellan';
```

returns rows in which the lastName column value is either "McClellan" or "MacClellan"

firstName	lastName	yearOfBirth
Midge	McClellan	1965
Mike	MacClellan	1945
Mabel	MacClellan	1945
Marcel	McClellan	1958

The % wildcard in that query stands for "zero or more unspecified characters."

Linking Tables with Inner Joins

Joins inspire joy in the hearts of database people the way navigational charts thrill sailors and pilots. Anyone who's read a general-interest book about relational databases is aware that joins have to do with extracting data from related tables, but it's generally only those who actually work with databases who can perform a join with any sort of alacrity. Anyone can write a single-table SELECT statement; it takes some experience to craft a join.

That said, joins aren't that complicated. They're really just slightly more complicated SELECT queries. As is the case with ordinary single-table SELECT queries, you write a query by nominating the tables and columns that interest you, and specifying the Boolean rules that determine which rows should be selected. The syntax is just slightly longer because there are more tables involved.

Imagine there is a company table that was created with this statement:

```
CREATE TABLE 'company'
('id' int NOT NULL AUTO_INCREMENT,
'name' varchar(30) NOT NULL DEFAULT ",
PRIMARY KEY ('id'))
TYPE=InnoDB;
```

and which looks like this:

id	name
1	AlphaCo
2	BoBoCo
3	CapCorp

Further suppose we have a contact table that was created with this statement:

```
CREATE TABLE 'contact'
('id' int NOT NULL AUTO_INCREMENT,
'name' varchar(30) NOT NULL DEFAULT ",
'companyID' int NOT NULL DEFAULT ",
```

```
PRIMARY KEY ('id'),
INDEX (companyID),
FOREIGN KEY (companyID)
REFERENCES company(id)
ON UPDATE CASCADE ON DELETE RESTRICT)
TYPE=InnoDB;
```

and which looks like this:

id	name	companyID
1	Alice	2
2	Bob	3
3	Camille	1
4	Dov	3

Note that, as discussed in Chapter 6, we're using the InnoDB table type because it provides strict enforcement of relationships.

We want a query that returns the name field from the contact table, next to the corresponding name field from the company table. First, we specify the columns that interest us, using a dot notation to be explicit about which table each column comes from:

```
SELECT contact.name AS contactName, company.name AS companyName
```

The two AS clauses ("AS contactName" and "AS companyName") are necessary because both tables have columns called name, and we need to differentiate them in the results of the query.

Then, we have to explicitly name the tables in the FROM clause:

```
FROM contacts, company
```

It is in the WHERE clause that we take advantage of the foreign key in contacts, requiring that it match the primary key column in company:

```
WHERE contacts.companyID=company.id
```

The query in its entirety looks like this:

```
SELECT contact.name AS contactName, company.name AS companyName
FROM contact, company
WHERE contact.companyID=company.id;
```

It yields the results we want:

contactName	companyName
Alice	BoBoCo
Bob	CapCorp
Camille	AlphaCo
Dov	CapCorp

The function of an inner join is to take two tables, each with a number of rows, and return the data in all columns of both tables, but only for those rows for which specified conditions are true. Typically, you'll use inner joins in conjunction with a foreign key to access related data stored in another table.

One could say that data integrity comes about when you spread data across many tables, eliminating duplication and reducing the opportunity for semantic errors in which multiple pieces of data stand for the same logical thing (e.g., Boeing Corporation versus Boeing Aircraft Corporation). Informational integrity, on the other hand, in which your database (and the system you use for accessing it) is able to quickly and automatically indicate links between related table rows, comes from effective use of joins, particularly inner joins.

Inner joins are tremendously powerful, enabling you to create virtual tables (really, result sets that come from combining multiple tables), and they're the most frequently used variety of join. More often than not, you'll use an inner join when pulling information out of your database in multi-tier applications. No row is an island, and your application will be far more powerful if you can access all related pieces of data at the same time. Note that it's appropriate to do this at the accessor level, with SQL queries, because the database server can process joins very quickly. Joins are not calculations, which should happen in the business logic layer. Joins are just slightly more complicated methods of accessing data.

The generic SQL syntax for an inner join is this:

```
SELECT columns
FROM table1
INNER JOIN table2
ON conditions
```

To demonstrate the behavior of inner joins with an example, let's suppose we have the same tables we worked with earlier in this chapter. One table contains information about companies, another contains information about contacts at those companies, as well as some people who aren't affiliated with a particular organization.

First, the company table, which was created with this SQL statement:

```
CREATE TABLE 'company'
('id' int NOT NULL AUTO_INCREMENT,
'name' varchar(30) NOT NULL DEFAULT ",
PRIMARY KEY ('id'))
TYPE=InnoDB
```

holds these contents:

id	name
1	AlphaCo
2	BoBoCo
3	CapCorp
4	DingDingLtd
5	EEEEK Inc.

The other table, contact, came about as a result of this SQL statement:

```
CREATE TABLE 'contact'
('id' int NOT NULL AUTO_INCREMENT,
'name' varchar(30) NOT NULL DEFAULT '',
'companyID' int NULL,
PRIMARY KEY ('id'),
INDEX (companyID),
FOREIGN KEY (companyID)
REFERENCES company(id))
TYPE=InnoDB
```

and holds these data:

id	name	companyID
1	Alice	2
2	Bob	3
3	Camille	1
4	Dov	3
5	Edgar	[NULL]
6	Francine	[NULL]
7	Gaylord	[NULL]
8	Hongbin	[NULL]

The id column in the company table is the primary key there, and the companyID column in the contact table is an integer that refers to the id column in the owner table—it's a foreign key. The foreign key may be null, indicating that there can be contacts with no associated company.

If we wanted a result set that contained full details of all companies and their employees, we'd use an inner join query like this one:

```
SELECT company.name AS companyName, contact.name AS contactName
FROM company
INNER JOIN contact
ON contact.companyID=company.id;
```

These are the results of this query:

companyName	contactName
BoBoCo	Alice
CapCorp	Bob
AlphaCo	Camille
CapCorp	Dov

If you like, you can use AND and OR to specify multiple conditions in the ON clause. The Boolean operators work just like they do in WHERE clauses.

Speaking of WHERE clauses, isn't this INNER JOIN syntax the same as the more advanced SELECT syntax we saw earlier in this chapter? Indeed it is. This query:

```
SELECT company.name AS companyName, contact.name AS contactName
FROM company, contact
WHERE contact.companyID=company.id;
```

is functionally the same as the INNER JOIN query we just tried out.

Linking Tables with Outer Joins

In contrast to inner joins, outer joins exist because there's often not a one-to-one relationship between rows in different tables. Often, you'll have people in your contacts table without corresponding companies in your companies table, or customer listings in the customers table without corresponding orders in the orders table. Similarly, a pet owner might have more than one pet, and a customer might have more than one order.

Outer joins differ from inner joins in that they return all rows in one table, combined with only certain rows in another table. Depending on whether you want to return all rows in the first table specified in your query, or all rows from the second, you could choose a left outer join (otherwise known as a left join) or a right outer join (a right join), respectively.

As with any query that is meant to return all rows in any table, you should use outer joins with care. If they are run on a large table, outer joins can require a lot of processing time and generate unwieldy result sets.

Left joins consider two tables, as do all joins. A left join, though, returns all rows in the first table, and only those rows in the second table that have relational links to the first table. The generic syntax for a left join is this:

```
SELECT columns
FROM left_table
LEFT [OUTER] JOIN right_table
ON conditions
```

Consider our contacts-and-companies example again. It's completely reasonable to think that our database would contain both companies at which we have no specific contacts, and contacts that are not associated with a company. Here is the company table:

id	name
1	AlphaCo
2	BoBoCo
3	CapCorp
4	DingDingLtd
5	EEEEK Inc.

And here is the contact table:

id	name	companyID
1	Alice	2
2	Bob	3
3	Camille	1
4	Dov	3
5	Edgar	[NULL]
6	Francine	[NULL]
7	Gaylord	[NULL]
8	Hongbin	[NULL]

Suppose we require an accessor function that returns a list of all companies in the company table, as well as contacts for those companies where they exist in the contact table. This is an appropriate application for a left join in which the company table is the left table, and the contact table is the right. Here's the query we'd use:

```
SELECT company.name AS companyName, contact.name AS contactName
FROM company
LEFT JOIN contact
ON company.id=contact.companyID;
```

The results of that query are exactly what we want:

companyName	contactName
AlphaCo	Camille
BoBoCo	Alice
CapCorp	Bob
CapCorp	Dov
DingDingLtd	[NULL]
EEEEK Inc.	[NULL]

Note that Edgar, Francine, Gaylord, and Hongbin, who are in the contact table but who have no company association, appear nowhere in the result set. Also note that DingDingLtd and EEEEK Inc., which appear in the company table but have no associated contacts, are listed in the result set, but with null values in the columns where the contact information should go.

Right joins, as you might expect, are the opposite of left joins. A right join returns all rows in the second table, and only those rows in the first table that have relational links to the second table. The generic syntax for a right join is as follows:

```
SELECT columns
FROM left_table
RIGHT [OUTER] JOIN right_table
ON conditions
```

A right join, applied to our companies-and-contacts database, would return all contacts regardless of whether they had associated companies, and would return only those company rows with associated contacts. The syntax specific to this application is:

```
SELECT contact.name AS contactName, company.name AS companyName
FROM company
RIGHT JOIN contact
ON company.id=contact.companyID;
```

It's nearly the same as the statement we used in the left join demonstration, with the exception of the keyword RIGHT. The results, however, are significantly different:

contactName	companyName
Alice	BoBoCo
Bob	CapCorp
Camille	AlphaCo
Dov	CapCorp
Edgar	[NULL]
Francine	[NULL]
Gaylord	[NULL]
Hongbin	[NULL]

Note that null values again appear in the company.name column for contacts that do not have associated company rows. Note also (again) that the contact table was listed in its entirety—a potentially risky phenomenon in situations in which the table contained many rows.

7.1.2   SELECT Queries for Currawong Accounting

In our multicurrency accounting application, we need a number of accessor-layer programs based on SELECT queries. Specifically, we need classes that will do the following tasks:

- Return all payees,
- Return all bank accounts,
- Return all currencies,
- Return all institutions,
- Return all accounts,
- Return all account types,
- Return all transactions,
- Return an account for which an id value is specified,
- Return an account type for which an id value is specified,

- Return a bank account for which an id value is specified,
- Return a currency for which an id value is specified,
- Return an institution for which an id value is specified,
- Return a payee for which an id value is specified,
- Return a transaction for which an id value is specified,
- Return a transaction type for which an id value is specified,
- Return the balance of a bank account on a specific date, given the account's id value and the date,
- Return the average balance of an account during a specified number of days prior to a specified date, given the account's id value, the date, and a number of days (this will be used for moving-average calculations), and
- Return a range of transactions from a specified account, given the account's id value, a start date, and an end date.

Most of these require only a simple SELECT statement, but others require that joins be used. The last eight items in this list are functionally very similar. They're all dealt with in the section titled, "Return a Specified Row from a Specified Table." Let's examine solutions to each of the requirements in turn.

Return All Payees

To return all payees, we obviously need a SELECT statement that draws all columns out of the ACCT_payee table. Because ACCT_payee has no foreign keys, extracting its data is a simple matter of sending a straightforward SELECT statement to the database server via a PEAR DB connection. Let's examine getPayees.php line by line to see how this is done.

```
require_once('nusoap-0.6/nusoap.php');
require_once('configuration.php');

// Establish NuSOAP soap_server object
// and register function as Web Service...

$s = new soap_server;
$s->register('getPayees');
$s->service($HTTP_RAW_POST_DATA);
```

The first order of business is to import the PEAR DB classes, the NuSOAP classes, and dbDetails.php, which contain information about the database server and security credentials for it. Then, we register the getPayees function—to be defined momentarily—as a SOAP service. Refer to Chapters 4 and 5 for further information on NuSOAP and Web services.

```
function getPayees() {

// Make globals from configuration.php available within function scope.
global $phptype;    // Type of database server.
global $hostspec;   // Hostname of database server.
global $database;   // Database name.
global $username;   // Database username.
global $password;   // Database password.
```

In the function definition, these five global variables must be declared in order for them to be accessible. Their values are assigned in dbDetails.php, which was imported at the beginning of the program.

```
// Assemble Data Source Name (DSN) and connect, allowing for errors...

$dsn = "$phptype://$username:$password@$hostspec/$database";

$db = DB::connect($dsn);

if (DB::isError($db)) {
   die ($db->getMessage());
   }
```

Using the standard PEAR DB procedure (see Chapter 5 for more details), we connect to the database server. The program checks for an error condition.

```
// Assemble and send SQL statement, allowing for errors...

$sql = "select id, name, streetAddress, city, state, postcode, country
from ACCT_payee";
```

That's the SQL query that is to be sent to the database server. Note that we specify the columns, even though it's all of them. That way we know what order the columns will be in when results come back.

```
$result = $db->query($sql);

if (DB::isError($result))
   {
   $errorMessage = $result->getMessage();
   die ($errorMessage);
   }
```

The program sends the query to the database and checks to see if an error message comes back.

```
$returnArray = array();
```

```
// Extract rows from query results, fitting pieces of data into
// $returnArray (an associative array) for returning.

while ($row = $result->fetchRow())
   {
   $id = $row[0];
   $name = $row[1];
   $streetAddress = $row[2];
   $city = $row[3];
   $state = $row[4];
   $postcode = $row[5];
   $country = $row[6];


   $returnArray[] = array('id' => $id, 'name' => $name, 'streetAddress' =>
   $streetAddress, 'city' => $city, 'state' => $state, 'postcode' =>
   $postcode, 'country' => $country);
   }

// Disconnect from database and return $returnArray...

$db->disconnect();

return $returnArray;


}
```

The remainder of the program involves setting up an array—$returnArray—and filling it with a series of subarrays (in other words, $returnArray is a two-dimensional array). The subarrays are associative arrays in which the keys correspond to database column names and values come from each row of results that comes out of $result by way of fetchRow().

Return All Bank Accounts

In order to return a list of all bank accounts, the database server will need to perform several joins. This is because the ACCT_bank_account table, which contains information on individual accounts maintained by the customer, has a number of foreign keys. Other than the complex SQL query, though, the accessor-layer program that retrieves account information is similar to other accessor-layer programs.

Here's a listing of getBankAccounts.php, which handles account-list retrieval.

```
require_once('nusoap-0.6/nusoap.php');
require_once('configuration.php');

// Establish NuSOAP soap_server object
```

```
// and register function as Web Service...

$s = new soap_server;
$s->register('getBankAccounts');
$s->service($HTTP_RAW_POST_DATA);

function getBankAccounts() {

// Make globals from configuration.php available within function scope.
global $phptype;      // Type of database server.
global $hostspec;     // Hostname of database server.
global $database;     // Database name.
global $username;     // Database username.
global $password;     // Database password.

// Assemble Data Source Name (DSN) and connect, allowing for errors...

$dsn = "$phptype://$username:$password@$hostspec/$database";

$db = DB::connect($dsn);

if (DB::isError($db)) {
   die ($db->getMessage());
   }

// Assemble and send SQL statement, allowing for errors...

$sql = <<<EOQ
SELECT
ACCT_bank_account.id,
ACCT_institution.institutionName AS institution,
ACCT_bank_account.number,
ACCT_currency.abbreviation AS currency,
ACCT_currency.id AS currencyId,
ACCT_acct_type.name AS type,
ACCT_bank_account.description
FROM ACCT_bank_account
LEFT JOIN ACCT_currency
ON ACCT_bank_account.currency=ACCT_currency.id
LEFT JOIN ACCT_acct_type
ON ACCT_acct_type.id=ACCT_bank_account.type
LEFT JOIN ACCT_institution
ON ACCT_institution.id=ACCT_bank_account.institution
```

```
EOQ;

$result = $db->query($sql);

if (DB::isError($result))
    {
    $errorMessage = $result->getMessage();
    die ($errorMessage);
    }

$returnArray = array();
// Extract rows from query results, fitting pieces of data into
// $returnArray (an associative array) for returning.

while ($row = $result->fetchRow())
    {
    $id = $row[0];
    $institution = $row[1];
    $number = $row[2];
    $currency = $row[3];
    $currencyId = $row[4];
    $type = $row[5];
    $description = $row[6];
    $returnArray[] = array('id' => $id, 'institution' => $institution,
    'number' => $number, 'currency' => $currency, 'currencyId' => $currencyId,
    'type' => $type, 'description' => $description);

    }

// Disconnect from database and return $returnArray...

$db->disconnect();

return $returnArray;

}
```

Again, this program bears a strong resemblance to other programs in the accessor layer, with the exception of this complicated SQL statement:

```
SELECT
ACCT_bank_account.id,
ACCT_institution.institutionName AS institution,
ACCT_bank_account.number,
```

```
ACCT_currency.abbreviation AS currency,
ACCT_currency.id AS currencyId,
ACCT_acct_type.name AS type,
ACCT_bank_account.description
FROM ACCT_bank_account
LEFT JOIN ACCT_currency
ON ACCT_bank_account.currency=ACCT_currency.id
LEFT JOIN ACCT_acct_type
ON ACCT_acct_type.id=ACCT_bank_account.type
LEFT JOIN ACCT_institution
ON ACCT_institution.id=ACCT_bank_account.institution
```

The statement specifies that seven columns are to be retrieved from four different tables. Not surprisingly, ACCT_bank_account is the main table, and the other three tables are left joined to it based on foreign key values in ACCT_bank_account. Performing multiple joins in a single query is not a problem. Note also that a number of retrieved columns are renamed with AS statements.

Return All Currencies

The requirement to return a list of all currencies stored in the database is handled by the code contained in getCurrencies.php. It's a straightforward query module with no joins or other unusual tricks. Here's a full listing:

```php
require_once('nusoap-0.6/nusoap.php');
require_once('configuration.php');

// Establish NuSOAP soap_server object
// and register function as Web Service...

$s = new soap_server;
$s->register('getCurrencies');
$s->service($HTTP_RAW_POST_DATA);

function getCurrencies() {

// Make globals from configuration.php available within function scope.
global $phptype;    // Type of database server.
global $hostspec;   // Hostname of database server.
global $database;   // Database name.
global $username;   // Database username.
global $password;   // Database password.

// Assemble Data Source Name (DSN) and connect, allowing for errors...
```

```php
$dsn = "$phptype://$username:$password@$hostspec/$database";

$db = DB::connect($dsn);

if (DB::isError($db)) {
    die ($db->getMessage());
    }

// Assemble and send SQL statement, allowing for errors...

$sql = <<<EOQ
select id,
abbreviation,
country,
name,
xRate,
DATE_FORMAT(updated,'%d %M %Y %T')
from ACCT_currency
EOQ;

// Note that the MySQL DATE_FORMAT() function is used to get the string into
the required format.

$result = $db->query($sql);

if (DB::isError($result))
    {
    $errorMessage = $result->getMessage();
    die ($errorMessage);
    }

// Extract rows from query results, fitting pieces of data into
// $returnArray (an associative array) for returning.

while ($row = $result->fetchRow())
    {
    $id = $row[0];
    $abbreviation = $row[1];
    $country = $row[2];
    $name = $row[3];
    $xRate = $row[4];
    $updated = $row[5];
```

```
      $returnArray[] = array('id' => $id, 'abbreviation' => $abbreviation,
      'country' => $country, 'name' => $name, 'xRate' => $xRate,
      'updated' => $updated);
      }

   // Disconnect from database and return $returnArray...

   $db->disconnect();

   return $returnArray;

   }
```

Simple enough. Again, the returned array—$returnArray—is a two-dimensional array in which the subarrays are associative.

Return All Institutions

Currawong Accounting must be able to return a list of all financial institutions with which the customer does business. Because the table that stores information about financial institutions, ACCT_institutions, has no foreign keys, there are no joins to be set up. The accessor program simply connects via PEAR DB, runs a simple query, and returns the results in an array. Here is a full listing of getInstitutions.php:

```
   require_once('nusoap-0.6/nusoap.php');
   require_once('configuration.php');

   // Establish NuSOAP soap_server object
   // and register function as Web Service...

   $s = new soap_server;
   $s->register('getInstitutions');
   $s->service($HTTP_RAW_POST_DATA);

   function getInstitutions() {

   // Make globals from configuration.php available within function scope.
   global $phptype;     // Type of database server.
   global $hostspec;    // Hostname of database server.
   global $database;    // Database name.
   global $username;    // Database username.
   global $password;    // Database password.

   // Assemble Data Source Name (DSN) and connect, allowing for errors...

   $dsn = "$phptype://$username:$password@$hostspec/$database";
```

```
$db = DB::connect($dsn);

if (DB::isError($db)) {
   die ($db->getMessage());
   }

// Assemble and send SQL statement, allowing for errors...

$sql = "select id, institutionName AS name, streetAddress, city, state,
postcode, country from ACCT_institution";

$result = $db->query($sql);

if (DB::isError($result))
   {
   $errorMessage = $result->getMessage();
   die ($errorMessage);
   }

$returnArray = array();


// Extract rows from query results, fitting pieces of data into
// $returnArray (an associative array) for returning.

while ($row = $result->fetchRow())
   {
   $id = $row[0];
   $name = $row[1];
   $streetAddress = $row[2];
   $city = $row[3];
   $state = $row[4];
   $postcode = $row[5];
   $country = $row[6];
   $returnArray[] = array('id' => $id, 'name' => $name, 'streetAddress' =>
   $streetAddress, 'city' => $city, 'state' => $state, 'postcode' =>
   $postcode, 'country' => $country);

}

// Disconnect from database and return $returnArray...

$db->disconnect();
```

```
   return $returnArray;

}
```

This is an accessor program like many others for Currawong Accounting. The SQL statement is simple, and the results are made available via a Web service in the form of an array of associative arrays.

Return All Accounts

Currawong Accounting must be able to return the names of all accounts—that is to say, all "accounting accounts," not all bank accounts in this case. This is a very simple operation, requiring only an uncomplicated SELECT query and the usual NuSOAP and array-returning infrastructure. Here is a full listing of getAccounts.php:

```php
require_once('nusoap-0.6/nusoap.php');
require_once('configuration.php');

// Establish NuSOAP soap_server object
// and register function as Web Service...

$s = new soap_server;
$s->register('getAccounts');
$s->service($HTTP_RAW_POST_DATA);


function getAccounts() {

// Make globals from configuration.php available within function scope.
global $phptype;      // Type of database server.
global $hostspec;     // Hostname of database server.
global $database;     // Database name.
global $username;     // Database username.
global $password;     // Database password.

// Assemble Data Source Name (DSN) and connect, allowing for errors...

$dsn = "$phptype://$username:$password@$hostspec/$database";

$db = DB::connect($dsn);

if (DB::isError($db)) {
   die ($db->getMessage());
   }
```

```
// Assemble and send SQL statement, allowing for errors...

$sql = "select id, name from ACCT_account";

$result = $db->query($sql);

if (DB::isError($result))
    {
    $errorMessage = $result->getMessage();
    die ($errorMessage);
    }


// Extract rows from query results, fitting pieces of data into
// $returnArray (an associative array) for returning.

while ($row = $result->fetchRow())
    {
    $id = $row[0];
    $name = $row[1];
    $returnArray[] = array('id' => $id, 'name' => $name);
    }

// Disconnect from database and return $returnArray...

$db->disconnect();

return $returnArray;

}
```

Again, quite simple. The program runs an unadorned SELECT statement:

```
SELECT id, name from ACCT_account
```

and returns the resultant rows in an indexed array of associative arrays.

Return All Account Types

The requirement to return a list of all account types stored in the database is handled by the code contained in getAcctTypes.php. It's a straightforward query module. Here's a full listing:

```
getAcctTypes.php

require_once('nusoap-0.6/nusoap.php');
```

```php
require_once('configuration.php');

// Establish NuSOAP soap_server object
// and register function as Web Service...

$s = new soap_server;
$s->register('getAcctTypes');
$s->service($HTTP_RAW_POST_DATA);

function getAcctTypes() {

// Make globals from configuration.php available within function scope.
global $phptype;     // Type of database server.
global $hostspec;    // Hostname of database server.
global $database;    // Database name.
global $username;    // Database username.
global $password;    // Database password.

// Assemble Data Source Name (DSN) and connect, allowing for errors...

$dsn = "$phptype://$username:$password@$hostspec/$database";

$db = DB::connect($dsn);

if (DB::isError($db)) {
   die ($db->getMessage());
   }

// Assemble and send SQL statement, allowing for errors...

$sql = "select id, name from ACCT_acct_type";

$result = $db->query($sql);

if (DB::isError($result))
   {
   $errorMessage = $result->getMessage();
   die ($errorMessage);
   }

$returnArray = array();


// Extract rows from query results, fitting pieces of data into
// $returnArray (an associative array) for returning.
```

```
while ($row = $result->fetchRow())
   {
   $id = $row[0];
   $name = $row[1];

   $returnArray[] = array('id' => $id, 'name' => $name);
   }

// Disconnect from database and return $returnArray...

$db->disconnect();

return $returnArray;

}
```

The core of this module is a simple SELECT statement that returns two columns, id and name, from every row in the table.

Return All Transactions

The program is required to return all transactions stored in the ACCT_register table. Although the requirement is easily satisfied with a SELECT query, the query must include a couple of JOIN operations because ACCT_register includes several foreign keys. Here is the complete listing of getTransactions.php, the file that handles the work:

```
require_once('nusoap-0.6/nusoap.php');
require_once('configuration.php');

// Establish NuSOAP soap_server object
// and register function as Web Service...

$s = new soap_server;
$s->register('getTransactions');
$s->service($HTTP_RAW_POST_DATA);

function getTransactions() {

// Make globals from configuration.php available within function scope.
global $phptype;    // Type of database server.
global $hostspec;   // Hostname of database server.
global $database;   // Database name.
global $username;   // Database username.
```

```
global $password;    // Database password.

// Assemble Data Source Name (DSN) and connect, allowing for errors...

$dsn = "$phptype://$username:$password@$hostspec/$database";

$db = DB::connect($dsn);

if (DB::isError($db)) {
   die ($db->getMessage());
   }

// Assemble and send SQL statement, allowing for errors...


$sql = <<<EOQ
SELECT
ACCT_register.id,
ACCT_register.date,
ACCT_register.number,
ACCT_payee.name AS payee,
ACCT_register.amount,
ACCT_account.name AS account
FROM ACCT_register
LEFT JOIN ACCT_payee
ON ACCT_register.payee=ACCT_payee.id
LEFT JOIN ACCT_account
ON ACCT_register.account=ACCT_account.id
EOQ;

$result = $db->query($sql);

if (DB::isError($result))
   {
   $errorMessage = $result->getMessage();
   die ($errorMessage);
   }

$returnArray = array();


// Extract rows from query results, fitting pieces of data into
// $returnArray (an associative array) for returning.

while ($row = $result->fetchRow())
```

```
{
$id = $row[0];
$date = $row[1];
$number = $row[2];
$payee = $row[3];
$amount = $row[4];
$account = $row[5];

$returnArray[] = array('id' => $id, 'date' => $date, 'number' => $number,
'payee' => $payee, 'amount' => $amount, 'account' => $account);
}


// Disconnect from database and return $returnArray...

$db->disconnect();

return $returnArray;

}
```

The unusual aspect of this program is the elaborate SELECT statement, which involves two left joins:

```
SELECT
ACCT_register.id,
ACCT_register.date,
ACCT_register.number,
ACCT_payee.name AS payee,
ACCT_register.amount,
ACCT_account.name AS account
FROM ACCT_register
LEFT JOIN ACCT_payee
ON ACCT_register.payee=ACCT_payee.id
LEFT JOIN ACCT_account
ON ACCT_register.account=ACCT_account.id
```

The two joins correspond to the two foreign keys in ACCT_register, which have to do with the payee and the accounting account involved in the transaction.

Return a Specified Row from a Specified Table

The Currawong specification requires a number of accessor-layer programs for similar purposes. These all take the primary key value (id) of some row in some table and return all or most column values from that row. Here's a list of all accessor-layer programs that do that kind of work:

- Return a specified account (getSpecifiedAccount.php)
- Return a specified account type (getSpecifiedAcctType.php)
- Return a specified bank account (getSpecifiedBankAccount.php)
- Return a specified currency (getSpecifiedCurrency.php)
- Return a specified institution (getSpecifiedInstitution.php)
- Return a specified payee (getSpecifiedPayee.php)
- Return a specified transaction (getSpecifiedTransaction.php)
- Return a specified transaction type (getSpecifiedTransType.php)

All of these programs are essentially the same, differing only in the tables against which their queries run. Let's have a look at getSpecifiedBankAccount.php, which can exemplify the bunch:

```
getSpecifiedBankAccount.php

require_once('DB.php');
require_once('nusoap-0.6/nusoap.php');
require_once('configuration.php');

// Establish NuSOAP soap_server object
// and register function as Web Service...

$s = new soap_server;
$s->register('getSpecifiedBankAccount');
$s->service($HTTP_RAW_POST_DATA);

function getSpecifiedBankAccount($id) {

// Make globals from configuration.php available within function scope.
global $phptype;    // Type of database server.
global $hostspec;   // Hostname of database server.
global $database;   // Database name.
global $username;   // Database username.
global $password;   // Database password.

// Assemble Data Source Name (DSN) and connect, allowing for errors...

$dsn = "$phptype://$username:$password@$hostspec/$database";
$db = DB::connect($dsn);
```

```
if (DB::isError($db)) {
    die ($db->getMessage());
    }

// Assemble and send SQL statement, allowing for errors...

$sql = <<<EOQ
SELECT
ACCT_bank_account.id,
ACCT_institution.institutionName AS institution,
ACCT_institution.id AS institutionId,
ACCT_bank_account.number,
ACCT_currency.abbreviation AS currency,
ACCT_currency.id AS currencyId,
ACCT_acct_type.name AS type,
ACCT_acct_type.id AS acctTypeId,
ACCT_bank_account.description
FROM ACCT_bank_account
LEFT JOIN ACCT_currency
ON ACCT_bank_account.currency=ACCT_currency.id
LEFT JOIN ACCT_acct_type
ON ACCT_acct_type.id=ACCT_bank_account.type
LEFT JOIN ACCT_institution
ON ACCT_institution.id=ACCT_bank_account.institution
WHERE
ACCT_bank_account.id="$id"
EOQ;

$result = $db->query($sql);

if (DB::isError($result))
    {
    $errorMessage = $result->getMessage();
    die ($errorMessage);
    }

$returnArray = array();


// Extract rows from query results, fitting pieces of data into
// $returnArray (an associative array) for returning.

while ($row = $result->fetchRow())
```

```
    {
    $idRedux = $row[0];
    $institution = $row[1];
    $institutionId = $row[2];
    $number = $row[3];
    $currency = $row[4];
    $currencyId = $row[5];
    $type = $row[6];
    $acctTypeId = $row[7];
    $description = $row[8];

    $returnArray[] = array('id' => $idRedux, 'institution' => $institution,
    'institutionId' => $institutionId, 'number' => $number, 'currency' =>
    $currency, 'currencyId' => $currencyId, 'type' => $type, 'acctTypeId' =>
    $acctTypeId, 'description' => $description);
    }

// Disconnect from database and return $returnArray...

$db->disconnect();

return $returnArray;

}
```

Essentially, that program makes the same query against ACCT_bank_account as getBankAccounts.php (which returns all bank accounts), except that this program contains a WHERE clause:

```
WHERE
ACCT_bank_account.id="$id"
```

Because $id arrived as a parameter, it can be used to grab the details of only the account required by the remote tier.

Return the Balance of an Account

The accessor layer has to be able to return the balance of a bank account on a specific date, given the account's id value and the date. This job is handled by getSpecifiedBankAccount-Balance.php, listed here:

```
getSpecifiedBankAccountBalance.php


require_once('nusoap-0.6/nusoap.php');
require_once('configuration.php');
```

```php
// Establish NuSOAP soap_server object
// and register function as Web Service...

$s = new soap_server;
$s->register('getSpecifiedBankAccountBalance');
$s->service($HTTP_RAW_POST_DATA);

function getSpecifiedBankAccountBalance($id, $date) {

// Make globals from configuration.php available within function scope.
global $phptype;     // Type of database server.
global $hostspec;    // Hostname of database server.
global $database;    // Database name.
global $username;    // Database username.
global $password;    // Database password.

// Assemble Data Source Name (DSN) and connect, allowing for errors...

$dsn = "$phptype://$username:$password@$hostspec/$database";
$db = DB::connect($dsn);

if (DB::isError($db)) {
   die ($db->getMessage());
   }

// Assemble and send SQL statement, allowing for errors...

$sql = <<<EOQ
SELECT
sum(amount) as balance
FROM
acct_register
WHERE
bank_account="$id"
AND
date < "$date"
EOQ;

$result = $db->query($sql);

if (DB::isError($result))
   {
   $errorMessage = $result->getMessage();
   die ($errorMessage);
```

```
            }

    $returnArray = array();


    // Extract rows from query results, fitting pieces of data into
    // $returnArray (an associative array) for returning.

    while ($row = $result->fetchRow())
        {
        $balance = $row[0];

        $returnArray[] = array('balance' => $balance);
        }

    // Disconnect from database and return $returnArray...

    $db->disconnect();

    return $returnArray;

    }
```

That program accepts the id (primary key value) of the account to be examined as a parameter, as well as the date for which the balance is to be calculated. The date value has to be in MySQL format (YYYY-MM-DD) when it arrives as a parameter; no verification of its format is done or conversion made.

The id and date values are used in a query:

```
SELECT
sum(amount) as balance
FROM
acct_register
WHERE
bank_account="$id"
AND
date < "$date"
```

There, sum() is a MySQL function that totals all values in a specified column (amount, in this case). The query is further limited by the WHERE clause, which imposes limits based on both id and date.

Return the Average Balance of an Account over Time

Currawong Accounting needs a module on the accessor layer that will return the average balance of an account during a specified number of days prior to a specified date, given the account's id value, the date, and a number of days. The idea is that the user can specify an account, a date, and a number of days (typically 60 or 90) and see the average balance (based on weekly samples) for that account during the preceding number of days specified. For example, if the user specified account 2 (that's an id value), today's date, and the value 60, this module should calculate the mean balance of account 2 during the past 60 days.

This work is carried out by getAverageBalance.php.

```
getAverageBalance.php

require_once('nusoap-0.6/nusoap.php');
require_once('configuration.php');
require_once('dateConv.php');


// Establish NuSOAP soap_server object
// and register function as Web Service...

$s = new soap_server;
$s->register('getAverageBalance');
$s->service($HTTP_RAW_POST_DATA);

function getAverageBalance($account, $date, $days) {
//$date comes in MySQL YYYY-MM-DD format
// Make globals from configuration.php available within function scope.
global $phptype;      // Type of database server.
global $hostspec;     // Hostname of database server.
global $database;     // Database name.
global $username;     // Database username.
global $password;     // Database password.

$date = mysql_datetime_to_timestamp($date);
$midDate = $date - ($days * 24 * 60 * 60);

$total = 0;
$n = 0;

// Assemble Data Source Name (DSN) and connect, allowing for errors...

$dsn = "$phptype://$username:$password@$hostspec/$database";
$db = DB::connect($dsn);

if (DB::isError($db))
    {
    die ($db->getMessage());
    }
```

```
while ($midDate < $date)
   {

$midDate = timestamp_to_mysql_date($midDate);

// Assemble and send SQL statement, allowing for errors...

$sql = <<<EOQ
SELECT
sum(amount) as balance
FROM
acct_register
WHERE
bank_account="$account"
AND
date < "$midDate"
EOQ;
$result = $db->query($sql);

if (DB::isError($result))
   {
   $errorMessage = $result->getMessage();
   die ($errorMessage);
   }


// Extract rows from query results, fitting pieces of data into
// $returnArray (an associative array) for returning.

while ($row = $result->fetchRow())
   {
   $balance = $row[0];
   $total += $balance;
   }

   $n++;
   $midDate = mysql_datetime_to_timestamp($midDate);
   $midDate += 604800;

   }

   $movingAverage = $total / $n;

   // Disconnect from database and return $returnArray...
```

```
$db->disconnect();

    return $movingAverage;

}
```

Note that getAverageBalance.php makes use of an unusual feature of PHP syntax in enclosing its SQL statement. The following sequence of characters is the functional equivalent of a double quotation mark (") in the opening position (that is, at the beginning of a quoted string).

```
<<<EOQ
```

Its complement is this:

```
EOQ;
```

That is the equivalent of a double quotation mark (") at the end of a quoted string. Between the two sequences you can have as many line breaks as you like; the PHP interpreter ignores them. The EOQ sequences allow you to break up long strings and thus make your source code more readable.

This program works by taking the provided date value, converting it to a Unix-standard timestamp, and subtracting from it a value equal to the number of seconds in the period for which an average value is required:

```
$date = mysql_datetime_to_timestamp($date);
$midDate = $date - ($days * 24 * 60 * 60);
```

Then, a loop gets the balance at the end of every seven-day period between that calculated starting point and the original date value. On each pass through the loop, the balance is added to a running total, and $n is incremented so the total number of samples is known:

```
while ($midDate < $date)
    {

$midDate = timestamp_to_mysql_date($midDate);

$sql = <<<EOQ
SELECT
sum(amount) as balance
FROM
acct_register
WHERE
bank_account="$account"
AND
date < "$midDate"
EOQ;

$result = $db->query($sql);
```

```
if (DB::isError($result))
   {
   $errorMessage = $result->getMessage();
   die ($errorMessage);
   }

while ($row = $result->fetchRow())
   {
   $balance = $row[0];
   $total += $balance;
   }

   $n++;
   $midDate = mysql_datetime_to_timestamp($midDate);
   $midDate += 604800;


   }
```

After the loop terminates, the average of all the samples is computed:

```
$movingAverage = $total / $n;
```

and returned:

```
return $movingAverage;
```

Return a Range of Transactions

In order for the presentation layer to be able to depict an account register, it has to be able to retrieve a series of transactions from an account of interest. The module contained in getSpecifiedTransactions.php will return a range of transactions from a specified account, given the account's id value, a start date, and an end date.

```
getSpecifiedTransactions.php


require_once('DB.php');
require_once('nusoap-0.6/nusoap.php');
require_once('configuration.php');

// Establish NuSOAP soap_server object
// and register function as Web Service...

$s = new soap_server;
$s->register('getSpecifiedTransactions');
$s->service($HTTP_RAW_POST_DATA);

function getSpecifiedTransactions($startDate, $endDate, $account) {
```

```php
// Make globals from configuration.php available within function scope.
global $phptype;      // Type of database server.
global $hostspec;     // Hostname of database server.
global $database;     // Database name.
global $username;     // Database username.
global $password;     // Database password.

// Assemble Data Source Name (DSN) and connect, allowing for errors...

$dsn = "$phptype://$username:$password@$hostspec/$database";

$db = DB::connect($dsn);

if (DB::isError($db)) {
   die ($db->getMessage());
   }

// Assemble and send SQL statement, allowing for errors...

$sql = <<<EOQ
SELECT
ACCT_register.id,
ACCT_register.date,
ACCT_register.number,
ACCT_register.memo,
ACCT_payee.name AS payee,
ACCT_register.amount,
ACCT_account.name AS account,
ACCT_trans_type.name AS type
FROM ACCT_register
LEFT JOIN ACCT_payee
ON ACCT_register.payee=ACCT_payee.id
LEFT JOIN ACCT_account
ON ACCT_register.account=ACCT_account.id
LEFT JOIN ACCT_trans_type
ON ACCT_register.type=ACCT_trans_type.id
WHERE
ACCT_register.date
BETWEEN
"$startDate" AND "$endDate"
AND
ACCT_register.bank_account="$account"
EOQ;

$result = $db->query($sql);
```

```
if (DB::isError($result))
   {
   $errorMessage = $result->getMessage();
   die ($errorMessage);
   }

$returnArray = array();


// Extract rows from query results, fitting pieces of data into
// $returnArray (an associative array) for returning.

while ($row = $result->fetchRow())
   {
   $id = $row[0];
   $date = $row[1];
   $number = $row[2];
   $memo = $row[3];
   $payee = $row[4];
   $amount = $row[5];
   $account = $row[6];
   $type = $row[7];

   $returnArray[] = array('id' => $id, 'date' => $date, 'number' => $number,
   'memo' => $memo, 'payee' => $payee, 'amount' => $amount, 'account' =>
   $account, 'type' => $type);
   }


// Disconnect from database and return $returnArray...

$db->disconnect();

return $returnArray;

}
```

This is not a complicated program. Its SQL query simply retrieves all fields in the ACCT_register table that have the right account value and fit within the date parameters:

```
SELECT
ACCT_register.id,
ACCT_register.date,
ACCT_register.number,
```

```
ACCT_register.memo,
ACCT_payee.name AS payee,
ACCT_register.amount,
ACCT_account.name AS account,
ACCT_trans_type.name AS type
FROM ACCT_register
LEFT JOIN ACCT_payee
ON ACCT_register.payee=ACCT_payee.id
LEFT JOIN ACCT_account
ON ACCT_register.account=ACCT_account.id
LEFT JOIN ACCT_trans_type
ON ACCT_register.type=ACCT_trans_type.id
WHERE
ACCT_register.date
BETWEEN
"$startDate" AND "$endDate"
AND
ACCT_register.bank_account="$account"
```

As is typical of the software in this layer, the retrieved values are then fitted into a two-dimensional associative array that's returned to the sender.

7.2 Adding Data to the Database

Another important function of the database is to take additions—to store information. Currawong Accounting, although not expected to handle a high volume of transactions, will need to store information about transactions, as well as information about new payees, currencies, accounts, and other aspects of accounting that will be added over time.

Generally speaking, adding data to databases is accomplished through the use of SQL INSERT queries (as well as UPDATE and other queries). This section deals with INSERT queries as both pure SQL and as part of the accessor layer of our imaginary client's multicurrency accounting application.

7.2.1 Using INSERT Queries

You should use INSERT queries to add new rows to the database. The simplest INSERT query presumes knowledge of the column headers and their sequence in the table. Assume that, at the starting point, the demo table contains this:

id	lastName	firstName	yearOfBirth
1	Baldoni	Burt	1956
2	Carey	Casey	1982
3	Delaney	Dave	1977

4	Estacio	Elena	1934
5	Farquhar	Fred	1961
6	Ghiotto	Gail	1966
7	Hertenberger	Hal	1954
8	Imrie	Iggy	1957
9	Jindi	Jerry	1957
10	Karakis	Kelly	1988
11	Loudoun	Laurie	1971
12	McClellan	Midge	1965
13	MacClellan	Mike	1945
14	MacClellan	Mabel	1945
15	McClellan	Marcel	1958
16	Nacelle	Nancy	1962
17	Odd	Otis	1962

Then, you run this SQL statement against the database:

```
INSERT INTO demo (lastName, firstname, yearOfBirth) VALUES
('Lawrence', 'Larry', 1966);
```

Afterwards, the demo table contains this:

id	lastName	firstName	yearOfBirth
1	Baldoni	Burt	1956
2	Carey	Casey	1982
3	Delaney	Dave	1977
4	Estacio	Elena	1934
5	Farquhar	Fred	1961
6	Ghiotto	Gail	1966
7	Hertenberger	Hal	1954
8	Imrie	Iggy	1957
9	Jindi	Jerry	1957
10	Karakis	Kelly	1988
11	Loudoun	Laurie	1971
12	McClellan	Midge	1965
13	MacClellan	Mike	1945
14	MacClellan	Mabel	1945
15	McClellan	Marcel	1958
16	Nacelle	Nancy	1962
17	Odd	Otis	1962
18	Lawrence	Larry	1966

Note that the id column, which was configured with the AUTO_INCREMENT modifier, fills itself in. In this case, the id column contains integers and serves as the primary key for the demo table.

This statement...

```
INSERT INTO demo (lastName, firstname, yearOfBirth) VALUES
('Lawrence', 'Larry', 1966);
```

... is the functional equivalent of this one:

```
INSERT INTO demo (firstname, lastName, yearOfBirth) VALUES
('Larry', 'Lawrence', 1966);
```

The column sequence is important, and it's a good idea to specify it explicitly.

When you run an INSERT query, the database server typically returns a message indicating the number of rows affected by the statement—in other words, the number of rows inserted.

MySQL, for example, returns a success statement like this:

```
Query OK, 1 row affected (0.01) sec
```

If there's a problem, the database server says so. The text message from MySQL varies according to the nature of the error, but it looks something like this:

```
[db2] ERROR 1054: Unknown column 'Year-o-Birth' in 'field list'
```

More importantly, the PEAR DB class can detect when errors occur. You should build error testing into your accessor classes, and later in this chapter you'll see how.

7.2.2 INSERT Queries for Currawong Accounting

Currawong Accounting needs to be able to accumulate and store various kinds of information. When data is added to the database, one of several PHP programs involving INSERT queries handles the job. The INSERT programs the accessor layer accomplish a number of important tasks, including:

- Add a currency to table ACCT_currency,

- Add an account type to table ACCT_acct_type,

- Add an account to table ACCT_account,

- Add an institution to table ACCT_institution,

- Add a payee to table ACCT_payee, and

- Add a transaction type to table ACCT_trans_type.

Add a Currency to Table ACCT_currency

To add a currency to the database, the user has to specify a collection of information that includes the currency name, country, abbreviation, and value relative to the U.S. dollar.

An INSERT statement then handles the addition of this data to the ACCT_currency data to the database as a new row. The addCurrency.php file contains the relevant code:

```php
require_once('nusoap-0.6/nusoap.php');
require_once('configuration.php');

// Establish NuSOAP soap_server object
// and register function as Web Service...

$s = new soap_server;
$s->register('addCurrency');
$s->service($HTTP_RAW_POST_DATA);

function addCurrency($abbreviation, $country, $name, $xRate) {

// $country = String, name of country in form "South Africa".
// $name = String, name of currency in form "Rand".
// $abbreviation = String, Oanda.com abbreviation in form "ZAR".
// $xRate = Real, value of currency relative to United States Dollar.
The xRate is the ratio by which you
// multiply one USD to get one of the currency represented by the row.
If a unit of currency is worth half
// as much as a USD, its xRate is 0.50.

// The other columns in the row, id and updated, are filled automatically by
the DBMS and should not be
// touched programmatically.

// Make globals from configuration.php available within function scope.
global $phptype;    // Type of database server.
global $hostspec;   // Hostname of database server.
global $database;   // Database name.
global $username;   // Database username.
global $password;   // Database password.

// Assemble Data Source Name (DSN) and connect, allowing for errors...

$dsn = "$phptype://$username:$password@$hostspec/$database";

$db = DB::connect($dsn);

if (DB::isError($db)) {
   die ($db->getMessage());
   }
```

```
// Assemble and send SQL statement, allowing for errors...

$sql = "INSERT INTO ACCT_currency (country, name, abbreviation, xRate) VALUES
('$country', '$name', '$abbreviation', '$xRate')";

$result = $db->query($sql);

if (DB::isError($result))
   {
   $returnArray['result'] = $result->getMessage();
   die ($errorMessage);
   }
   else $returnArray['result'] = "Query completed okay.";


// Disconnect from database and return $returnArray...

$db->disconnect();

return $returnArray;

}
```

The core of this program is an SQL statement:

```
INSERT INTO ACCT_currency (country, name, abbreviation, xRate) VALUES
('$country', '$name', '$abbreviation', '$xRate')
```

It's a simple INSERT statement that presumes knowledge of the column names that exist in ACCT_currency. The SQL statement either fails and returns an error, or succeeds and does not. Note that the values ($country, $name, and so on) are contained in quotes. This is necessary in order for the SQL to be valid.

Add an Account Type to Table ACCT_acct_type

Adding an account type requires only that the name of the new account type be sent to function addAcctType, contained in file addAcctType.php. Here is a listing:

```
require_once('nusoap-0.6/nusoap.php');
require_once('configuration.php');

// Establish NuSOAP soap_server object
// and register function as Web Service...

$s = new soap_server;
$s->register('addAcctType');
```

```
$s->service($HTTP_RAW_POST_DATA);

function addAcctType($name) {

// $name = String, the name of the new account type, in form "Mortgage".

// The other column in the row, id, is filled automatically by the DBMS and
should not be
// touched programmatically.

// Make globals from configuration.php available within function scope.
global $phptype;    // Type of database server.
global $hostspec;   // Hostname of database server.
global $database;   // Database name.
global $username;   // Database username.
global $password;   // Database password.

// Assemble Data Source Name (DSN) and connect, allowing for errors...

$dsn = "$phptype://$username:$password@$hostspec/$database";

$db = DB::connect($dsn);

if (DB::isError($db)) {
   die ($db->getMessage());
   }

// Assemble and send SQL statement, allowing for errors...

$sql = "INSERT INTO ACCT_acct_type (name) VALUES ('$name')";

$result = $db->query($sql);

if (DB::isError($result))
   {
   $returnArray['result'] = $result->getMessage();
   die ($errorMessage);
   }
   else $returnArray['result'] = "Query completed okay.";


// Disconnect from database and return $returnArray...

$db->disconnect();
```

```
        return $returnArray;

    }
```

The INSERT query is simple:

```
    INSERT INTO ACCT_acct_type (name) VALUES ('$name')
```

The database server assigns an appropriate value to the id column automatically.

Add an Account to Table ACCT_account

Adding an account to the ACCT_account table is as easy as adding an account type to the ACCT_acct_type table. Only the name of the new account is specified. File addAccount.php contains the relevant code:

```
    require_once('nusoap-0.6/nusoap.php');
    require_once('configuration.php');

    // Establish NuSOAP soap_server object
    // and register function as Web Service...

    $s = new soap_server;
    $s->register('addAccount');
    $s->service($HTTP_RAW_POST_DATA);

    function addAccount($name) {

    // $name = String, the name of the new account, in form "revolving credit".

    // The other important column in the row, id, is filled automatically by the
    DBMS and should not be
    // touched programmatically. The parent column exists only for future expansion.

    // Make globals from configuration.php available within function scope.
    global $phptype;     // Type of database server.
    global $hostspec;    // Hostname of database server.
    global $database;    // Database name.
    global $username;    // Database username.
    global $password;    // Database password.

    // Assemble Data Source Name (DSN) and connect, allowing for errors...

    $dsn = "$phptype://$username:$password@$hostspec/$database";

    $db = DB::connect($dsn);
```

```
if (DB::isError($db)) {
   die ($db->getMessage());
   }

// Assemble and send SQL statement, allowing for errors...

$sql = <<<EOQ
INSERT INTO
ACCT_account (name)
VALUES
('$name')
EOQ;
$result = $db->query($sql);

if (DB::isError($result))
   {
   $returnArray['result'] = $result->getMessage();
   die ($errorMessage);
   }
   else $returnArray['result'] = "Query completed okay.";



// Disconnect from database and return $returnArray...

$db->disconnect();

return $returnArray;

}
```

The INSERT statement is a virtual clone of the one used in addAcctType:

```
INSERT INTO ACCT_account (name) VALUES ('$name')
```

Add an Institution to Table ACCT_institution

In order to add a new financial institution to the database, we equip the program with
addInstitution.php. This accessor-layer program takes values for all attributes in the
ACCT_institution table as arguments and runs an INSERT query to add them to the table.
Here is the full listing:

```
require_once('nusoap-0.6/nusoap.php');
require_once('configuration.php');
```

```
// Establish NuSOAP soap_server object
// and register function as Web Service...

$s = new soap_server;
$s->register('addInstitution');
$s->service($HTTP_RAW_POST_DATA);


function addInstitution($institutionName, $streetAddress, $city, $state,
$postcode, $country) {

// $institutionName = String, name of the financial institution in form
"First Pomposity Bank".
// $streetAddress = String, street number and street name
// $city = String, city in form "Liverpool"
// $state = String, state or other division if any, in form "OH".
// $postcode = String, postcode in form "L3 4BL".
// $country = String, country in form "United Kingdom"

// The other important column in the row, id, is filled automatically
// touched programmatically. The contact column exists for future expansion

// Make globals from configuration.php available within function scope.
global $phptype;    // Type of database server.
global $hostspec;   // Hostname of database server.
global $database;   // Database name.
global $username;   // Database username.
global $password;   // Database password.

// Assemble Data Source Name (DSN) and connect, allowing for errors...

$dsn = "$phptype://$username:$password@$hostspec/$database";


$db = DB::connect($dsn);

if (DB::isError($db)) {
   die ($db->getMessage());
   }

// Assemble and send SQL statement, allowing for errors...

$sql = <<<EOQ
INSERT INTO ACCT_institution
(institutionName, streetAddress, city, state, postcode, country) VALUES
```

```
                 ('$institutionName', '$streetAddress', '$city', '$state', '$postcode', '$country')
                 EOQ;

                 $result = $db->query($sql);

                 if (DB::isError($result))
                    {
                    $returnArray['result'] = $result->getMessage();
                    die ($errorMessage);
                    }
                    else $returnArray['result'] = "Query completed okay.";


                 // Disconnect from database and return $returnArray...

                 $db->disconnect();

                 return $returnArray;

                 }
```

Again, this isn't a complicated program. Its core is an INSERT statement that explicitly spells out how the arguments correspond to table columns:

```
INSERT INTO ACCT_institution
(institutionName, streetAddress, city, state, postcode, country) VALUES
('$institutionName', '$streetAddress', '$city', '$state', '$postcode', '$country')
```

Add a Payee to Table ACCT_payee

To add a payee to the ACCT_payee table, Currawong Accounting must once again be endowed with an accessor-layer program that uses an INSERT statement to pop a new row in to the table. The code in addPayee.php does the job:

```
require_once('nusoap-0.6/nusoap.php');
require_once('configuration.php');

// Establish NuSOAP soap_server object
// and register function as Web Service...

$s = new soap_server;
$s->register('addPayee');
$s->service($HTTP_RAW_POST_DATA);
```

```php
function addPayee($name, $streetAddress, $city, $state, $postcode, $country) {

// $name = String, name of the person in form "Lassie Comehome".
// $streetAddress = String, street number and street name.
// $city = String, city in form "Newcastle"
// $state = String, state or other division if any, in form "NSW".
// $postcode = String, postcode in form "2200".
// $country = String, country in form "Australia"

// The other important column in the row, id, is filled automatically by the
DBMS and should not be
// touched programmatically. The contact column exists for future expansion
only and is not yet used.

// Make globals from configuration.php available within function scope.
global $phptype;    // Type of database server.
global $hostspec;   // Hostname of database server.
global $database;   // Database name.
global $username;   // Database username.
global $password;   // Database password.

// Assemble Data Source Name (DSN) and connect, allowing for errors...

$dsn = "$phptype://$username:$password@$hostspec/$database";

$db = DB::connect($dsn);

if (DB::isError($db)) {
   die ($db->getMessage());
   }

// Assemble and send SQL statement, allowing for errors...

$sql = <<<EOQ
INSERT INTO ACCT_payee
(name, streetAddress, city, state, postcode, country) VALUES
('$name', '$streetAddress', '$city', '$state', '$postcode', '$country')
EOQ;

$result = $db->query($sql);

if (DB::isError($result))
```

```
    {
    $returnArray['result'] = $result->getMessage();
    die ($errorMessage);
    }
    else $returnArray['result'] = "Query completed okay.";


    // Disconnect from database and return $returnArray...

    $db->disconnect();

    return $returnArray;

    }
```

Once again, it's all based on an INSERT statement that explicitly aligns the values that come in as arguments with the columns in the database table.

Add a Transaction Type to Table ACCT_trans_type

To add a new transaction type to the ACCT_trans_type database, a short program (contained in addTransType.php) takes the name of the new transaction type as an argument and fits it into an INSERT query. The INSERT query, runs via PEAR DB, handles the insertion into the database. Here is the full listing:

```
    require_once('nusoap-0.6/nusoap.php');
    require_once('configuration.php');

    // Establish NuSOAP soap_server object
    // and register function as Web Service...

    $s = new soap_server;
    $s->register('addTransType');
    $s->service($HTTP_RAW_POST_DATA);

    function addTransType($name) {

    // $name = String, the name of the new transaction type, in form "dividend
    // received". The other column in the row, id, is filled automatically by the
    // DBMS and should not be touched programmatically.

    // Make globals from configuration.php available within function scope.
    global $phptype;    // Type of database server.
    global $hostspec;   // Hostname of database server.
    global $database;   // Database name.
```

```
global $username;   // Database username.
global $password;   // Database password.

// Assemble Data Source Name (DSN) and connect, allowing for errors...

$dsn = "$phptype://$username:$password@$hostspec/$database";

$db = DB::connect($dsn);

if (DB::isError($db)) {
   die ($db->getMessage());
   }

// Assemble and send SQL statement, allowing for errors...

$sql = "INSERT INTO ACCT_trans_type (name) VALUES ('$name')";

$result = $db->query($sql);

if (DB::isError($result))
   {
   $returnArray['result'] = $result->getMessage();
   die ($errorMessage);
   }
   else $returnArray['result'] = "Query completed okay.";


// Disconnect from database and return $returnArray...

$db->disconnect();

return $returnArray;

}
```

7.3 Modifying Data in the Database

When you want to change certain records that already exist in the database, you want to use an UPDATE statement. UPDATE statements don't create new records, and they don't display any records. They just change specified existing records. The trick is in how you specify the records you want to change.

7.3.1   Using UPDATE Queries

The simplest UPDATE statement sets a particular column in a specified row equal to a specified value. Say we had a table called demo that contained this set of data:

id	lastName	firstName	yearOfBirth
1	Baldoni	Burt	1956
2	Carey	Casey	1982
3	Delaney	Dave	1977
4	Estacio	Elena	1934
5	Farquhar	Fred	1961
6	Ghiotto	Gail	1966
7	Hertenberger	Hal	1954
8	Imrie	Iggy	1957
9	Jindi	Jerry	1957
10	Karakis	Kelly	1988
11	Loudoun	Laurie	1971
12	McClellan	Midge	1965
13	MacClellan	Mike	1945
14	MacClellan	Mabel	1945
15	McClellan	Marcel	1958
16	Nacelle	Nancy	1962
17	Odd	Otis	1962
18	Lawrence	Larry	1966
20	Sprinkleton	Sid	1928

We want to change the firstName column in the Sid Sprinkleton row to equal his nickname, "Junior." The syntax for accomplishing this is not complicated:

```
UPDATE demo SET firstName='Junior' WHERE lastName='Sprinkleton';
```

That statement would alter the table, just the one row, really, to look like this:

id	lastName	firstName	yearOfBirth
1	Baldoni	Burt	1956
2	Carey	Casey	1982
3	Delaney	Dave	1977
4	Estacio	Elena	1934
5	Farquhar	Fred	1961
6	Ghiotto	Gail	1966
7	Hertenberger	Hal	1954
8	Imrie	Iggy	1957
9	Jindi	Jerry	1957
10	Karakis	Kelly	1988

11	Loudoun	Laurie	1971
12	McClellan	Midge	1965
13	MacClellan	Mike	1945
14	MacClellan	Mabel	1945
15	McClellan	Marcel	1958
16	Nacelle	Nancy	1962
17	Odd	Otis	1962
18	Lawrence	Larry	1966
20	Sprinkleton	Junior	1928

In running that query, you'd change the firstName column values of all records in which the lastName column value equaled "Sprinkleton" (if there were more than one), so you would have to be sure that either you wanted that effect or that you had only one Sprinkleton in the database.

This is one application of primary keys. If you run an UPDATE statement and specify a value for the primary key column in the WHERE clause, you're absolutely guaranteed to get (at most) one match and thereby change the row you want to change.

Another use of the UPDATE command involves using AND, a Boolean operator, to specify multiple conditions in the WHERE clause. Such a statement could look like this:

```
UPDATE demo SET firstName='Junior' WHERE lastName='Sprinkleton'
AND firstName='Sid';
```

Note that the WHERE conditions apply to values *before* the execution of the UPDATE command, and so it's possible to use the "old" value of the column value to be changed as a condition of the UPDATE statement's execution. If you're not using the primary key to uniquely identify a row, at least try to use multiple WHERE conditions to make sure you have the right row.

7.3.2 UPDATE Queries for Currawong Accounting

Currawong Accounting must be able to carry out four tasks related to changing values stored in the database. These tasks are:

1. Update the names of accounts,
2. Update currencies,
3. Update institutions, and
4. Update payees.

Each of these jobs is handled by an UPDATE statement. The four UPDATE-oriented programs in Currawong Accounting's accessor layer are strikingly similar.

Update the Names of Accounts

In updating rows in the ACCT_account table, the application needs only to change the contents of the name column. To identify the row to be modified, however, the function must take an id value as an argument. Presumably, the correct id value would be provided by a user interface that correlated the name with the id. See Chapter 9 for information on how this is done.

Here is a listing of updateAccount.php, which handles the update work:

```
require_once('DB.php');
require_once('nusoap-0.6/nusoap.php');
require_once('configuration.php');

// Establish NuSOAP soap_server object
// and register function as Web Service...

$s = new soap_server;
$s->register('updateAccount');
$s->service($HTTP_RAW_POST_DATA);

function updateAccount($id, $name) {

// This service modifies the row in table ACCT_account whose id
// column equals $id.
// It changes the name column (to the value in $name) only.

// Make globals from configuration.php available within function scope.
global $phptype;    // Type of database server.
global $hostspec;   // Hostname of database server.
global $database;   // Database name.
global $username;   // Database username.
global $password;   // Database password.

// Assemble Data Source Name (DSN) and connect, allowing for errors...

$dsn = "$phptype://$username:$password@$hostspec/$database";

$db = DB::connect($dsn);

if (DB::isError($db)) {
   die ($db->getMessage());
   }

// Assemble and send SQL statement, allowing for errors...

$sql = <<<EOQ
UPDATE ACCT_account SET name='$name' WHERE id=$id
EOQ;

$result = $db->query($sql);
```

```
if (DB::isError($result))
    {
    $returnArray['result'] = $result->getMessage();
    die ($errorMessage);
    }
    else $returnArray['result'] = "Query completed okay.";


// Disconnect from database and return $returnArray...

$db->disconnect();

return $returnArray;

}
```

The key piece of this program is the SQL statement:

```
UPDATE ACCT_account SET name='$name' WHERE id=$id
```

It matches the id that comes in as a parameter, and, where a match is found (there should be only one because id is the primary key) the name column is altered.

Update Currencies

In updating the ACCT_currency table, Currawong Accounting must be able to change the values contained in any of the columns of the table (except the timestamp, which the database server updates automatically whenever a change takes place). Aside from the more extensive array of arguments, though, the code contained in updateCurrency.php uses the same strategy as all the other UPDATE modules in the accessor layer. Here is a complete listing:

```
require_once('nusoap-0.6/nusoap.php');
require_once('configuration.php');

// Establish NuSOAP soap_server object
// and register function as Web Service...

$s = new soap_server;
$s->register('updateCurrency');
$s->service($HTTP_RAW_POST_DATA);

function updateCurrency($id, $abbreviation, $country, $name, $xRate) {

// $id = Integer, primary key value
// $country = String, name of country in form "South Africa".
// $name = String, name of currency in form "Rand".
```

```
// $abbreviation = String, Oanda.com abbreviation in form "ZAR".
// $xRate = Real, value of currency relative to United States Dollar.
// The xRate is the ratio by which you
// multiply one USD to get one of the currency represented by the row. If a
// unit of currency is worth half
// as much as a USD, its xRate is 0.50.

// This service modifies the row in table ACCT_currency whose id column equals $id.
// It can potentially modify all columns except id and changed (changed is the
// timestamp).

// Make globals from configuration.php available within function scope.
global $phptype;     // Type of database server.
global $hostspec;    // Hostname of database server.
global $database;    // Database name.
global $username;    // Database username.
global $password;    // Database password.

// Assemble Data Source Name (DSN) and connect, allowing for errors...

$dsn = "$phptype://$username:$password@$hostspec/$database";


$db = DB::connect($dsn);

if (DB::isError($db)) {
   die ($db->getMessage());
   }

// Assemble and send SQL statement, allowing for errors...

$sql = "UPDATE ACCT_currency SET country='$country', name='$name',
abbreviation='$abbreviation', xRate=$xRate WHERE id=$id";

$result = $db->query($sql);

if (DB::isError($result))
   {
   $returnArray['result'] = $result->getMessage();
   die ($errorMessage);
   }
   else $returnArray['result'] = "Query completed okay.";


// Disconnect from database and return $returnArray...
```

```
$db->disconnect();

return $returnArray;

}
```

As is typical of the UPDATE functions, the key is an UPDATE statement in which id matching takes place in a WHERE clause.

```
UPDATE ACCT_currency SET country='$country', name='$name',
abbreviation='$abbreviation', xRate=$xRate WHERE id=$id
```

Update Institutions

To update stored data having to do with financial institutions, the relevant function in the accessor layer must take a lot of values as arguments. The key one, no pun intended, is the id argument, which should match one of the values in the id column of the table. With that value matched, the other columns can be changed to agree with the other received arguments. Here is a listing of updateInstitution.php, which contains the relevant code:

```
require_once('nusoap-0.6/nusoap.php');
require_once('configuration.php');

// Establish NuSOAP soap_server object
// and register function as Web Service...

$s = new soap_server;
$s->register('updateInstitution');
$s->service($HTTP_RAW_POST_DATA);

function updateInstitution($id, $institutionName, $streetAddress, $city, $state,
$postcode, $country) {

// $id = Integer, primary key value
// $institutionName = String, name of the financial institution in form
// "First Pomposity Bank".
// $streetAddress = String, street number and street name in form "101 Rainbow Way".
// $city = String, city in form "Liverpool"
// $state = String, state or other division if any, in form "OH".
// $postcode = String, postcode in form "L3 4BL".
// $country = String, country in form "United Kingdom"

// This service modifies the row in table ACCT_institution whose id column
// equals $id.
```

```
// It can potentially modify all columns except id.

// Make globals from configuration.php available within function scope.
global $phptype;     // Type of database server.
global $hostspec;    // Hostname of database server.
global $database;    // Database name.
global $username;    // Database username.
global $password;    // Database password.

// Assemble Data Source Name (DSN) and connect, allowing for errors...

$dsn = "$phptype://$username:$password@$hostspec/$database";

$db = DB::connect($dsn);

if (DB::isError($db)) {
   die ($db->getMessage());
   }

// Assemble and send SQL statement, allowing for errors...

$sql = <<<EOQ
UPDATE ACCT_institution
SET
institutionName='$institutionName',
streetAddress='$streetAddress',
city='$city',
state='$state',
postcode='$postcode',
country='$country'
WHERE
id=$id
EOQ;

$result = $db->query($sql);

if (DB::isError($result))
   {
   $returnArray['result'] = $result->getMessage();
   die ($errorMessage);
   }
   else $returnArray['result'] = "Query completed okay.";


// Disconnect from database and return $returnArray...
```

```
$db->disconnect();

return $returnArray;

}
```

The matching of the id values takes place in the WHERE clause of the UPDATE statement:

```
UPDATE ACCT_institution
SET
institutionName='$institutionName',
streetAddress='$streetAddress',
city='$city',
state='$state',
postcode='$postcode',
country='$country'
WHERE
id=$id
```

Update Payees

The strategy for updating payee data should be familiar by now. A whole collection of data comes in as arguments for the exposed function. Of these, one matches a value in the id column of the table to be updated—ACCT_payee in this case. Then everything else is altered to match the other values that came in as arguments. The file updatePayee.php contains the code:

```
require_once('nusoap-0.6/nusoap.php');
require_once('configuration.php');

// Establish NuSOAP soap_server object
// and register function as Web Service...

$s = new soap_server;
$s->register('updatePayee');
$s->service($HTTP_RAW_POST_DATA);

function updatePayee($id, $name, $streetAddress, $city, $state, $postcode,
$country) {

// $id = Integer, primary key value
// $name = String, name of the person in form "Lassie Comehome".
// $streetAddress = String, street number and street name.
// $city = String, city in form "Newcastle"
// $state = String, state or other division if any, in form "NSW".
```

```
// $postcode = String, postcode in form "2200".
// $country = String, country in form "Australia"

// This service modifies the row in table ACCT_payee whose id column
// equals $id.
// It can potentially modify all columns except id.

// Make globals from configuration.php available within function scope.
global $phptype;    // Type of database server.
global $hostspec;   // Hostname of database server.
global $database;   // Database name.
global $username;   // Database username.
global $password;   // Database password.

// Assemble Data Source Name (DSN) and connect, allowing for errors...

$dsn = "$phptype://$username:$password@$hostspec/$database";

$db = DB::connect($dsn);

if (DB::isError($db)) {

   die ($db->getMessage());
   }

// Assemble and send SQL statement, allowing for errors...

$sql = <<<EOQ
UPDATE ACCT_payee
SET
name='$name',
streetAddress='$streetAddress',
city='$city',
state='$state',
postcode='$postcode',
country='$country'
WHERE
id=$id
EOQ;

$result = $db->query($sql);

if (DB::isError($result))
```

```
{
$returnArray['result'] = $result->getMessage();
die ($errorMessage);
}
else $returnArray['result'] = "Query completed okay.";


// Disconnect from database and return $returnArray...

$db->disconnect();

return $returnArray;

}
```

The SQL statement in that program is almost identical to the one in updateInstitution.php.

7.4 Deleting Data from the Database

A DELETE query is for removing one or more rows, or possibly all of them, from a table, without altering the underlying table structure. DELETE should not be confused with DROP (which is not relevant to our application and so is not covered in this book), which removes a table body from a database, erasing column names, datatypes, and all contents.

7.4.1 Delete Queries in General

If you're not careful, a DELETE query will remove all data from the named table. The following statement removes all rows from the demo database (again, leaving the column names and other structural elements in place).

```
DELETE FROM demo;
```

Unqualified DELETE statements result in empty tables.

More useful is the qualified DELETE statement, in which a WHERE clause is used to limit the rows that are eliminated. Suppose we had a table that looked like this:

id	lastName	firstName	yearOfBirth
1	Baldoni	Burt	1956
2	Carey	Casey	1982
3	Delaney	Dave	1977

4	Estacio	Elena	1934
5	Farquhar	Fred	1961
6	Ghiotto	Gail	1966
7	Hertenberger	Hal	1954
8	Imrie	Iggy	1957
9	Jindi	Jerry	1957
10	Karakis	Kelly	1988
11	Loudoun	Laurie	1971
12	McClellan	Midge	1965
13	MacClellan	Mike	1945
14	MacClellan	Mabel	1945
15	McClellan	Marcel	1958
16	Nacelle	Nancy	1962
17	Odd	Otis	1962
18	Lawrence	Larry	1966
20	Sprinkleton	Junior	1928

To the database containing that table, we sent this SQL statement:

```
DELETE FROM demo WHERE lastName='Imrie';
```

The results are the same table, minus the row for Iggy Imrie:

id	lastName	firstName	yearOfBirth
1	Baldoni	Burt	1956
2	Carey	Casey	1982
3	Delaney	Dave	1977
4	Estacio	Elena	1934
5	Farquhar	Fred	1961
6	Ghiotto	Gail	1966
7	Hertenberger	Hal	1954
9	Jindi	Jerry	1957
10	Karakis	Kelly	1988
11	Loudoun	Laurie	1971
12	McClellan	Midge	1965
13	MacClellan	Mike	1945
14	MacClellan	Mabel	1945
15	McClellan	Marcel	1958
16	Nacelle	Nancy	1962
17	Odd	Otis	1962
18	Lawrence	Larry	1966
20	Sprinkleton	Junior	1928

You can use multiple conditions with the AND operator in this situation, too.

7.4.2 DELETE Queries in Currawong Accounting

There's only one DELETE-centric function in the entire accounting application. It exists for the purpose of eliminating individual transactions. The logic is that a transaction might be entered in error and need to be deleted, but a currency, institution, or payee could be referenced in other tables and therefore needs to exist long after it stopped being in active service.

Furthermore, because we set up our foreign keys (see Chapter 6) with ON DELETE CASCADE statements, a deletion of a row in a parent table (like ACCT_currency) will cause dependent rows in other tables (like ACCT_register) to be deleted. This could throw everything off. Therefore, it's best to make deletions possible only in a child table: ACCT_register.

The code that handles deletions in ACCT_register is contained in the file deleteTransaction.php. Here is a full listing:

```
require_once('DB.php');
require_once('nusoap-0.6/nusoap.php');
require_once('configuration.php');

// Establish NuSOAP soap_server object
// and register function as Web Service...

$s = new soap_server;
$s->register('deleteTransaction');
$s->service($HTTP_RAW_POST_DATA);

function deleteTransaction($id) {

// This service goes into the ACCT_register table and eliminates the row
// whose id column value is equal to $id
// (id and $id are integers).

// Make globals from configuration.php available within function scope.
global $phptype;    // Type of database server.
global $hostspec;   // Hostname of database server.
global $database;   // Database name.
global $username;   // Database username.
global $password;   // Database password.

// Assemble Data Source Name (DSN) and connect, allowing for errors...

$dsn = "$phptype://$username:$password@$hostspec/$database";

$db = DB::connect($dsn);
```

```
if (DB::isError($db)) {
   die ($db->getMessage());
   }

// Assemble and send SQL statement, allowing for errors...

$sql = "DELETE FROM ACCT_register WHERE id='$id'";

$result = $db->query($sql);

if (DB::isError($result))
   {
   $returnArray['result'] = $result->getMessage();
   die ($errorMessage);
   }
   else $returnArray['result'] = "Query completed okay.";


// Disconnect from database and return $returnArray...

$db->disconnect();

return $returnArray;

}
```

The code could not be much simpler. The key element is the SQL statement, which matches
the id value sent as an argument to a row in the ACCT_register table.

```
DELETE FROM ACCT_register WHERE id='$id'
```

The row in which the id values match is deleted.

A PHP Web Service Test Utility Because the accessor classes described in this chapter
make use of the NuSOAP library to expose functions as Web services and have no
easily visible user interface, it may be handy to have a little application available for
sending values to the accessor functions.

The Web service tester listed here presents an HTML document—a Web page—
with two columns of input boxes. In the left column, you should enter the names of
arguments the service is expecting. For example, if you were testing the addCurrency
service described in this chapter, you would enter country, name, abbreviation, and

xRate into individual boxes in the left column. The right column would contain corresponding values. To continue the example, the right column boxes might contain Mexico, Peso, MXN, and 0.092. The Service uniform resource locator (URL) box contains the HTTP address of the service to be tested, and the Function Name box holds the name of the exposed (registered) Web service.

Figure 7.1 illustrates the program in use.

Upon clicking the Go button, the form's contents are submitted to the specified service. When the service returns a value—an array in almost all cases discussed in this chapter—the Web page shows the resultant data. It can handle returned simple values, arrays, and two-dimensional arrays. Here is a listing of the Web service tester:

```
<html>

<head>
<title>Service Tester</title>
</head>

<body>

<H1>Service Tester</H1>


require_once('nusoap-0.6/nusoap.php');

if ($serviceURL != "")

{

$parameters = array($name1=>$value1, $name2=>$value2, $name3=>$value3,
$name4=>$value4, $name5=>$value5, $name6=>$value6, $name7=>$value7,
$name8=>$value8, $name9=>$value9);

$soapclient = new soapclient($serviceURL);

$result = $soapclient->call($functionName,$parameters);

echo "<H2>Results of call to $functionName";
echo "<BR>at $serviceURL</H2>";

$datatype = gettype($result);
```

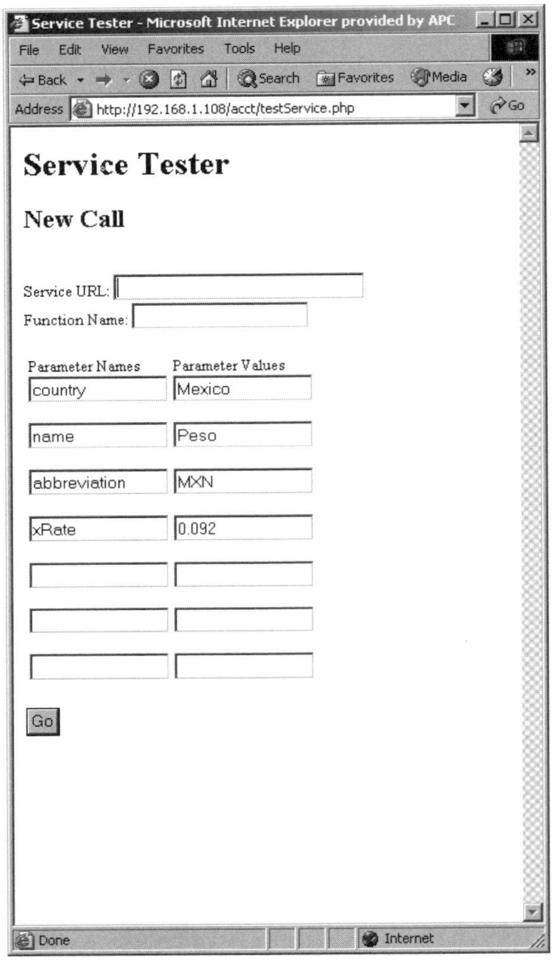

Figure 7.1: The Web service tester helps verify that the accessor-layer classes are working properly.

```
if ($datatype != "array")

  {

  // Sole result
  echo "Sole value: $result";

  }
```

```
else {

$keys = array_keys($result);

$datatype = gettype($result[$keys[0]]);

if ($datatype = "array")
    {

    // Array of arrays

    foreach ($result as $key => $subarray)

    {

    echo "<P>*********** New Element! ***********";
    echo "<BR>Key: $key";


    foreach ($subarray as $subkey => $subvalue)

        {

        echo "<P>Subkey: $subkey";
        echo "<BR>Subvalue: $subvalue";

        }

    }


}

else

  {

  // Simple array

  foreach ($result as $key3 => $value)
```

```
        {
        echo "$result[$key3] => $value";
        }

        $keys = array_keys($result);

        foreach ($keys as $key)
        {
        echo "<P>Key: $key";
        echo "<BR>Value: $result[$key]";
        }
        }

}

}


<H2>New Call</H2>

<P>

<form action="<?php echo $_SERVER['$PHP_SELF']; ?>" method="post">

<BR>Service URL: <input type="text" name="serviceURL" value="" size=30>

<BR>Function Name: <input type="text" name="functionName" value=""
size=20>

<P>
<P>

<TABLE COLS=2>

<TR>

<TD>
Parameter Names
<BR><input type="text" name="name1" value="" size=15>
<BR><input type="text" name="name2" value="" size=15>
```

```
<BR><input type="text" name="name3" value="" size=15>
<BR><input type="text" name="name4" value="" size=15>
<BR><input type="text" name="name5" value="" size=15>
<BR><input type="text" name="name6" value="" size=15>
<BR><input type="text" name="name7" value="" size=15>
<BR><input type="text" name="name8" value="" size=15>
<BR><input type="text" name="name9" value="" size=15>
</TD>

<TD>
Parameter Values
<BR><input type="text" name="value1" value="" size=15>
<BR><input type="text" name="value2" value="" size=15>
<BR><input type="text" name="value3" value="" size=15>
<BR><input type="text" name="value4" value="" size=15>
<BR><input type="text" name="value5" value="" size=15>
<BR><input type="text" name="value6" value="" size=15>
<BR><input type="text" name="value7" value="" size=15>
<BR><input type="text" name="value8" value="" size=15>
<BR><input type="text" name="value9" value="" size=15>

</TD>
</TR>

</TABLE>

<P><input type="submit" value="Go">

</form>

</body>

</html>
```

7.5 Questions and Exercises

1. Why are DELETE statements risky in a relational database, particularly when ON DELETE CASCADE statements were used in establishing the foreign keys? Why could this really throw off an accounting application?

2. Can you make an argument for using, as is generally the case in this chapter, "get" functions (based on SELECT statements) that retrieve whole rows from the database and leave it to other layers to pick out needed elements? Can you make an argument for the alternate strategy of having many more accessor-layer functions that pull out much smaller subsets of data?

3. Can you see an advantage to having all of your accessor-layer functions combined into a single large file? Can you see any disadvantages to that strategy?

4. How might you go about protecting the dbDetails.php file, which in Currawong Accounting is the file that contains details about how to access the database?

chapter **8**

Business Logic

This chapter unpacks the business-logic portion of Currawong Accounting. Most of its software modules are very simple—little more than bridges between hypertext transport protocol (HTTP) requests (of the GET and POST varieties) and simple object access protocol (SOAP) queries to the accessor layer. A few of its elements are quite exciting, though. These have to do with taking raw business data and converting it to graphical form.

8.1 Inserting, Updating, and Deleting

In insert, update, and delete operations, in which activity on the presentation layer, usually in the form of a human user manipulating an hypertext markup language (HTML) form in some way, the business logic layer acts as an intermediary between the presentation layer and the accessor layer. The programs of the business logic layer receive HTTP GET or POST requests from the presentation layer, and in this implementation do little more than repackage the values received as the elements of a parameters array that's transmitted to the relevant Web service on the accessor layer.

Because the insert, update, and delete modules on the business logic layer are so similar, only a single typical example of each is shown in this chapter.

8.1.1 Inserting a Row

Several interface pages on the presentation layer are concerned with adding rows to the Currawong Accounting database. For example, the enterBankAccount.php program (covered in depth in Chapter 9) presents the user with an HTML form, which is meant to be filled with the details of a bank account. This form ultimately gets submitted according to this directive:

```
<FORM name='addBankAccount' METHOD='POST' ACTION='http://" . $blHost .
"/acct/bl/blEnterBankAccount.php'>
```

That means that the contents of the form are submitted by HTTP POST to a program called blEnterBankAccount.php on the business logic layer. Here's what that file looks like:

```
blEnterAccount.php

require_once('nusoap-0.6/nusoap.php');
require_once('configuration.php');

// Convert $_POST array to $parameters for clarity.

foreach ($_POST as $key => $value)

    {

    $parameters[$key] = $value;

    }

// BL-level processing of submission could go here.
// Establish NuSOAP soapclient object and make call to Web Service

$soapclient = new soapclient("http://" . $accessorHost . "/acct/accessor/
addAccount.php");

$result = $soapclient->call('addAccount',$parameters);

// Refresh the page to show updated data.

$URL = "http://" . $presentationHost . "/acct/presentation/enterAccount.php";
$locationHeader = "Location: " . $URL;

header($locationHeader);
```

The core of this program is a loop that examines $_POST, which contains the submitted form's contents:

```
// Convert $_POST array to $parameters for clarity.

foreach ($_POST as $key => $value)

    {
```

```
$parameters[$key] = $value;

}
```

The entire contents of the $_POST array are transferred to a new array called $parameters. It's true that a direct assignment could have accomplished the same thing, and even that $_POST itself could be submitted to the accessor layer (as shown shortly), but this approach makes the assignment process more obvious, and there's a clear place to put further processing logic if some is needed in the future.

With $parameters defined, a call is made to the accessor layer:

```
$soapclient = new soapclient("http://" . $accessorHost . "/acct/accessor/
addAccount.php");

$result = $soapclient->call('addAccount',$parameters);
```

Finally, the page is made to refresh, via a manipulation of the local page's HTTP header:

```
// Refresh the page to show updated data.

$URL = "http://" . $presentationHost .
"/acct/presentation/enterAccount.php";

$locationHeader = "Location: " . $URL;
header($locationHeader);
```

Other modules on the business-logic layer that are functionally similar to this one are:

- blEnterAccount.php,
- blEnterAcctType.php,
- blEnterCurrency.php,
- blEnterInstitution.php,
- blEnterPayee.php,
- blEnterTransaction.php, and
- blEnterTransType.php.

8.1.2 Updating a Row

The logic involved in updating a row is very similar to that of inserting a row, at least at the business-logic layer (significant differences exist at the presentation layer, and especially at the accessor layer). The incoming $_POST array becomes the input for an update program on the accessor layer. The program blUpdateAccount.php, used for modifying the characteristics of accounting categories, is typical of the "blUpdate" modules.

blUpdateAccount.php

```php
require_once('nusoap-0.6/nusoap.php');
require_once('configuration.php');

$parameters = array();

// Convert $_POST array to $parameters for clarity.

foreach ($_POST as $key => $value)

    {

    $parameters[$key] = $value;

    }

// BL-level processing of submission could go here.
// Establish NuSOAP soapclient object and make call to Web Service

$soapclient = new soapclient("http://" . $accessorHost . "/acct/accessor/
updateAccount.php");

$result = $soapclient->call('updateAccount',$parameters);

// Refresh the page to show updated data.

$URL = "http://" . $blHost . "/acct/bl/reloadAndClose.html";

$locationHeader = "Location: " . $URL;

header($locationHeader);
```

The most significant difference here is in the "page refresh" functionality at the end, shown here again:

```php
// Refresh the page to show updated data.

$URL = "http://" . $blHost . "/acct/bl/reloadAndClose.html";

$locationHeader = "Location: " . $URL;

header($locationHeader);
```

The page that's loaded is reloadAndClose.html. That's because the pieces of the presentation layer related to update activity run in a window that's separate from the main window. Let's have a look at reloadAndClose.html.

```
reloadAndClose.html

<HTML>
<HEAD>

<SCRIPT LANGUAGE="JavaScript">
function reloadAndClose() {

// Reload the contents of the window that opened this one...

opener.location.reload();

// ...then close this window.

window.close();

}

</SCRIPT>

</HEAD>

<BODY onLoad="reloadAndClose()">

<H1>Succeeded.</H1>

</BODY>

</HTML>
```

The functionality here is implemented entirely with JavaScript. When the page loads, the onLoad event handler (noted in the opening BODY tag) fires. In doing so, it calls the reloadAndClose() function. It uses the document object model (DOM) to refer to the location of the window that opened the current window (opener.location) and invoke its reload() method. It then invokes window.close(), thus closing its own window.

Other modules on the business-logic layer that resemble blUpdateAccount.php are:

- blUpdateAcctType.php,
- blUpdateBankAccount.php,
- blUpdateCurrency.php,
- blUpdateInstitution.php,
- blUpdatePayee.php,

- blUpdateTransaction.php, and
- blUpdateTransType.php.

8.1.3   Deleting a Row

At the business-logic layer, the deletion of a row is very similar to the insertion or modification of a row. Once again, the $_POST array is repackaged as an array of parameters for a module on the accessor layer.

There's only one business-logic-layer program concerned with deletions. That is blDeleteTransaction, php.

```
blDeleteTransaction

require_once('nusoap-0.6/nusoap.php');
require_once('configuration.php');

$parameters=array();

// Convert $_POST array to $parameters for clarity.

foreach ($_POST as $key => $value)

    {

    $parameters[$key] = $value;

    }

// BL-level processing of submission could go here.

// Establish NuSOAP soapclient object and make call to Web Service
$soapclient = new soapclient("http://" . $accessorHost . "/acct/accessor/
deleteTransaction.php");

$result = $soapclient->call('deleteTransaction',$parameters);

// Refresh the page to show updated data.

$URL = "http://" . $blHost . "/acct/bl/reloadAndClose.html";

$locationHeader = "Location: " . $URL;

header($locationHeader);
```

This program is functionally identical to those concerned with update capabilities, right down to the use of reloadAndClose.html (discussed in the previous section) for refreshing the parent frame.

8.2 Reporting

The most important functions of the business-logic layer in Currawong Accounting are the reporting functions. These enable the user to view summary information about the managed bank accounts, and therefore have a better idea of what is happening with his or her money.

The reporting capabilities discussed here comprise a tabular summary page that displays the contents of any group of specified accounts, as well as a series of graphs. There are three graphs:

1. A bar graph showing the value of a specified account in its native currency, with weekly sampling.
2. A similar bar graph with a supplementary line depicting the 60-day moving average of the account's balance.
3. A bar graph showing, simultaneously, the values of several accounts, with all values shown in U.S. dollars for consistency. This graph also employs weekly sampling.

The graphing modules make use of a bar- and line-graph generating class written by Herman Veluwenkamp of New Zealand and released under the lesser GNU public license (LGPL), which means we're free to make use of it as a library here. That's why the graphing modules import graph.php—Veluwenkamp's class—and devote code to manipulating an instance of it.

8.2.1 Generating an Accounts Summary

Currawong Accounting needs a summary page that shows the individual values of all existing accounts. The page, generated by blAccountsReport.php, takes no input from the presentation layer. It always displays information about all accounts.

```
blAccountsReport.php

<html>

<head>
<title>View Transactions</title>

</head>

<body>
```

```
<H1>Summary of Accounts</H1>


require_once('nusoap-0.6/nusoap.php');
require_once('configuration.php');


// Get list of bank accounts

$parameters = array();

$soapclient = new soapclient('http://' . $accessorHost . '/acct/accessor/
getBankAccounts.php');
$result = $soapclient->call('getBankAccounts',$parameters);

// Get today's date.
$today = date("Y-m-d");

$totalUSDBalance = 0;

// Generate a table containing accounts and their balances.

echo '<TABLE BORDER="1" CELLPADDING="5">';
echo '<TR>';

echo '<TD>';
echo '<B>Description</B>';
echo '</TD>';
echo '<TD>';
echo '<B>Institution</B>';
echo '</TD>';
echo '<TD>';
echo '<B>Number</B>';
echo '</TD>';
echo '<TD>';
echo '<B>Currency</B>';
echo '</TD>';
echo '<TD>';
echo '<B>Native Balance</B>';
echo '</TD>';
echo '<TD>';
echo '<B>USD Balance</B>';
```

```
echo '</TD>';
echo '</TR>';


foreach ($result as $key => $subarray)
   {
   echo '<TR>';

   echo '<TD>';
   echo $subarray['description'];
   echo '</TD>';

   echo '<TD>';
   echo $subarray['institution'];
   echo '</TD>';

   echo '<TD>';
   echo $subarray['number'];
   echo '</TD>';

   echo '<TD>';
   echo $subarray['currency'];
   echo '</TD>';

   // For each account, get balance as of today.

   echo '<TD>';
   $parameters = array('id'=>$subarray['id'], 'date'=>$today);
   $soapclient = new soapclient('http://' . $accessorHost .
   '/acct/accessor/getSpecifiedBankAccountBalance.php');
   $result2 = $soapclient->call('getSpecifiedBankAccountBalance',
   $parameters);
   echo round(($result2[0]['balance'] + 0),2);
   echo '</TD>';

   // For each account, get relevant currency xRate -- the latest in the
   application's currency table.
   echo '<TD>';
   $parameters = array();
   $parameters['id'] = $subarray['currencyId'];
   $soapclient = new soapclient('http://' . $accessorHost .
   '/acct/accessor/getSpecifiedCurrency.php');
   $result = $soapclient->call('getSpecifiedCurrency',
   $parameters);
   $xRate = $result[0]['xRate'];
```

```
$usdBalance = $xRate * $result2[0]['balance'];
echo round($usdBalance,2);
echo '</TD>';
echo '</TR>';

// Add to overall USD (converted balance) for later display.

$totalUSDBalance += $usdBalance;

}

echo '</TABLE>';

echo "<P>";
echo "Total Value of Accounts (USD): ";
echo round($totalUSDBalance,2);
echo "<P>";
echo date("d F Y H:i T");

</body>

</html>
```

The program begins its operation by retrieving all details of all bank accounts:

```
// Get list of bank accounts

$parameters = array();
$soapclient = new soapclient('http://' . $accessorHost .
'/acct/accessor/getBankAccounts.php');
$result = $soapclient->call('getBankAccounts',$parameters);
```

The results of this call to the accessor layer are then used to populate a table. Some of the values require further queries and some manipulation, though. To get the balance of a given account, for example, the program must make another query to the accessor layer:

```
$parameters = array('id'=>$subarray['id'],
'date'=>$today);
$soapclient = new soapclient('http://' . $accessorHost .
'/acct/accessor/getSpecifiedBankAccountBalance.php');
$result2 = $soapclient->call('getSpecifiedBankAccountBalance',
$parameters);
echo round(($result2[0]['balance'] + 0),2);
```

That yields the account's balance in its native currency. Notice that 0 is added to the balance figure so that something is displayed in the event that the balance comes back null, and that round() is used to make sure that two decimal places are displayed.

Further queries yield the relative value of the account's native currency to the U.S. dollar:

```
$parameters = array();
$parameters['id'] = $subarray['currencyId'];
$soapclient = new soapclient('http://' . $accessorHost .
'/acct/accessor/getSpecifiedCurrency.php');
$result = $soapclient->call('getSpecifiedCurrency',
$parameters);
$xRate = $result[0]['xRate'];
```

This is then used to convert the account's balance to U.S. dollar terms:

```
$usdBalance = $xRate * $result2[0]['balance'];
```

In the foreach loop, the program accumulates a running total U.S. dollar value for the account, which is then displayed at the bottom of the information table. A date is rendered, as well:

```
echo date("d F Y H:i T");
```

The letters provided as an argument dictate how the date is rendered (Figure 8.1 shows a depiction and see the date() function documentation for other options). Figure 8.1 shows the accounts summary page.

8.2.2 Graphing the Balance of a Single Account over Time

In order to provide Currawong Accounting users with a bar graph that shows the balance of a specified account every seven days for a designated period of time, blBarGraphAccountWeekly.php exists. It takes input from viewBarGraphSingleAccount-Weekly.php on the presentation layer. Specifically, it receives three values:

- account. An integer corresponding to the id value of a row in the ACCT_bank_account table.

- startDate. A date, in YYYY-MM-DD form (the MySQL standard form) that represents the first day in the period to be graphed.

- endDate. A date, in YYYY-MM-DD form (the MySQL standard form) that represents the last day in the period to be graphed.

A bit of background about dates: MySQL date columns (such as the one that appears in the ACCT_bank_account table) use the YYYY-MM-DD format. However, it's hard to do calculations on dates in that form. It's much easier to do math on dates in the Unix time-stamp form, in which a date is represented as a number of seconds since midnight on

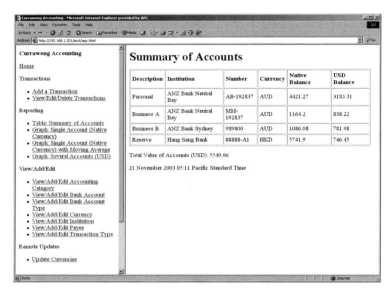

Figure 8.1: Currawong Accounting's summary of accounts.

January 1, 1970. Because this program (and the other graphing programs in the business-logic layer) need to do date math, we need some utility functions for converting back and forth between Unix timestamp format and MySQL format. Those functions appear in dateConv.php.

dateConv.php

```
function mysql_datetime_to_timestamp($dt)
{
    $yr=strval(substr($dt,0,4));
    $mo=strval(substr($dt,5,2));
    $da=strval(substr($dt,8,2));
    $hr=strval(substr($dt,11,2));
    $mi=strval(substr($dt,14,2));
    $se=strval(substr($dt,17,2));

    return mktime($hr,$mi,$se,$mo,$da,$yr);
}

function timestamp_to_mysql_date($ts)
{

    $d=getdate($ts);
```

```
        $yr=$d["year"];
        $mo=$d["mon"];
        $da=$d["mday"];

        return sprintf("%04d-%02d-%02d",$yr,$mo,$da);
    }
```

It's all done with substring and date-manipulation functions, but the key thing to know is that mysql_datetime_to_timestamp() makes one conversion, and timestamp_to_mysql_date() goes the other way. We'll need both functions to make the graph we want.

With that background out of the way, we can examine blBarGraphAccountWeekly.php itself.

blBarGraphAccountWeekly.php

```
include 'graph.php';
require_once('configuration.php');
require_once('nusoap-0.6/nusoap.php');
require_once('dateConv.php');
require_once('rounder.php');
require_once('standardGraphFormat.php');

// Instantiate a graph object.

$graph = new graph(700,480);

// Initialize relevant dates...

$startDate = mysql_datetime_to_timestamp($_POST['startDate']);
$endDate = mysql_datetime_to_timestamp($_POST['endDate']);

$midDate = $startDate;

$xLabelArray = array();
$yDataArray = array();
$minValue = 0;
$maxValue = 0;

$graph->y_order=array();

// For every chosen account, get the current balance...
```

```php
foreach ($_POST['accounts'] as $account)

{

$arrayOfValues = array();0

while ($midDate < $endDate)
    {

    $formattedMidDate = timestamp_to_mysql_date($midDate);

    $xLabelArray[] = $formattedMidDate;

    $parameters = array('id' => $account, 'date' =>
    $formattedMidDate);
    $soapclient = new soapclient('http://' . $accessorHost .
    '/acct/accessor/getSpecifiedBankAccountBalance.php');

    $result = $soapclient->call('getSpecifiedBankAccountBalance',
    $parameters);
    $balance = $result[0]['balance'];

    // Do some range-setting, so the graph is the right size...

    if ($balance < $minValue)
        {
        $minValue = $balance;
        }

    elseif ($balance > $maxValue)
        {
        $maxValue = $balance;
        }

    // Add balance to arrayOfValues (which is to be graphed)
    // Requires round() below, or no sub-zero range in graph.
    $arrayOfValues[] = round($balance);

    // Advance $midDate by seven days for another check

    $midDate += 604800;

    }
```

```
// Assign arrayOfValues to y_data (an associative array) under the
$account key...

$graph->y_data[$account] = $arrayOfValues;


}


$graph->y_order = array();

$availableColours = array('maroon','olive','green','navy','purple','gray',
'red','lime','yellow','blue','fuchsia','aqua','black');
$useColour=0;

// For each account being graphed, get the description for the
legend, and associate a color.

foreach ($_POST['accounts'] as $account)
{
$parameters2 = array();
$parameters2['id'] = $account;
$soapclient2 = new soapclient('http://' . $accessorHost .
'/acct/accessor/getSpecifiedBankAccount.php');
$result2 = $soapclient2->call('getSpecifiedBankAccount',
$parameters2);

$accountName = $result2[0]['description'];
$accountCurrency = $result2[0]['currency'];

$graph->y_format[$account] = array('colour' =>
$availableColours[$useColour], 'bar' => 'fill', 'legend' =>
"$accountName ($accountCurrency)");
$graph->y_order[] = $account;
$useColour++;
}
// Set the size and granulatity of the graph...

$minValue = round($minValue*1.5);
$maxValue = round($maxValue*1.5);

$minValue = abs($minValue);
$minValue = round_to_nearest($minValue, 50);
$minValue = $minValue * -1;
```

```
$maxValue = round_to_nearest($maxValue, 50);

// ************************

// Do final formatting and draw the graph...

formatGraph();
$graph->parameter['title'] = 'Weekly Balance of Account (in
local currency)';
$graph->parameter['y_label'] = 'Balance';

$graph->x_data = $xLabelArray;

$graph->parameter['y_min_left'] = $minValue;
$graph->parameter['y_max_left'] = $maxValue;

$graph->draw();
```

The program begins with a long series of variable initializations, among them the instantiation of the graph object (available from the imported graph.php) that will ultimately represent an image file containing the bar graph:

```
$graph = new graph(700,480);
```

The business of getting values to graph takes place inside a pair of loops. The outer foreach loop guarantees that we get data for each account specified in the HTTP POST request that kicked off execution:

```
foreach ($_POST['accounts'] as $account)
```

And the inner while loop performs the weekly sampling on the balance of that account:

```
while ($midDate < $endDate)
```

Bear in mind that there should be only one account in the $_POST array in this case, and that this program is designed to be adaptable to multiaccount applications covered later in this chapter.

Within the inner while loop, we add a label to $xLabelArray, which contains the dates that appear along the x-axis:

```
$xLabelArray[] = $formattedMidDate;
```

We also make a call to the accessor layer to get the balance for the current account on the date specified by $formattedMidDate:

```
$parameters = array('id' => $account, 'date' =>
$formattedMidDate);
$soapclient = new soapclient('http://' . $accessorHost .
```

```
'/acct/accessor/getSpecifiedBankAccountBalance.php');
$result = $soapclient->call('getSpecifiedBankAccountBalance',
$parameters);
$balance = $result[0]['balance'];
```

A bit of ranging comes next, to make sure that the y-axis is high and low enough to accommodate the most extreme balance values (positive and negative):

```
if ($balance < $minValue)
    {
    $minValue = $balance;
    }

elseif ($balance > $maxValue)
    {
    $maxValue = $balance;
    }
```

Then, arrayOfValues has the balance appended to it as a new element:

```
$arrayOfValues[] = round($balance);
```

The variable $midDate is then advanced by 684,800, which equals 60*60*24*7, or the number of seconds in a week:

```
$midDate += 604800;
```

Before leaving the loop, the two-dimensional associative array y_data gets a new element, which has the current account id number as its key and $arrayOfValues as its value:

```
$graph->y_data[$account] = $arrayOfValues;
```

The process repeats for all accounts contained in the $_POST array.

The program then loops through the specified accounts one more time to populate the y_format property of the $graph object with details about the color in which each account's bars are to be rendered. Note that there's a call to getSpecifiedBankAccount.php on the accessor layer to convert the account's id number to a name (description, actually) and get its native currency for the graph legend, as well.

```
foreach ($_POST['accounts'] as $account)
    {
    $parameters2 = array();
    $parameters2['id'] = $account;
    $soapclient2 = new soapclient('http://' . $accessorHost .
    '/acct/accessor/getSpecifiedBankAccount.php');
    $result2 = $soapclient2->call('getSpecifiedBankAccount',
    $parameters2);
```

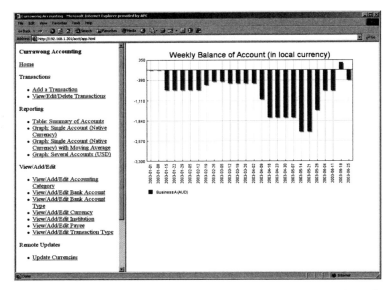

Figure 8.2: Currawong Accounting's single-account bar graph performs weekly balance sampling over a specified time range.

```
$accountName = $result2[0]['description'];
$accountCurrency = $result2[0]['currency'];

$graph->y_format[$account] = array('colour' =>
$availableColours[$useColour], 'bar' => 'fill', 'legend' =>
"$accountName ($accountCurrency)");
$graph->y_order[] = $account;
$useColour++;
}
```

A bit more ranging takes place—the code makes the top and bottom of the y-axis 50 percent greater than each actual extreme, just so the graph looks more comfortable—and the settings are applied to the $graph object with a series of assignments. Finally, there's a call to $graph->draw(), which causes a PCX graphic file to be generated based on the calculated specifications. Figure 8.2 shows the single-currency bar graph.

8.2.3   Graphing the Balance of a Single Account over Time, with a Moving Average

A bar graph of account values every seven days during a specified time period is useful, but it would be better if there were a line showing the changes in a 60-day moving average each week. With such a line visible, the user of Currawong Accounting could see whether the balance of the account was, overall, tending to increase or decrease. In blBarGraph-SingleAccountWeeklyWithMA.php, some modifications are made to the program discussed in the preceding section to enable the addition of such a trend line.

This program takes its input from viewBarGraphSingleAccountWeeklyWithMA.php on the presentation layer. That program provides three values in an HTTP POST request:

- account. An integer corresponding to the id value of a row in the ACCT_bank_account table.

- startDate. A date, in YYYY-MM-DD form (the MySQL standard form) that represents the first day in the period to be graphed.

- endDate. A date, in YYYY-MM-DD form (the MySQL standard form) that represents the last day in the period to be graphed.

Here's the program that takes those values.

```
blBarGraphSingleAccountWeeklyWithMA.php
```

```php
include 'graph.php';
require_once('configuration.php');
require_once('nusoap-0.6/nusoap.php');
require_once('dateConv.php');
require_once('rounder.php');
require_once('standardGraphFormat.php');
// Instantiate a graph object.

$graph = new graph(700,480);

// Initialize relevant dates...

$startDate = mysql_datetime_to_timestamp($_POST['startDate']);
$endDate = mysql_datetime_to_timestamp($_POST['endDate']);

$midDate = $startDate;

$xLabelArray = array();
$yDataArray = array();
$minValue = 0;
$maxValue = 0;

$graph->y_order=array();

// For every chosen account, get the current balance...
```

```php
foreach ($_POST['accounts'] as $account)

{

$arrayOfValues = array();
$arrayOfMovingAverageValues = array();

// ...for each specified $midDate value...

while ($midDate < $endDate)
    {

    $formattedMidDate = timestamp_to_mysql_date($midDate);

    $xLabelArray[] = $formattedMidDate;

    $parameters = array('id' => $account, 'date' => $formattedMidDate);
    $soapclient = new soapclient('http://' . $accessorHost .
    '/acct/accessor/getSpecifiedBankAccountBalance.php');
    $result = $soapclient->call('getSpecifiedBankAccountBalance',
    $parameters);
    $balance = $result[0]['balance'];

    if ($balance < $minValue)
        {
        $minValue = $balance;
        }

    elseif ($balance > $maxValue)
        {
        $maxValue = $balance;
        }

    // Requires round() below, or no sub-zero range in graph.

    $arrayOfValues[] = round($balance);

    // Calculate 60-day moving average as of current $midDate...

    $parameters = array('id' => $account, 'date' => $formattedMidDate, 60);

    $soapclient = new soapclient('http://' . $accessorHost .
    '/acct/accessor/getAverageBalance.php');
```

```
$movingAverage = $soapclient->call('getAverageBalance',
$parameters);

// Add moving average value to its own array...

$arrayOfMovingAverageValues[] = round($movingAverage);
$midDate += 604800;

}


// Add each array of account-balance values to the y_data
(associative) array, using the account as a key...

$graph->y_data[$account] = $arrayOfValues;

// Add the array of overall moving-average values values to the
y_data array, using 'Moving Average' as a key...

$graph->y_data['Moving Average'] = $arrayOfMovingAverageValues;

}
$graph->y_order = array();

$availableColours = array('maroon','olive','green','navy','purple','gray',
'red','lime', 'yellow','blue','fuchsia','aqua','black');
$useColour=0;

// For each graphed account, choose a color and get a
description to use in the legend.

foreach ($_POST['accounts'] as $account)
{
$parameters2 = array();
$parameters2['id'] = $account;
$soapclient2 = new soapclient('http://' . $accessorHost .
'/acct/accessor/getSpecifiedBankAccount.php');
$result2 = $soapclient2->call('getSpecifiedBankAccount',
$parameters2);
$accountName = $result2[0]['description'];
$accountCurrency = $result2[0]['currency'];
```

```
$graph->y_format[$account] = array('colour' =>
$availableColours[$useColour], 'bar' => 'fill', 'legend' =>
"$accountName ($accountCurrency)");
$graph->y_order[] = $account;
$useColour++;
}

$graph->y_format['Moving Average'] = array('colour' =>
$availableColours[$useColour], 'line' => 'brush', 'legend' =>
"60-Day Moving Average");

$graph->y_order[] = 'Moving Average';



$minValue = round($minValue*1.5);
$maxValue = round($maxValue*1.5);


$minValue = abs($minValue);
$minValue = round_to_nearest($minValue, 50);
$minValue = $minValue * -1;


$maxValue = round_to_nearest($maxValue, 50);
// ***********************

// Do some final formatting and generate the graph image:

formatGraph();

$graph->parameter['title'] = 'Weekly Balance of Account (in local currency)';
$graph->parameter['y_label'] = 'Balance';
$graph->x_data = $xLabelArray;

$graph->parameter['y_min_left'] = $minValue;
$graph->parameter['y_max_left'] = $maxValue;

$graph->draw();
```

The chief innovation of this program is a second call to the accessor layer to get the 60-day
moving average for every $formattedMidDate looped through:

```
$parameters = array('id' => $account, 'date' =>
$formattedMidDate, 60);
$soapclient = new soapclient('http://' . $accessorHost .
```

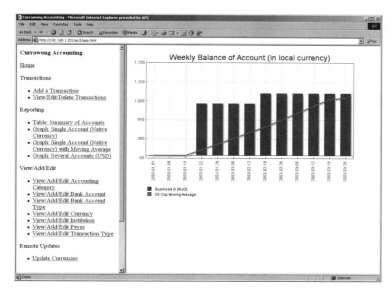

Figure 8.3: The 60-day moving average line adds a lot to the value of the account-balance graph.

```
'/acct/accessor/getAverageBalance.php');
$movingAverage = $soapclient->call('getAverageBalance',
$parameters);
$arrayOfMovingAverageValues[] = round($movingAverage);
```

When the loop is done, $arrayOfMovingAverageValues is another data series that can be formatted for depiction as a line:

```
$graph->y_format['Moving Average'] = array('colour' =>
$availableColours[$useColour], 'line' => 'brush', 'legend' =>
"60-Day Moving Average");
```

and graphed with the bar data showing the weekly balances. Figure 8.3 shows the graph with a moving average.

8.2.4 Graphing the Balance of Multiple Accounts over Time

The requirement to equip Currawong Accounting with a graphing function that shows a clustered bar graph of all accounts' values in U.S. dollar terms requires another adaptation of the graphing program used twice already. The module blBarGraphMultiAccountWeekly-USD.php has no moving average, but it converts each account's balance to U.S. dollars before adding it to an array of values to be rendered in graphical form.

This program receives input from viewBarGraphMultiAccountWeeklyUSD.php on the presentation layer. It sends two discrete data values and one array:

- account. An array of integers corresponding to the id value of a rows in the ACCT_bank_account table, representing the accounts to be included in the graph.
- startDate. A date, in YYYY-MM-DD form (the MySQL standard form) that represents the first day in the period to be graphed.
- endDate. A date, in YYYY-MM-DD form (the MySQL standard form) that represents the last day in the period to be graphed.

A problem with Currawong Accounting in this area is its lack of any historical exchange rate information. As a result, the historical balances depicted by the graphs that result from this program are converted to U.S. dollars based on the latest available exchange rate. The extreme case would be a graph showing balances for a six-month period three years ago, with conversion to U.S. dollars according to today's exchange rate! It's a weakness that can be fixed with an additional database table.

```
blBarGraphMultiAccountWeeklyUSD.php

include 'graph.php';
require_once('configuration.php');
require_once('nusoap-0.6/nusoap.php');
require_once('dateConv.php');
require_once('rounder.php');
require_once('standardGraphFormat.php');

set_time_limit(0);

$graph = new graph(700,480);

$startDate = mysql_datetime_to_timestamp($_POST['startDate']);
$endDate = mysql_datetime_to_timestamp($_POST['endDate']);

//$midDate = $startDate;

$xLabelArray = array();
$yDataArray = array();

$minValue = 0;
$maxValue = 0;

$graph->y_order=array();

// Get details of all selected bank accounts...
```

```php
foreach ($_POST['accounts'] as $account)

{

$midDate = $startDate;

$arrayOfValues = array();

$parameters = array();
$parameters['id'] = $account;
$soapclient = new soapclient('http://' . $accessorHost.
'/acct/accessor/getSpecifiedBankAccount.php');
$result = $soapclient->call('getSpecifiedBankAccount',
$parameters);
$currency = $result[0]['currencyId'];

$parameters = array();
$parameters['id'] = $currency;
$soapclient = new soapclient('http://' . $accessorHost .
'/acct/accessor/getSpecifiedCurrency.php');
$result = $soapclient->call('getSpecifiedCurrency',$parameters);
$xRate = $result[0]['xRate'];

$xLabelArray = array();

// Get the balance as of the current $midDate...

while ($midDate <= $endDate)
   {

   $formattedMidDate = timestamp_to_mysql_date($midDate);
   $xLabelArray[] = $formattedMidDate;

// Get balance and convert to USD...

   $parameters = array('id' => $account, 'date' =>
   $formattedMidDate);
   $soapclient = new soapclient('http://' . $accessorHost .
   '/acct/accessor/getSpecifiedBankAccountBalance.php');
   $result = $soapclient->call('getSpecifiedBankAccountBalance',
   $parameters);
   $balance = $result[0]['balance'] * $xRate;
```

```php
// Do some range-setting...

   if ($balance < $minValue)
      {
      $minValue = $balance;
      }

   elseif ($balance > $maxValue)
      {
      $maxValue = $balance;
      }

   // Requires round() below, or no sub-zero range in graph.
   $arrayOfValues[] = round($balance);
   $midDate += 604800;


   }

$graph->y_data[$account] = $arrayOfValues;

}


$graph->y_order = array();

$availableColours = array('maroon','olive','green','navy','purple','gray',
'red','lime','yellow','blue','fuchsia','aqua','black');
$useColour=0;

// For each account, get a description and choose a color...

foreach ($_POST['accounts'] as $account)
{
$parameters2 = array();
$parameters2['id'] = $account;
$soapclient2 = new soapclient('http://' . $accessorHost .
'/acct/accessor/getSpecifiedBankAccount.php');
$result2 = $soapclient2->call('getSpecifiedBankAccount',$parameters2);
$accountName = $result2[0]['description'];
$accountCurrency = $result2[0]['currency'];

$graph->y_format[$account] = array('colour' =>
$availableColours[$useColour], 'bar' => 'fill', 'legend' =>
"$accountName ($accountCurrency converted to USD)");
```

```
$graph->y_order[] = $account;
$useColour++;
}

// Do some more formatting...

$minValue = round($minValue*1.5);
$maxValue = round($maxValue*1.5);

$minValue = abs($minValue);

$minValue = round_to_nearest($minValue, 50);
$minValue = $minValue * -1;

$maxValue = round_to_nearest($maxValue, 50);

// ***********************

// Assign titles and generate the image...

formatGraph();

$graph->parameter['title'] = 'Weekly Balance of Accounts (in current USD)';
$graph->parameter['y_label'] = 'Balance';

$graph->x_data = $xLabelArray;

$graph->parameter['y_min_left'] = $minValue;
$graph->parameter['y_max_left'] = $maxValue;

$graph->draw();
```

What's new in this program? Primarily, this, the call to getSpecifiedCurrency.php on the accessor layer to determine the rate of exchange to U.S. dollars:

```
$parameters = array();
$parameters['id'] = $currency;
$soapclient = new soapclient('http://' . $accessorHost .
'/acct/accessor/getSpecifiedCurrency.php');
$result = $soapclient->call('getSpecifiedCurrency',
$parameters);
$xRate = $result[0]['xRate'];
```

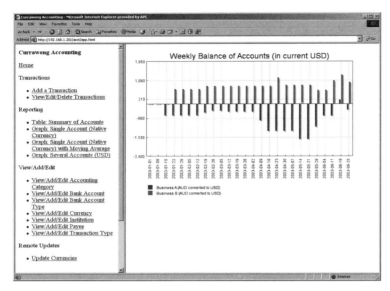

Figure 8.4: Currawong Accounting can standardize the value of several accounts in U.S. dollars for combined reporting.

With that available, the balance of each account is converted before being added to the two-dimensional y_data array:

```
$balance = $result[0]['balance'] * $xRate;
```

Figure 8.4 shows an example of the graph with those results.

8.3 Questions and Exercises

1. What validation functions could you build into the simple business-logic modules covered in this chapter?

2. What are the relative merits of doing validation in PHP on the business-logic layer and doing it in JavaScript (or another client-side language) on the presentation layer?

3. The three graphing programs in this chapter bear a lot of similarity to one another. Try combining them into a single, multipurpose class or procedural program.

4. There are some classes, available under LGPL on the Web, that will generate pie charts (the French call them Camembert charts, no kidding). Create a new reporting module that shows the relative values of all accounts in such a format.

chapter **9**

The Presentation Layer

The presentation layer of an application that uses multi-tier software architecture is concerned with providing the public fact of that application. It is the programs of the presentation layer that generate interfaces of various kinds.

An interface may be a human interface, such as a command-line syntax, or a graphical user interface (GUI). Most often, these will take the form of hypertext markup language (HTML) pages. Alternately, a GUI can be in the form of some sort of special client that's particular to your operating system. Either way, it's important to separate, as fully as possible, the people who do the accessor- and logic-layer work from the designers who concern themselves primarily with the visual appearance of data. Lots of tools exist to help you achieve this goal, notably the PHP-based Smarty templating engine (read its nutshell tutorial here: http://smarty.php.net/crashcourse.php).

Alternately, the presentation layer may provide an interface that's suitable for inter-pretation only by a machine. It's possible that you would create a presentation layer that generates extensible markup language (XML) documents for consumption by some remote computing resource.

In this chapter, we'll endow Currawong Accounting with a front end in the form of a collection of HTML pages. These documents will deliver information to and extract information (and commands) from the application's user.

9.1 Frameworks and Resources

In creating an HTML-based presentation layer, we'll need to create a couple of resources up front. First among these is a basic system of HTML frames, one of which acts as a navigation bar with which to call up the various presentation-layer programs (it also acts as a sort of "to-do" list as you work toward implementing all of the features you want your application to have). We'll also need to create a library that makes it easier to include standard HTML features, such as list boxes containing the names of all recorded payees, in our pages.

9.1.1   An HTML Display Framework

The first thing we're going to need is an HTML framework in which to display our information. The basic design is a single window with two frames: a small navigation strip down the left side and the remainder of the window for displaying the results of PHP programs. Setting this up isn't hard; the job requires only a single master framing document, a links document to fill the navigation strip, and a default page that displays when the master framing document is loaded (i.e., before any links in the navigation strip have been clicked).

The master framing document is called app.html, and it looks like this:

app.html

```
<!DOCTYPE HTML PUBLIC "-//W3C//DTD HTML 4.0 Transitional//EN">

<html>

<head>

<title>Currawong Accounting</title>

</head>

<frameset COLS="30%,*">

<frame name="controls" src="acctLinks.html">
<frame name="display" src="welcome.html">

</frameset>
</html>
```

The key bit is the frameset element, which defines two columnar frames in a 30–70 allocation. Then, it defines the two frames themselves, giving them each a name and some initial contents: acctLinks.html and welcome.html. It's important to note that the name of the right-hand frame is display, because we'll have to make PHP programs render there in a moment.

With those columns established, let's look at the documents they're defined as containing. Here's acctLinks.html:

acctLinks.html

```
<!DOCTYPE HTML PUBLIC "-//W3C//DTD HTML 4.0 Transitional//EN">

<html>

<head>

<title>Currawong Accounting</title>

</head>

<body>

<H4>Currawong Accounting</H4>

<P> <A HREF="welcome.html" TARGET="display">Home</A>

<P>Transactions
<UL>
<LI><A HREF="/acct/presentation/enterTransaction.php"
TARGET="display">Add a Transaction</A>
<LI><A HREF="/acct/presentation/viewTransactions.html"
TARGET="display">View/Edit/Delete Transactions</A>
</UL>

<P>Reporting
<UL>
<LI><A HREF="/acct/bl/blAccountsReport.php"
TARGET="display">Table: Summary of Accounts</A>
<LI><A HREF="/acct/presentation/viewBarGraphSingleAccountWeekly.php"
TARGET="display">Graph: Single Account (Native Currency)</A>
<LI><A HREF="/acct/presentation/viewBarGraphSingleAccountWeeklyWithMA.php"
TARGET="display">Graph: Single Account (Native Currency) with Moving
Average</A>
<LI><A HREF="/acct/presentation/viewBarGraphMultiAccountWeeklyUSD.php"
TARGET="display">Graph: Several Accounts (USD)</A>
</UL>

<P> View/Add/Edit
<UL>
<LI> <A HREF="/acct/presentation/enterAccount.php"
TARGET="display">View/Add/Edit Accounting Category</A>
<LI> <A HREF="/acct/presentation/enterBankAccount.php"
```

```
                   TARGET="display">View/Add/Edit Bank Account</A>
                   <LI> <A HREF="/acct/presentation/enterAcctType.php"
                   TARGET="display">View/Add/Edit Bank Account Type</A>
                   <LI> <A HREF="/acct/presentation/enterCurrency.php"
                   TARGET="display">View/Add/Edit Currency</A>
                   <LI> <A HREF="/acct/presentation/enterInstitution.php"
                   TARGET="display">View/Add/Edit Institution</A>
                   <LI> <A HREF="/acct/presentation/enterPayee.php"
                   TARGET="display">View/Add/Edit Payee</A>
                   <LI> <A HREF="/acct/presentation/enterTransType.php"
                   TARGET="display">View/Add/Edit Transaction Type</A>
                   </UL>

                   <P> Remote Updates
                   <UL>
                   <LI> <A HREF="/acct/elsewhere/updateCurrencies.php"
                   TARGET="display">Update Currencies</A>
                   </UL>

                   <BR><BR><BR><BR><BR>

                   <center>

                   <IMAGE SRC="littleCurrawong.jpg">

                   </center>

                   </body>
                   </html>
```

Again, not even close to rocket science. The only interesting bits (and that is only if you're kind of out of touch with HTML) are the TARGET attributes of the A elements (the links). Notice that each of the links looks like this example:

```
<A HREF="/acct/presentation/enterPayee.php"
TARGET="display">View/Add/Edit Payee</A>
```

The TARGET="display" part of that line tells the browser that the document to which the link points should not be rendered in the frame that contains the link (the navigation strip), but rather in the frame named display. We defined the larger frame as having that name in the master framing document (app.html). It's a simple but important effect.

By default (because it's specified in app.html), the large frame contains a file called welcome.html. This is essentially the splash screen of Currawong Accounting, containing the applications name and a photo of Strepera graculina, the currawong. It's not a complex HTML file:

```
welcome.html

<!DOCTYPE HTML PUBLIC "-//W3C//DTD HTML 4.0 Transitional//EN">

<html>

<head>

<title>Currawong Accounting</title>

</head>

<body>

<CENTER>

<H2>Currawong Accounting</H2>
<H3>Multi-Currency Bookkeeping for Small Business</H3>

<IMAGE SRC="currawong.jpeg">

</CENTER>

</body>
</html>
```

Figure 9.1 illustrates the default appearance of Currawong Accounting.

9.1.2 Generating List Boxes

In generating HTML pages on the presentation layer, there will be a number of points at which we'll want to generate lists representing the contents of database tables. When presenting the user with the opportunity to record a transaction, for example, there will need to be list boxes containing the names of all existing bank accounts, all existing payees, and so on.

In HTML, list boxes look like this:

```
<select name='bankAccount'>
<option value='1'>Middleburg Bank Savings</option>
<option value='2'>Business A</option>
<option value='3'>Business B</option>
```

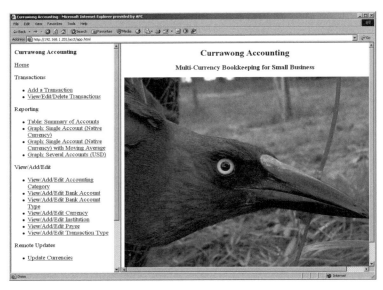

Figure 9.1: Currawong Accounting looks like this when it's first opened.

```
<option value='4'>Lloyds Retirement</option>
</select>
```

That's an actual example of a list box that's required for the Currawong Accounting presentation layer. Key parts of it include:

- The name, which in this case is "institution." A name allows JavaScript to manipulate the list box, among other things.

- The text enclosed by the option tags (such as "Middleburg Bank"), which is actually visible in the list box when it's rendered.

- The value attributes of the option elements, which are what can be manipulated programmatically and what goes to the server when the form is submitted.

In the case of Currawong Accounting, the text enclosed by option tags represents a value (usually the name or description column) from a row in a database table. The value attribute of the same option is the value of the primary key column of the same row (the primary key column is always the id column, in the database we set up in Chapter 6). That way, when the form is submitted, there's no need to resolve the name (or description) back to the id value. There's one less place for a mistake to appear.

In some cases, we'll want an option other than the first to be preselected. This will be the case, for example, when offering users the opportunity to edit something that already exists. In editing a transaction, say, the user should be able to change the account on which a check was drawn (it may have been entered in error originally), but should be able to see the details of the transaction as they were originally recorded). The HTML for this is straightforward:

```
<select name='bankAccount'>
<option value='1'>Middleburg Bank Savings</option>
<option value='2'>Business A</option>
<option value='3' SELECTED>Business B</option>
<option value='4'>Lloyds Retirement</option>
</select>
```

In that list box, the Hang Seng Bank option is shown selected when the list box is originally rendered.

A third possibility is a list box in which multiple elements may be selected. Such a list box looks like this:

```
<select MULTIPLE name='bankAccount'>
<option value='1'>Middleburg Bank Savings</option>
<option value='2'>Business A</option>
<option value='3' SELECTED>Business B</option>
<option value='4'>Lloyds Retirement</option>
</select>
```

The MULTIPLE attribute makes it possible to choose multiple elements.

For the Currawong application, we need a way to quickly generate HTML code like the above. We want to be able to import a library into our presentation-layer programs and use lines like this:

```
menuBankAccount('bankAccounts', 3, 0);
```

That would cause a list box of all existing bank accounts to be generated. It would have a name attribute of bankAccount, and the option with a value attribute equal to 3 would be shown selected. The final parameter, 0, indicates that it should not have a MULTIPLE attribute (a 1 in place of the 0 would indicate that a MULTIPLE attribute was required). In other words, we'd get precisely the same HTML code as was shown earlier:

```
<select name='bankAccount'>
<option value='1'>Middleburg Bank Savings</option>
<option value='2'>Business A</option>
<option value='3' SELECTED>Business B</option>
<option value='4'>Lloyds Retirement</option>
</select>
```

By the way, if you don't want a particular option preselected, you could call the function like this:

```
menuBankAccount('bankAccounts', 0, 0);
```

The library containing the code for generating selection lists is called listboxes.php. It contains seven functions, listed here:

```
menuBankAccounts()
menuAccount()
menuPayees()
menuTransTypes()
menuInstitutions()
menuAcctTypes()
menuCurrencies()
```

Most take two arguments (a name value and the id value of the element to be pre-selected) and all, except menuBankAccounts(), return selection lists with the value attribute equal to the id column and the visible text equal to the name column. In the case of menuBankAccounts(), the rendered text comes from the description column, which allows for the possibility that the user would have multiple accounts at the same bank. It's also the case that menuBankAccounts() takes a third parameter to allow the inclusion of the MULTIPLE attribute.

Because listboxes.php will have to make reference to the accessor layer, it has to import the usual libraries:

```
require_once('nusoap-0.6/nusoap.php');
require_once('configuration.php');
```

After that, the functions are defined. A typical example is menuBankAccounts():

```
function menuBankAccounts($listName, $selectedIndex, $multiple)

{

global $accessorHost;

$serviceURL = 'http://' . $accessorHost .
'/acct/accessor/getBankAccounts.php';
$functionName = "getBankAccounts";

$soapclient = new soapclient($serviceURL);

$parameters = array();

$result = $soapclient->call($functionName,$parameters);

$datatype = gettype($result);

if ($multiple==1)
```

```
        {
        echo "<select name='$listName' MULTIPLE>\n";
        }
        else
            {
            echo "<select name='$listName'>\n";
            }

    foreach ($result as $key => $subarray)
        {
        $id = $subarray['id'];
        $identifier = $subarray['description'];
        if ($id == $selectedIndex)
            {
            echo "<option value='$id' selected>$identifier</option>\n";
            }
            else
            {
            echo "<option value='$id'>$identifier</option>\n";
            }
        }

    echo "</select>\n";

    }
```

That function makes a call to a program on the accessor layer (getBankAccounts.php, in this case) and receives an array back. The array contains the contents of the ACCT_bankAccounts table (see Chapter 6 for more about the design of the database). The following line picks out each returned row as an array, and the code contained in its block pulls out the required elements by name.

```
    foreach ($result as $key => $subarray)
```

An if-else block determines if the element is one that's meant to be shown preselected, and the end result is that the HTML that represents the selection list is written with a series of echo commands.

The other six functions lack the capacity to add a MULTIPLE attribute to the generated list box. Function menuAccount() is typical:

```
    function menuAccount($listName, $selectedIndex)

    {

    global $accessorHost;
```

```
$serviceURL = "http://" . $accessorHost . "/acct/accessor/getAccounts.php";
$functionName = "getAccounts";

$soapclient = new soapclient($serviceURL);

$parameters = array();

$result = $soapclient->call($functionName,$parameters);

$datatype = gettype($result);

echo "<select name=$listName>\n";

foreach ($result as $key => $subarray)
   {
   $id = $subarray['id'];
   $identifier = $subarray['name'];
   if($id == $selectedIndex)
      {
      echo "<option value='$id' selected>$identifier</option>\n";
      }
         else
           {
           echo "<option value=\"$id\" >$identifier</option>\n";
           }
   }

echo "</select>\n";

}
```

The other five functions in listboxes.php are virtually identical to menuAccount(), and so are not listed here.

9.2   Viewing and Adding—Everything but Transactions

A key functional element of Currawong Accounting is the ability to view information stored in the database. The user needs to be able to extract lists of existing (i.e., already stored) currencies, payees, bank accounts, institutions, and the other business entities that are involved in managing the bookkeeping system. The user also has to be able to add to these lists, adding new payees, currencies, and so on. In other words, the user needs to be able to insert new rows into the tables in the database.

Specifically, we need user interfaces for the following purposes:

- Viewing and adding accounting categories,

- Viewing and adding bank accounts,

- Viewing and adding bank account types,

- Viewing and adding currencies,

- Viewing and adding institutions,

- Viewing and adding payees, and

- Viewing and adding transaction types.

As it happens, the programs in this category are very similar to one another. For that reason, this book does not include full listings of each one. There is a full listing of enterAccount.php, which is the presentation-level program used to view accounting categories, add new ones, and spawn the subwindow with which you edit existing categories. There's a full commentary on how enterAccount.php works, as well.

For the other programs in this section, you'll find only the parts that are significantly different (meaning, not the decorative HTML that surrounds the PHP code) listed here.

There is also a need for an interface with which to view and add transactions. However, because that requirement is handled differently, it's covered in a separate section at the end of this chapter.

9.2.1 Viewing and Adding Accounting Categories

The same presentation-layer program handles viewing and adding accounting categories. It's contained in a file called enterAccount.php.

Here's a listing of that file:

```
enterAccount.php

<html>

<head>
<title>Enter Account</title>

<SCRIPT LANGUAGE="JavaScript">

function openEditWindow(id)

{
```

```
var url = "editAccount.php?id=" + id;

var newWindow = window.open(url, "child", "HEIGHT=200, WIDTH=300");

}

</SCRIPT>

</head>

<body>

<H1>Enter Accounting Category</H1>


require_once('listboxes.php');
require_once('nusoap-0.6/nusoap.php');
require_once('configuration.php');

$parameters = array();

$soapclient = new soapclient('http://' . $accessorHost .
'/acct/accessor/getAccounts.php');

$result = $soapclient->call('getAccounts',$parameters);

echo "<P><B>Existing Accounts</B>\n";
echo "<BR>";

echo '<TABLE BORDER="1" CELLPADDING="5">';
echo '<TR>';
echo '<TD>';
echo '<B>Name</B>';
echo '</TD>';
echo '</TR>';


foreach ($result as $key => $subarray)
    {
    echo '<TR>';
    echo '<TD>';
    echo $subarray['name'];
    echo '</TD>';
```

```
        echo '<TD>';
        echo '<INPUT TYPE="BUTTON" onClick="openEditWindow('. $subarray['id'] . ')"
VALUE="Edit">';
        echo '</TD>';
    }

echo '</TABLE>';

echo '<FORM name="addAcct" METHOD="POST" ACTION="http://'
. $blHost . '/acct/bl/blEnterAccount.php">';

echo '<P><B>New Account</B>';

echo '<TABLE BORDER="1" CELLPADDING="5">';
echo '<TR>';
echo '<TD>';
echo '<B>Name</B>';
echo '</TD>';
echo '</TR>';

echo '<TR>';
echo '<TD>';
echo '<INPUT TYPE="TEXT" NAME="name" SIZE=15>';
echo '</TD>';
echo '</TR>';

echo '</TABLE>';

echo '<P><INPUT TYPE="SUBMIT" NAME="submit" VALUE="Submit">';

echo '</FORM>';

?>

</body>

</html>
```

In large part, this program is concerned with generating table code. The table is filled with data retrieved directly from the accessor layer, specifically getAccounts.php. The first interesting bit of code in the presentation-layer program presented here has to do with contacting getAccounts.php:

```
$parameters = array();
$soapclient = new soapclient('http://' . $accessorHost .
```

```
'/acct/accessor/getAccounts.php');
$result = $soapclient->call('getAccounts',$parameters);
```

Those three lines of code create a simple object access protocol (SOAP) client object (which is possible because the NuSOAP library is imported), which accesses the getAccounts.php file and sends it $parameters, an empty array (the accessor-layer program is defined as taking no parameters, as discussed in Chapter 7). After the call, $result contains a two-dimensional array representing the output of getAccounts().

That variable, $results, is used to generate the table of existing accounts. By using this construction:

```
foreach ($result as $key => $subarray)
```

each row in $result is split off individually (as $subarray) and can then be manipulated individually. The whole routine looks like this:

```
foreach ($result as $key => $subarray)
    {
    echo '<TR>';
    echo '<TD>';
    echo $subarray['name'];
    echo '</TD>';
    echo '<TD>';
    echo '<INPUT TYPE="BUTTON" onClick="openEditWindow(' . $subarray['id'] . ')"
    VALUE="Edit">';
    echo '</TD>';
    }
```

In the loop, $subarray['name'] represents the contents of the name element in that particular row (see the accessor-layer program that created the array in the first place for further explanation). The name element from each returned row gets inserted into a table.

The other interesting line in that block is this one:

```
echo '<INPUT TYPE="BUTTON" onClick="openEditWindow(' . $subarray['id'] . ')"
VALUE="Edit">';
```

It puts an Edit button in the table next to a row of data. When clicked, it calls a JavaScript function called openEditWindow(). To that function, it sends a single parameter: The value of the id column of the current row. That way, the JavaScript function knows what element it's working with.

The JavaScript function, openEditWindow(), is short. It looks like this:

```
function openEditWindow(id)
{
var url = "editAccount.php?rowToEdit=" + id;
var newWindow = window.open(url, "child", "HEIGHT=200,WIDTH=300");
}
```

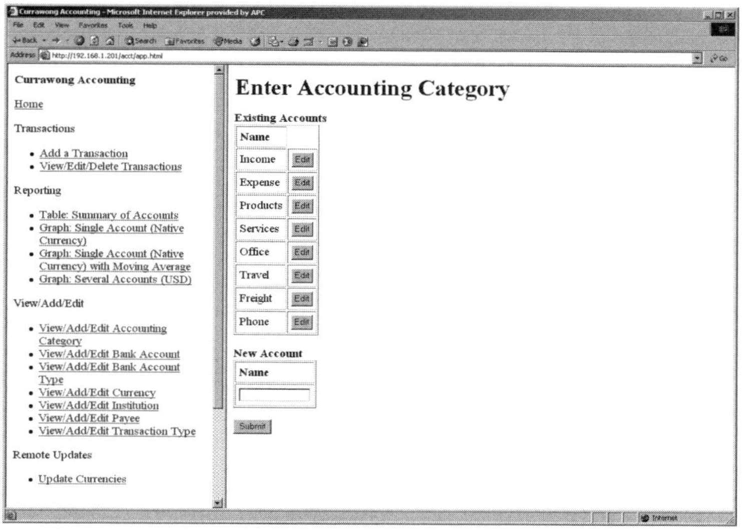

Figure 9.2: Viewing and adding accounting categories.

It takes the id value as an argument (note that JavaScript variables aren't preceded by $) and assembles a string using it. The string looks like this (using the id value 3 as an example):

```
editAccount.php?rowToEdit=3
```

That's a hypertext transport protocol (HTTP) GET statement. Indeed, this uniform resource locator (URL), when invoked by the final line of openEditWindow(), opens a new window containing HTML generated by editAccount.php (which is discussed in the editing section later in this chapter). That last line, by the way, opens a new window (using the window.open method) and calls the new window child. It's necessary to give the new window a name in JavaScript. Note also the unusual syntax of the HEIGHT and WIDTH specifications. These are different for the various child windows covered later in this chapter.

The second form generated by enterAccount.php is used to add a new row to the ACCT_accounts table, by way of insertAccount.php on the accessor layer. The call is made, however, to the business-logic layer:

```
echo '<FORM name="addAcct" METHOD="POST"
ACTION="http://' . $blHost . '/acct/bl/blEnterAccount.php">';
```

In Chapter 8, you saw that blEnterAccount.php receives the HTTP POST packet generated by the Submit button of this form and passes it on to the accessor layer via SOAP.

Figure 9.2 shows enterAccount.php.

9.2.2   Viewing and Adding Bank Accounts

The presentation-layer work of viewing and adding bank accounts takes place in enterBankAccount.php. Its design is very similar to that of enterAccount.php. However, the Web service call is different:

```
$parameters = array();
$soapclient = new soapclient("http://" . $accessorHost .
"/acct/accessor/getBankAccounts.php");
$result = $soapclient->call('getBankAccounts',$parameters);
```

Also, the table-generation code is a bit more elaborate, because more pieces of data come back from the accessor layer:

```
foreach ($result as $key => $subarray)
   {
   echo '<TR>';
   echo '<TD>';
   echo $subarray['institution'];
   echo '</TD>';
   echo '<TD>';
   echo $subarray['number'];
   echo '</TD>';
   echo '<TD>';
   echo $subarray['description'];
   echo '</TD>';
   echo '<TD>';
   echo $subarray['currency'];
   echo '</TD>';
   echo '<TD>';
   echo $subarray['type'];
   echo '</TD>';
   echo '<TD>';
   echo '<INPUT TYPE="BUTTON" onClick="openEditWindow(' . $subarray['id'] . ')"
   VALUE="Edit">';
   echo '</TD>';
   echo '</TR>';
   }
```

The table is just more of the same, though—all of the required returned elements are accessed as $subarray['columnName']. Plus, the "add new" form is submitted to a different program on the business-logic layer:

```
echo "<FORM name='addBankAccount' METHOD='POST'
ACTION='http://" . $blHost . "/acct/bl/blEnterBankAccount.php'>";
```

Figure 9.3 shows enterBankAccount.php, fully rendered.

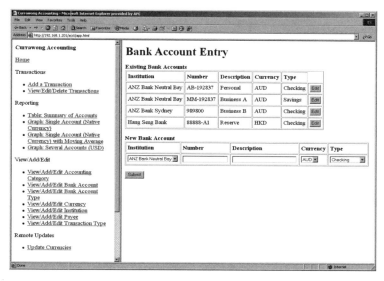

Figure 9.3: Viewing and adding bank accounts.

9.2.3   Viewing and Adding Bank Account Types

The presentation-layer program involved with viewing and adding bank account types is enterAcctType.php. It's similar in design to other programs covered in more detail earlier in this section.

The call to the accessor layer (to retrieve rows for display) looks like this:

```
$parameters = array();
$soapclient = new soapclient('http://' . $accessorHost .
'/acct/accessor/getAcctTypes.php');
$result = $soapclient->call('getAcctTypes',$parameters);
```

The table-generation code looks like this, involving only one column from the database:

```
foreach ($result as $key => $subarray)
  {
  echo '<TR>';
  echo '<TD>';
  echo $subarray['name'];
  echo '</TD>';
  echo '<TD>';
  echo '<INPUT TYPE="BUTTON" onClick="openEditWindow(' . $subarray['id'] . ')"
  VALUE="Edit">';
  echo '</TD>';
  }
```

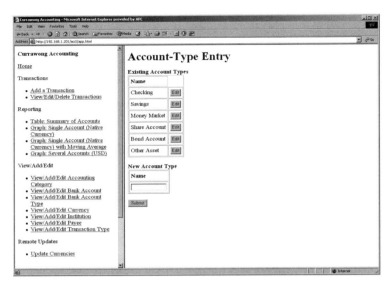

Figure 9.4: Viewing and adding bank account types.

Finally, the "add" form calls blEnterAccountType.php:

```
echo '<FORM name="addTransType" METHOD="POST"
ACTION="http://' . $blHost . '/acct/bl/blEnterAcctType.php">';
```

Figure 9.4 shows enterAcctType.php in action.

9.2.4   Viewing and Adding Currencies

The code for viewing and adding currencies is contained in enterCurrency.php. Its call to the accessor layer is unique:

```
$parameters = array();
$soapclient = new soapclient('http://' . $accessorHost .
'/acct/accessor/getCurrencies.php');
$result = $soapclient->call('getCurrencies',$parameters);
```

Its table-generator uses standard techniques to generate a custom look:

```
foreach ($result as $key => $subarray)
    {
    echo '<TR>';
    echo '<TD>';
    echo $subarray['abbreviation'];
    echo '</TD>';
```

```
echo '<TD>';
echo $subarray['country'];
echo '</TD>';
echo '<TD>';
echo $subarray['name'];
echo '</TD>';
echo '<TD>';
echo $subarray['xRate'];
echo '</TD>';
echo '<TD>';
echo $subarray['updated'];
echo '</TD>';
echo '<TD>';
echo '<INPUT TYPE="BUTTON" onClick="openEditWindow(' . $subarray['id'] . ')"
VALUE="Edit">';
echo '</TD>';
echo '</TR>';
}
```

Finally, the "Add Currency" form submits to a special program on the business layer:

```
echo '<FORM name="addCurrency" METHOD="POST" ACTION="http://' . $blHost .
'/acct/bl/blEnterCurrency.php">';
```

Figure 9.5 shows enterCurrency.php as it fits into the rest of the Currawong Accounting interface.

9.2.5 Viewing and Adding Institutions

The presentation-layer code for viewing and adding financial institutions is contained in enterInstitution.php. Its call to the accessor layer refers to getInstitutions.php:

```
$parameters = array();
$soapclient = new soapclient("http://" . $accessorHost .
"/acct/accessor/getInstitutions.php");
$result = $soapclient->call('getInstitutions',$parameters);
```

The institution-related table-generation code is fairly complicated, but it uses the standard echo $subarray['columnName'] technique repeatedly:

```
foreach ($result as $key => $subarray)
    {
    echo '<TR>';
    echo '<TD>';
    echo $subarray['name'];
```

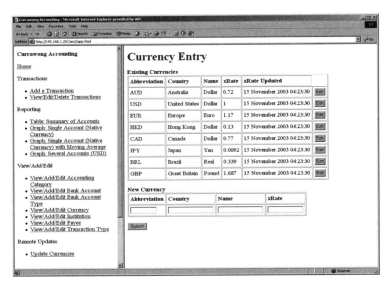

Figure 9.5: Viewing and adding currencies.

```
echo '</TD>';
echo '<TD>';
echo $subarray['streetAddress'];
echo '</TD>';
echo '<TD>';
echo $subarray['city'];
echo '</TD>';
echo '<TD>';
echo $subarray['state'];
echo '</TD>';
echo '<TD>';
echo $subarray['postcode'];
echo '</TD>';
echo '<TD>';
echo $subarray['country'];
echo '</TD>';
echo '<TD>';
echo '<INPUT TYPE="BUTTON" onClick="openEditWindow(' . $subarray['id'] . ')"
VALUE="Edit">';
echo '</TD>';
echo '</TR>';
}
```

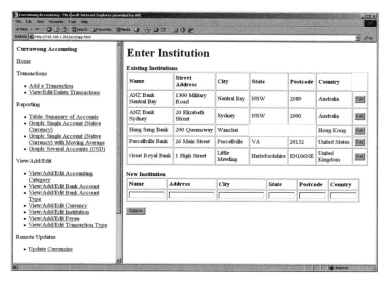

Figure 9.6: Viewing and adding institutions.

Its "Add Institution" form submits to blEnterInstitution.php:

```
echo '<FORM name="addInstitution" METHOD="POST" ACTION="http://' . $blHost .
'/acct/bl/blEnterInstitution.php">';
```

Figure 9.6 shows enterInstitution.php ready for use.

9.2.6 Viewing and Adding Payees

The job of viewing and adding payees on the presentation layer falls to enterPayee.php.
Its SOAP client looks like this:

```
$parameters = array();
$soapclient = new soapclient("http://" . $accessorHost .
"/acct/accessor/getPayees.php");
$result = $soapclient->call('getPayees',$parameters);
```

Its table generator is moderately long but not complex:

```
foreach ($result as $key => $subarray)
  {
  echo '<TR>';
  echo '<TD>';
  echo $subarray['name'];
```

```
echo '</TD>';
echo '<TD>';
echo $subarray['streetAddress'];
echo '</TD>';
echo '<TD>';
echo $subarray['city'];
echo '</TD>';
echo '<TD>';
echo $subarray['state'];
echo '</TD>';
echo '<TD>';
echo $subarray['postcode'];
echo '</TD>';
echo '<TD>';
echo $subarray['country'];
echo '</TD>';
echo '<TD>';
echo '<INPUT TYPE="BUTTON" onClick="openEditWindow(' . $subarray['id'] . ')"
VALUE="Edit">';
echo '</TD>';
echo '</TR>';
}
```

And, its "Add Payee" form submits to a specialized program on the business-logic layer:

```
echo "<FORM name='addPayee' METHOD='POST' ACTION='http://" . $blHost .
"/acct/bl/blEnterPayee.php'>";
```

Figure 9.7 shows enterPayee.php at work within the rest of the bookkeeping application.

9.2.7 Viewing and Adding Transaction Types

The portion of the presentation layer concerned with viewing and adding transaction types is contained in enterTransType.php. The call to the accessor layer (to retrieve existing transaction types) looks like this:

```
$parameters = array();
$soapclient = new soapclient("http://" . $accessorHost .
"/acct/accessor/getTransTypes.php");
$result = $soapclient->call('getTransTypes',$parameters);
```

The code that displays the retrieved transaction types is simple:

```
foreach ($result as $key => $subarray)
    {
    echo '<TR>';
```

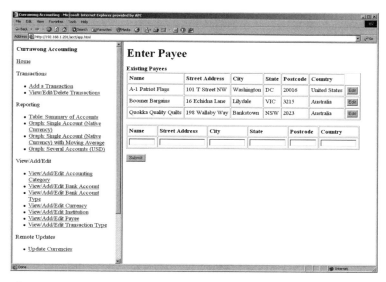

Figure 9.7: Viewing and adding payees.

```
echo '<TD>';
echo $subarray['name'];
echo '</TD>';
echo '<TD>';
echo '<INPUT TYPE="BUTTON" onClick="openEditWindow(' . $subarray['id'] . ')"
VALUE="Edit">';
echo '</TD>';
}
```

The "Add New Transaction Type" form submits to blEnterTransType.php on the business-logic layer:

```
echo "<FORM name='addTransType' METHOD='POST' action='http://" . $blHost .
"/acct/bl/blEnterTransType.php'>\n";
```

Figure 9.8 shows enterTransType.php as a user would see it.

9.3 Editing—Everything but Transactions

In the programs having to do with viewing and adding business entities (dealt with in the preceding section), you saw that each view/add page included an Edit button for each

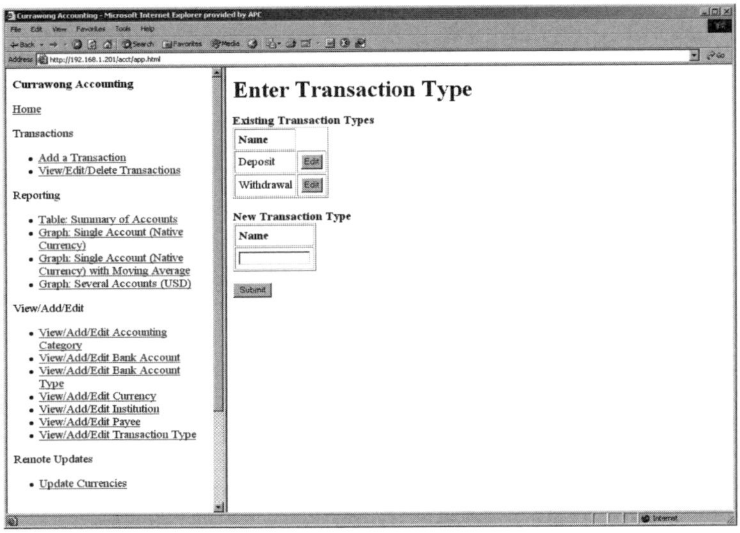

Figure 9.8: Viewing and adding transaction types.

element extracted from the database. The Edit buttons, in each case, triggered a JavaScript function, which in turn spawned a child window of some specified size. The child windows displayed the results of PHP programs. Those PHP programs are the subject of this discussion.

The editing programs on the presentation layer are concerned with extracting a particular row from a particular table in the database, and presenting the data in that row in a way that makes editing possible.

There are seven editing programs, each concerned with a different table. They correspond exactly to the seven view/add programs. They are:

1. Editing accounting categories,
2. Editing bank accounts,
3. Editing bank account types,
4. Editing currencies,
5. Editing institutions,
6. Editing payees, and
7. Editing transaction types.

Because the seven programs are so similar, this section explains only the first in detail, then highlights the slight differences of the others.

9.3.1 Editing Accounting Categories

In editing accounting categories, Currawong Accounting is concerned with extracting the values contained in a specified row of the ACCT_accounts table. The whole idea of multi-tier software design is that we don't need to know the name of the table, so we refer only to the relevant accessor-layer program: getAccounts.php.

The work of extracting a database row, displaying it in a useful form, and allowing the user to submit a change is handled by editAccount.php. Here is a full listing:

```
editAccount.php

<html>

<head>
<title>Edit Account</title>

</head>

<body>

<H1>Edit Account</H1>

<?php

require_once('listboxes.php');
require_once('nusoap-0.6/nusoap.php');
require_once('configuration.php');

$parameters = array();

foreach ($_GET as $key => $value)

   {
   $parameters[$key] = $value;
   }

$soapclient = new soapclient('http://' . $accessorHost .
'/acct/accessor/getSpecifiedAccount.php');

$result = $soapclient->call('getSpecifiedAccount',$parameters);

echo '<FORM name="addTransType" METHOD="POST"
ACTION="http://' . $blHost . '/acct/bl/blUpdateAccount.php">';
echo "\n";
```

```php
echo '<P>Modify Existing Accounting Account';
echo "\n";
echo '<P><INPUT TYPE="HIDDEN" NAME="id" VALUE="' .
$result[0]['id'] . '" SIZE=15>';
echo "\n";
echo '<P>Name:<INPUT TYPE="TEXT" NAME="name" VALUE="' .
$result[0]['name'] . '" SIZE=15>';
echo "\n";
echo '<P><INPUT TYPE="SUBMIT" NAME="submit" VALUE="Submit">';
echo "\n";
echo '</FORM>';

?>


</body>

</html>
```

Remember that editAccount.php is called with a full HTTP GET statement, such as this:

```
editAccount.php?rowToEdit=3
```

That means that the rowToEdit value is available within the program. Depending on which version of PHP Currawong is running under, the value submitted as part of the GET statement is accessible in one of two ways:

1. As $_GET['rowToEdit']. This works only under PHP 4.3 and newer. Note that the $_GET array is a "superglobal" array that does not need to be declared in order to be available within functions.

2. As an ordinary global variable with a name that matches the value in the GET statement: $rowToEdit.

If you're using a version of PHP prior to version 4.3, you will need to set register_globals equal to On in php.ini, and edit the code so that it refers to the GET variables by name rather than through $_GET. It's probably easier to upgrade, if you can.

The $_GET array is used to populate the $parameters array, which is used in a call to the accessor layer:

```php
$parameters = array();

foreach ($_GET as $key => $value)

   {
   $parameters[$key] = $value;
   }
```

Figure 9.9: Editing accounting categories.

```
$soapclient = new soapclient('http://' . $accessorHost .
'/acct/accessor/getSpecifiedAccount.php');

$result = $soapclient->call('getSpecifiedAccount',$parameters);
```

With that call made, $result holds a two-dimensional array of only one row—it's effectively an array containing a single subarray. That's why the form-generation code pulls values from it like this:

```
echo '<P><INPUT TYPE="HIDDEN" NAME="id" VALUE="' .
$result[0]['id'] . '" SIZE=15>';
```

All results are referred to as $result[0]['columnName']. Note also that this form submits to a program on the business-logic layer that's specific to updating accounts:

```
echo '<FORM name="addTransType" METHOD="POST"
ACTION="http://' . $blHost . '/acct/bl/blUpdateAccount.php">';
```

There's a screen shot of editAccount.php in Figure 9.9.

9.3.2 Editing Bank Accounts

For editing bank accounts, Currawong Accounting relies on editBankAccount.php. It's very similar to editAccount.php. Its call to the accessor layer looks like this:

```
$parameters = array();
```

```
foreach ($_GET as $key => $value)

  {
  $parameters[$key] = $value;
  }

$soapclient = new soapclient('http://' . $accessorHost .
'/acct/accessor/getSpecifiedBankAccount.php');

$result = $soapclient->call('getSpecifiedBankAccount',$parameters);
```

Its table-generation code looks like this:

```
echo '<TR>';
echo '<TD>';
menuInstitutions("institution",$result[0]['institutionId']);
echo '</TD>';
echo '<TD>';
echo '<INPUT TYPE="TEXT" NAME="number" VALUE="' .
$result[0]['number'] . '" SIZE=20>';
echo '</TD>';
echo '<TD>';
echo '<INPUT TYPE="TEXT" NAME="description" VALUE="' .
$result[0]['description'] . '" SIZE=30>';
echo '</TD>';
echo '<TD>';
menuCurrencies("currency",$result[0]['currencyId']);
echo '</TD>';
echo '<TD>';
menuAcctTypes("type",$result[0]['acctTypeId']);
echo '</TD>';
echo '</TR>';
```

The interesting elements of the table-generation code are the calls to the functions in the listbox.php library. These make use of the second argument to specify which element in the generated list box should be shown and preselected. A typical example is this:

```
menuAcctTypes("type",$result[0]['acctTypeId']);
```

That tells the menuAcctTypes function (in listboxes.php) to generate a list of available account types, with the account type whose id value is equal to $result[0]['acctTypeId'] selected. That is, the list box should show the current bank account's account type preselected. Figure 9.10 shows how this editing script looks in the wild.

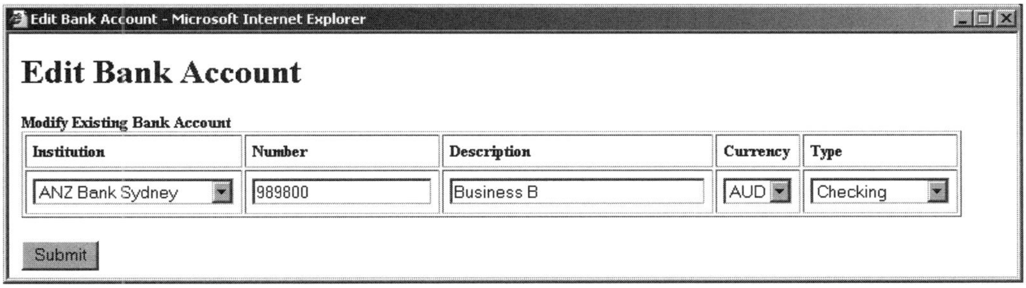

Figure 9.10: Editing bank accounts.

9.3.3 Editing Bank Account Types

For editing bank account types, users of Currawong accounting use editAcctType.php. It works like most of the other editing programs. Its call to the accessor layer, in which an HTTP GET value is used as a parameter, looks like this:

```
$parameters = array();

foreach ($_GET as $key => $value)

    {
    $parameters[$key] = $value;
    }

$soapclient = new soapclient('http://' . $accessorHost .
'/acct/accessor/getSpecifiedAcctType.php');

$result = $soapclient->call('getSpecifiedAcctType',$parameters);
```

Its table-generation code looks like this:

```
echo '<FORM name="addTransType" METHOD="POST"
ACTION="http://' . $blHost . '/acct/bl/blUpdateAcctType.php">';
echo "\n";
echo '<P>Modify Existing Account Type';
echo "\n";
echo '<P><INPUT TYPE="HIDDEN" NAME="id" VALUE="' .
$result[0]['id'] . '" SIZE=15>';
echo "\n";
echo '<P>Name:<INPUT TYPE="TEXT" NAME="name" VALUE="' .
$result[0]['name'] . '" SIZE=15>';
echo "\n";
```

Figure 9.11: Editing bank account types.

```
echo '<P><INPUT TYPE="SUBMIT" NAME="submit" VALUE="Submit">';
echo "\n";
echo '</FORM>';
```

Note that it submits the form contents to blUpdateAcctType.php, a special-purpose program on the business-logic layer. Figure 9.11 shows how this program looks when rendered in a browser window.

9.3.4   Editing Currencies

The program contained in editCurrency.php handles the work of modifying the character-istics of a currency. Functionally, this program is much the same as others.

To retrieve details from the accessor layer, the program makes a SOAP client call:

```
$parameters = array();

foreach ($_GET as $key => $value)

  {
  $parameters[$key] = $value;
  }
$soapclient = new soapclient('http://' . $accessorHost .
'/acct/accessor/getSpecifiedCurrency.php');

$result = $soapclient->call('getSpecifiedCurrency',$parameters);
```

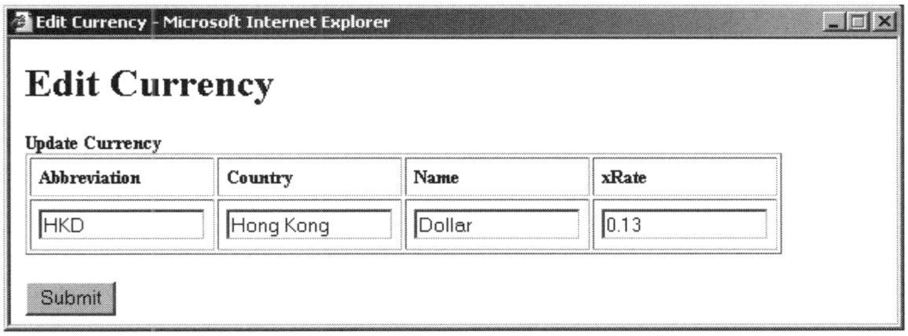

Figure 9.12: Editing currencies.

It then uses the results, literally, the array $result, to generate a form containing the existing values:

```
echo '<FORM name="editCurrency" METHOD="POST"
ACTION="http://' . $blHost . '/acct/bl/blUpdateCurrency.php">';
echo '<TR>';
echo '<TD>';
echo '<INPUT TYPE="TEXT" NAME="abbreviation" VALUE="' .
$result[0]['abbreviation'] . '" SIZE=15>';
echo '</TD>';
echo '<TD>';
echo '<INPUT TYPE="TEXT" NAME="country" VALUE="' .
$result[0]['country'] . '" SIZE=15>';
echo '</TD>';
echo '<TD>';
echo '<INPUT TYPE="TEXT" NAME="name" VALUE="'.$result[0]['name'].'" SIZE=15>';
echo '</TD>';
echo '<TD>';
echo '<INPUT TYPE="TEXT" NAME="xRate" VALUE="' .
$result[0]['xRate'] . '" SIZE=15>';
echo '</TD>';
echo '</TR>';
```

Figure 9.12 shows how Microsoft Internet Explorer renders this program.

9.3.5 Editing Institutions

To edit the attributes of an institution that's already been recorded in the database, Currawong Accounting uses editInstitution.php. Like other editing programs, editInstitution.php makes a call to the accessor layer:

```
$parameters = array();
```

```
foreach ($_GET as $key => $value)

    {
    $parameters[$key] = $value;
    }

$soapclient = new soapclient('http://' . $accessorHost .
'/acct/accessor/getSpecifiedInstitution.php');

$result = $soapclient->call('getSpecifiedInstitution',$parameters);
```

It then generates a form in a table, using the contents of $result to populate the fields with existing values:

```
echo "<FORM name='modifyExisitngInstitution' METHOD='POST'
ACTION='http://" . $blHost . "/acct/bl/blUpdateInstitution.php'>";

echo '<TR>';
echo '<TD>';
echo '<INPUT TYPE="TEXT" NAME="name" VALUE="' .
$result[0]['name'] . '" SIZE=15>';
echo '</TD>';
echo '<TD>';
echo '<INPUT TYPE="TEXT" NAME="streetAddress" VALUE="' .
$result[0]['streetAddress'] . '" SIZE=20>';
echo '</TD>';
echo '<TD>';
echo '<INPUT TYPE="TEXT" NAME="city" VALUE="' .
$result[0]['city'] . '" SIZE=20>';
echo '</TD>';
echo '<TD>';
echo '<INPUT TYPE="TEXT" NAME="state" VALUE="' .
$result[0]['state'] . '" SIZE=10>';
echo '</TD>';
echo '<TD>';
echo '<INPUT TYPE="TEXT" NAME="postcode" VALUE="' .
$result[0]['postcode'] . '" SIZE=10>';
echo '</TD>';
echo '<TD>';
echo '<INPUT TYPE="TEXT" NAME="country" VALUE="' .
$result[0]['country'] . '" SIZE=10>';
echo '</TD>';
echo '</TR>';
```

Figure 9.13 shows how this looks when rendered in a browser.

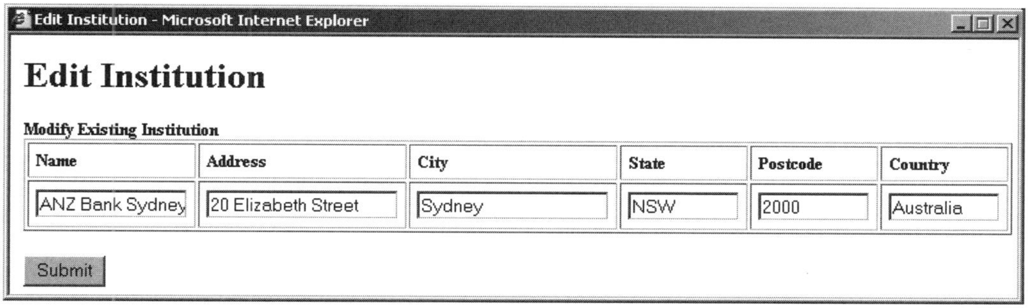

Figure 9.13: Editing institutions.

9.3.6 Editing Payees

The code in editPayee.php is involved in editing existing payees. Its call to the accessor layer looks like this:

```
$parameters = array();

foreach ($_GET as $key => $value)

    {
    $parameters[$key] = $value;
    }

$soapclient = new soapclient('http://' . $accessorHost .
'/acct/accessor/getSpecifiedPayee.php');

$result = $soapclient->call('getSpecifiedPayee',$parameters);
```

Its form-generation code looks like this:

```
echo "<FORM name='modifyExisitngPayee' METHOD='POST'
ACTION='http://" . $blHost . "/acct/bl/blUpdatePayee.php'>";
echo '<P><INPUT TYPE="HIDDEN" NAME="id" VALUE="' .
$result[0]['id'] . '" SIZE=15>';
echo '<P><B>Modify Existing Payee</B>';
echo '<TABLE BORDER="1" CELLPADDING="5">';
echo '<TR>';
echo '<TD>';
echo '<INPUT TYPE="TEXT" NAME="name" VALUE="' .
$result[0]['name'] . '" SIZE=15>';
echo '</TD>';
echo '<TD>';
```

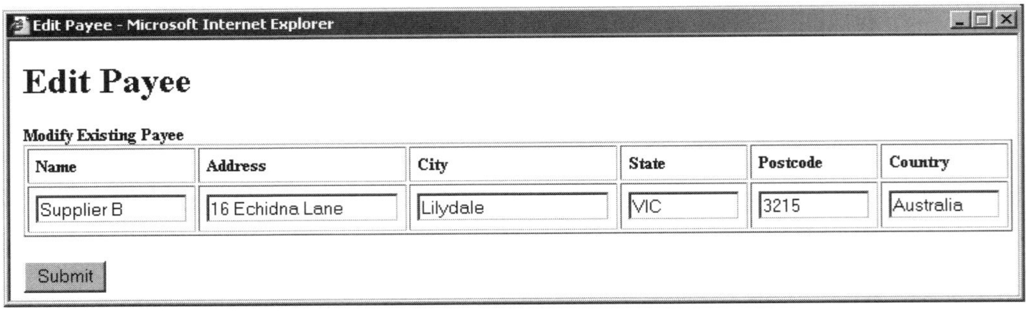

Figure 9.14: Editing Payees.

```
echo '<INPUT TYPE="TEXT" NAME="streetAddress" VALUE="' .
$result[0]['streetAddress'] . '" SIZE=20>';
echo '</TD>';
echo '<TD>';
echo '<INPUT TYPE="TEXT" NAME="city" VALUE="' .
$result[0]['city'] . '" SIZE=20>';
echo '</TD>';
echo '<TD>';
echo '<INPUT TYPE="TEXT" NAME="state" VALUE="' .
$result[0]['state'] . '" SIZE=10>';
echo '</TD>';
echo '<TD>';
echo '<INPUT TYPE="TEXT" NAME="postcode" VALUE="' .
$result[0]['postcode'] . '" SIZE=10>';
echo '</TD>';
echo '<TD>';
echo '<INPUT TYPE="TEXT" NAME="country" VALUE="' .
$result[0]['country'] . '" SIZE=10>';
echo '</TD>';
echo '</TR>';
```

When rendered in a browser, editPayee.php looks as shown in Figure 9.14.

9.3.7   Editing Transaction Types

To give the user the ability to edit existing transaction types, Currawong Accounting provides editTransType.php. It makes a SOAP call to getSpecifiedTransType.php on the accessor layer:

```
$parameters = array();
```

```
foreach ($_GET as $key => $value)

    {
    $parameters[$key] = $value;
    }

$soapclient = new soapclient('http://' . $accessorHost .
'/acct/accessor/getSpecifiedTransType.php');

$result = $soapclient->call('getSpecifiedTransType',$parameters);
```

It also generates a form containing the returned values and allows the user to submit changes to a dedicated program on the business-logic layer:

```
echo '<FORM name="addTransType" METHOD="POST"
ACTION="http://' . $blHost . '/acct/bl/blUpdateTransType.php">';
echo "\n";
echo '<P>Modify Existing Transaction Type';
echo "\n";
echo '<P><INPUT TYPE="HIDDEN" NAME="id" VALUE="' .
$result[0]['id'] . '" SIZE=15>';
echo "\n";
echo '<P>Name:<INPUT TYPE="TEXT" NAME="name" VALUE="' .
$result[0]['name'] . '" SIZE=15>';
echo "\n";
echo '<P><INPUT TYPE="SUBMIT" NAME="submit" VALUE="Submit">';
echo "\n";
echo '</FORM>';
```

Rendered, editTransType.php is shown in Figure 9.15.

Figure 9.15: Editing transaction types.

9.4 Transactions

Currawong Accounting handles the viewing, recording, and modifying of transactions in a way different from those in which it handles similar activities on other business entities. The application also allows for the deletion of transactions.

Transactions have to be treated as a special case because, for one thing, there can potentially be so many of them. If the program were to just retrieve and display all transactions on command, the resulting page would likely contain hundreds of transactions. There has to be a way to limit transaction retrieval and display to a specified date range.

Additionally, all transactions are stored in a single table—ACCT_register—in the database. Currawong Accounting needs to have a way to limit the display of transactions to those that affected a given account. There also has to be a way of presenting the balance of the account, both at the end of the specified time period and at the current date.

This section shows how view, add, edit, and delete operations affecting transactions are carried out on the presentation layer.

9.4.1 Special HTML Framework

For the purposes of controlling the display of transactions, the right-hand (display) windows is divided into two subframes when the "View/Edit/Delete Transactions" link in the main navigation strip is clicked. In other words, the "View/Edit/Delete Transactions" link fills the right-hand pane of the browser window with another framing document (viewTransactions.html), which in turn creates two subframes in the right pane. The code in viewTransactions.html looks like this:

```
viewTransactions.html

<!DOCTYPE HTML PUBLIC "-//W3C//DTD HTML 4.0 Transitional//EN">

<html>

<head>

<title>Currawong Accounting</title>

</head>

<frameset ROWS="20$% $,*">

<frame name="controls" src="viewControls.php">
<frame name="display" src="viewDefault.html">

</frameset>
</html>
```

It divides the right pane into two rows (along a 20–80 split). It populates the top pane with viewControls.php and the bottom pane with viewDefault.html. It happens that viewDefault.html is a blank page—it generates only whitespace. The top document, though, is much more interesting. It's discussed in the next section.

9.4.2 Specifying which Transactions to Display

The upper frame of the interface for viewing, editing, and deleting transactions contains viewControls.php, which generates the HTML form in which the user specifies the date range and account for which he or she wants to see transactions. Essentially, it comprises a selection box from which a bank account may be selected (by description) and two text boxes into which the user enters start and end dates. Here's viewControls.php:

```
viewControls.php

<!DOCTYPE HTML PUBLIC "-//W3C//DTD HTML 4.0 Transitional//EN">

<html>

<head>

<SCRIPT LANGUAGE="JavaScript">

function loadTransactions()

{

url = "viewTransactions.php?startDate=" + viewTransactions.start.value +
"&endDate=" + viewTransactions.end.value +
"&account=" + viewTransactions.bank_account.value;

parent.display.location=url;

}

</SCRIPT>

</head>

<H1>View/Edit/Delete Transactions</H1>

<?php

require_once('listboxes.php');
```

```
echo "<FORM name='viewTransactions' METHOD='POST' ACTION=''>\n";
echo '<TABLE BORDER="1" CELLPADDING="5">';
echo '<TR>';
echo '<TD>';
echo '<B>Account</B>';
echo '</TD>';
echo '<TD>';
echo '<B>Start</B>';
echo '</TD>';
echo '<TD>';
echo '<B>End</B>';
echo '</TD>';
echo '</TR>';

echo '<TR>';
echo '<TD>';
menuBankAccounts("bank_account",0,0);
echo '</TD>';
echo '<TD>';
echo '<input type="input" name="start" value="2003-01-01" size=15>';
echo '</TD>';
echo '<TD>';
echo '<input type="input" name="end" value="2003-12-31" size=15>';
echo '</TD>';

echo '<TD>';
echo '<input type="button" name="submitButton" value="Go
onClick="loadTransactions()">';
echo '</TD>';

echo '</TR>';

echo '</TABLE>';
echo '</FORM>';

?>

</html>
```

It's essentially a form that, using the functions made available in listboxes.php, collects details about which account the user wants to retrieve transactions from and what date range should be retrieved (there is, unfortunately, nothing here to catch errors in date format—the user has to enter dates in "YYYY-MM-DD" format). Note what happens when the form is submitted, though. Normally, you'd figure that out by looking at the opening FORM tag:

```
echo "<FORM name='viewTransactions' METHOD='POST' ACTION=">\n";
```

The ACTION attribute is null, so nothing would happen when the form was submitted. But look, there isn't even a proper SUBMIT button. It's a BUTTON button at the bottom of the form:

```
echo '<input type="button" name="submitButton" value="Go"
onClick="loadTransactions()">';
```

That's a general-purpose button with an onClick event handler attached. When the button is clicked, it runs the JavaScript function called loadTransactions(). Its code looks like this:

```
function loadTransactions()
{
url = "viewTransactions.php?startDate = " + viewTransactions.start.value +
"&endDate=" + viewTransactions.end.value +
"&account=" + viewTransactions.bank_account.value;

parent.display.location=url;
}
```

There are two lines: (1) a string concatenation operation, and (2) a pane-redirector. The string concatenator works by taking the values of three form elements and concatenating them into a single HTTP GET statement.

A typical example of a reference to a value contained in a form element is view-Transactions.start.value. That represents the contents of the element named start within the form named viewTransactions. In the case of viewTransactions.bank_account.value, the value is the value attribute (not the visible label) of the account selected in the section box.

In any case, the assembled URL looks something like this:

```
viewTransactions.php?startDate=2003-10-31&endDate=2003-12-31&account=3
```

That provides the input for the lower frame, in which the specified transactions are listed.

9.4.3 Viewing Transactions

The mechanism for viewing transactions takes input as name/value pairs provided in an HTTP GET statement (in other words, in a URL, as covered in the previous section). The provided values specify the date range of transactions to be shown, as well as the account from which transactions are to be shown.

The code for displaying transactions is contained in viewTransactions.php. Here is a full listing of that file:

```
viewTransactions.php

<html>

<head>
<title>View Transactions</title>

<SCRIPT LANGUAGE="JavaScript">

function openEditWindow(id)

{

var url = "editTransaction.php?id=" + id;

var newWindow = window.open(url, "child", "HEIGHT=300,WIDTH=800");

}

function openDeleteWindow(id)

{

var url = "deleteTransaction.php?id=" + id;

var newWindow = window.open(url, "child", "HEIGHT=350,WIDTH=800");

}

</SCRIPT>

</head>

<body>

<?php

require_once('listboxes.php');
require_once('nusoap-0.6/nusoap.php');
require_once('configuration.php');

$parameters = array();
```

```
foreach ($_GET as $key => $value)

   {

   $parameters[$key] = $value;

   }

$soapclient = new soapclient('http://' . $accessorHost .
'/acct/accessor/getSpecifiedTransactions.php');

$result = $soapclient->call('getSpecifiedTransactions',$parameters);


// Get acccount description

$parameters2 = array();

$parameters2['id'] = $_GET['account'];

$soapclient2 = new soapclient('http://' . $accessorHost .
'/acct/accessor/getSpecifiedBankAccount.php');

$result2 = $soapclient2->call('getSpecifiedBankAccount',$parameters2);

$accountName = $result2[0]['description'];


// Get acccount balance (at end of displayed period)

$parameters3 = array('id' => $_GET['account'], 'date' => $_GET['endDate']);

$soapclient3 = new soapclient('http://' . $accessorHost .
'/acct/accessor/getSpecifiedBankAccountBalance.php');

$result3 = $soapclient3->call('getSpecifiedBankAccountBalance',$parameters3);

$periodBalance = $result3[0]['balance'];


// Get acccount balance (as of today)

$today = date("Y-m-d");

$parameters4 = array('id' => $_GET['account'], 'date'=>$today);
```

```php
$soapclient4 = new soapclient('http://' . $accessorHost .
'/acct/accessor/getSpecifiedBankAccountBalance.php');

$result4 = $soapclient4->call('getSpecifiedBankAccountBalance',$parameters4);

$currentBalance = $result4[0]['balance'];

echo '<TABLE BORDER="1" CELLPADDING="5">';
echo '<TR>';
echo '<TD>';
echo '<B>Selected Account</B>';
echo '</TD>';
echo '<TD>';
echo '<B>Start Date</B>';
echo '</TD>';
echo '<TD>';
echo '<B>End Date</B>';
echo '</TD>';
echo '<TD>';
echo '<B>Balance at End of Period</B>';
echo '</TD>';
echo '<TD>';
echo '<B>Latest Balance</B>';
echo '</TD>';
echo '</TR>';

echo '<TR>';
echo '<TD>';


echo $accountName;
echo '</TD>';
echo '<TD>';
echo $_GET['startDate'];
echo '</TD>';
echo '<TD>';
echo $_GET['endDate'];
echo '</TD>';
echo '<TD>';
echo $periodBalance;
echo '</TD>';
echo '<TD>';
echo $currentBalance;
```

```
echo '</TD>';
echo '</TR>';

echo '</TABLE>';

echo '<P>';

echo '<TABLE BORDER="1" CELLPADDING="5">';
echo '<TR>';
echo '<TD>';
echo '<B>Date</B>';
echo '</TD>';
echo '<TD>';
echo '<B>Number</B>';
echo '</TD>';
echo '<TD>';
echo '<B>Payee</B>';
echo '</TD>';
echo '<TD>';
echo '<B>Amount</B>';
echo '</TD>';
echo '<TD>';
echo '<B>Account</B>';
echo '</TD>';
echo '<TD>';
echo '<B>Trans. Type</B>';
echo '</TD>';
echo '<TD>';
echo '<B>Memo</B>';
echo '</TD>';
echo '</TR>';


foreach ($result as $key => $subarray)
   {
   echo '<TR>';
   echo '<TD>';
   echo $subarray['date'];
   echo '</TD>';
   echo '<TD>';
   echo $subarray['number'];
   echo '</TD>';
   echo '<TD>';
```

```
       echo $subarray['payee'];
       echo '</TD>';
       echo '<TD>';
       echo $subarray['amount'];
       echo '</TD>';
       echo '<TD>';
       echo $subarray['account'];
       echo '</TD>';
       echo '<TD>';
       echo $subarray['type'];
       echo '</TD>';
       echo '<TD>';
       echo $subarray['memo'];
       echo '</TD>';
       echo '<TD>';
       echo '<INPUT TYPE="BUTTON" onClick="openEditWindow(' . $subarray['id'] . ')"
       VALUE="Edit">';
       echo '</TD>';
       echo '<TD>';
       echo '<INPUT TYPE="BUTTON"
       onClick="openDeleteWindow(' . $subarray['id'] . ')" VALUE="Delete">';
       echo '</TD>';
       echo '</TR>';
          }

    echo '</TABLE>';

    ?>

    </body>

    </html>
```

The first detail to notice is that this program makes four separate calls to the accessor layer. The first call looks like this:

```
    $parameters = array();

    foreach ($_GET as $key => $value)

       {

       $parameters[$key] = $value;

       }
```

```
$soapclient = new soapclient('http://' . $accessorHost .
'/acct/accessor/getSpecifiedTransactions.php');

$result = $soapclient->call('getSpecifiedTransactions',$parameters);
```

That's a standard call to getSpecifiedTransactions.php, which takes parameters specifying the start date, end date, and account of the transactions to be retrieved.

The second call to the accessor layer has to do with resolving the $_GET['account'] value to a meaningful name. It calls getSpecifiedBankAccount.php and extracts the description value from the array that comes back. This allows the presentation-layer program to include a meaningful text description (rather than an id number) of the account whose transactions are being shown. Here's the code for the second call:

```
$parameters2 = array();

$parameters2['id'] = $account;

$soapclient2 = new soapclient('http://' . $accessorHost .
'/acct/accessor/getSpecifiedBankAccount.php');

$result2 = $soapclient2->call('getSpecifiedBankAccount',$parameters2);

$accountName = $result2[0]['description'];
```

The third call to the accessor layer calls getSpecifiedBankAccountBalance.php, an accessor-layer program that returns the cumulative balance of a specified account as of a specified date. In this case, the presentation layer sends $_GET['endDate']—the end of the displayed period—to getSpecifiedBankAccountBalance.php. Here is the code:

```
$parameters3 = array('id' => $account, 'date' => $_GET['endDate']);

$soapclient3 = new soapclient('http://' . $accessorHost .
'/acct/accessor/getSpecifiedBankAccountBalance.php');

$result3 = $soapclient3->call('getSpecifiedBankAccountBalance',$parameters3);

$periodBalance = $result3[0]['balance'];
```

The final call to the accessor layer is very similar, except for the fact that it sends the current date, formatted as YYYY-MM-DD, to getSpecifiedBankAccountBalance.php. That ensures that the resulting value is the latest balance—the balance as of today. Here is the code:

```
$today = getdate("Y-m-d");

$parameters4 = array('id' => $account, 'date'=>'12-12-2003');
```

```
$soapclient4 = new soapclient('http://' . $accessorHost .
'/acct/accessor/getSpecifiedBankAccountBalance.php');

$result4 = $soapclient4->call('getSpecifiedBankAccountBalance',$parameters4);

$currentBalance = $result4[0]['balance'];
```

The table-creation code in this program is not unusual, but it's important to note that there are two separate JavaScript functions. The first handles the "edit transaction" operation and is called when the Edit button is clicked:

```
function openEditWindow(id)
{
var url = "editTransaction.php?rowToEdit=" + id;
var newWindow = window.open(url, "child", "HEIGHT=300, WIDTH=800");
}
```

It makes an HTTP GET call to editTransaction.php, which is discussed later in this section. The HTTP GET call sends the id of the transaction to be edited (the value of the id column in the relevant row of the ACCT_register table).

The other JavaScript function makes a similar HTTP GET reference to deleteTransaction.php, which is also discussed later in this section. Its code is very similar:

```
function openDeleteWindow(id)
{
var url = "deleteTransaction.php?rowToDelete=" + id;
var newWindow = window.open(url, "child", "HEIGHT=350,WIDTH=800");
}
```

Figure 9.16 shows a typical display of transactions.

9.4.4   Editing Transactions

When the Edit Transaction window pops up, it has (as a result of HTTP GET) the id value of the row in the ACCT_register table it is supposed to operate on. With that given, it is then the job of editTransaction.php to present the transaction to the user as it is, and allow him or her to make changes.

Here is what editTransaction.php looks like:

```
editTransaction.php

<html>

<head>
<title>Edit Transaction</title>

<SCRIPT LANGUAGE="JavaScript">
```

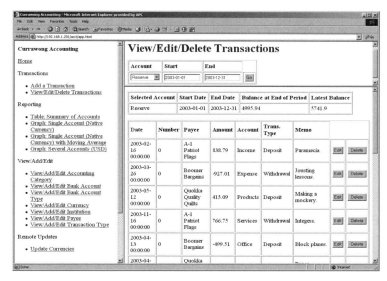

Figure 9.16: An account and a date range limit the display of transactions.

```
function calculateAmount()

{

transactionForm.amount.value = transactionForm.inflow.value -
transactionForm.outflow.value;

return true;

}

</SCRIPT>

</head>

<body>

<H1>Edit Transaction</H1>

<?php

require_once('listboxes.php');
require_once('configuration.php');
```

```php
// this is here for 4.0 compatibility

//$_POST = array('id' => $rowToEdit);

// end 4.0 *********

$parameters = array();

foreach ($_GET as $key => $value)

    {
    $parameters[$key] = $value;
    }


$soapclient = new soapclient('http://' . $accessorHost .'/acct/accessor/
    getSpecifiedTransaction.php');

$result = $soapclient->call('getSpecifiedTransaction',$parameters);

$id = $result[0]['id'];
$date = $result[0]['date'];
$bank_account = $result[0]['bank_account'];
$number = $result[0]['number'];
$memo = $result[0]['memo'];
$account = $result[0]['account'];
$payee = $result[0]['payee'];
$amount = $result[0]['amount'];
$type = $result[0]['type'];

if($amount<0)
    {
    $inflow = 0;
    $outflow = abs($amount);
    }
        elseif($amount>0)
        {
        $outflow = 0;
        $inflow = abs($amount);
        }
            else
            {
            $inflow=0;
            $outflow=0;
            }
```

```php
echo '<FORM name="transactionForm" method="POST" action="http://' . $blHost .
   '/acct/bl/blUpdateTransaction.php" onSubmit="return calculateAmount()">';

echo "<input type='hidden' name='id' value='" . $id . "' size=15>";

echo "<input type='hidden' name='amount' value=0 size=15>";

echo "<TABLE border=1 cellpadding=5>";

echo "<tr>";

echo "<td>";
echo "Date: <input type='input' name='date' value='" . $date . "'
   size=15>";
echo "</td>";

echo "<td>";
echo "Account: <BR>";
menuBankAccounts("bank_account", $bank_account, 0);
echo "</td>";

echo "<td>";
echo "Payee: <BR>";
menuPayees("payee", $payee);
echo "</td>";

echo "<td>";
echo "Inflow: <BR> <input type='input' name='inflow' value='" . $inflow . "'
size=15>\n";
echo "</td>";

echo "</tr>";

echo "<tr>";

echo "<td>";
echo "</td>";

echo "<td>";
echo "Trans. Type: <BR>";
menuTransTypes("type", $type);
echo "</td>";

echo "<td>";
```

```
echo "Acctg. Account: <BR>";
menuAccount("account", $account);
echo "</td>";

echo "<td>";
echo "Outflow: <BR> <input type='input' name='outflow'
value='" . $outflow . "' size=15>";
echo "</td>";
echo "</tr>";


echo "<tr>";

echo "<td>";
echo "</td>";

echo "<td colspan=5>";
echo "Memo: <input type='input' name='memo' value='" . $memo . "' size=100>";
echo "</td>";

echo "</tr>";


echo "<tr>";

echo "<td colspan=6 align='center'>";
echo "<input type='submit' name='submitButton' value='Submit'>\n";
echo "</td>";

echo "</tr>";

echo "</TABLE> \n";

echo "</FORM>";

?>

</body>

</html>
```

The first order of business is for the program to call the accessor layer, like this:

```
$parameters = array();
```

```
foreach ($_GET as $key => $value)

    {
    $parameters[$key] = $value;
    }

$soapclient = new soapclient('http://' . $accessorHost . '/acct/accessor/
getSpecifiedTransaction.php');

$result = $soapclient->call('getSpecifiedTransaction',$parameters);
```

The only element of $parameters is the id element, which represents the id of the row in
ACCT_register to be retrieved and presented for editing. When the SOAP response comes
back and $result is thus populated with the contents of the table row of interest, some
calculations are performed to determine whether the transaction represents an addition
to the bank account specified by the record, or a subtraction from it, or an account with
zero value and no net effect on the balance of the account:

```
if($amount<0)
    {
    $inflow = 0;
    $outflow = abs($amount);
    }
    elseif($amount>0)
    {
    $outflow = 0;
    $inflow = abs($amount);
    }
    else
    {
    $inflow=0;
    $outflow=0;
    }
```

At the end of that, two variables—$inflow and $outflow—are available for inclusion in
the table that's subsequently generated. The table generation isn't, for the most part,
remarkable, except that it makes repeated use of the listbox.php functions, particularly
their ability to render selection lists with specified options prehighlighted. The calls look
like this:

```
menuBankAccounts("bank_account", $bank_account, 0);
```

In that case and in others, $bank_account is an integer that corresponds to an id value.
The 0 indicates the MULTIPLE isn't needed in the resultant list box.

It's important to see that the form contains two input elements of type hidden. One of
these contains the id value of the record being edited and is submitted to the logic layer

like every other form element. This is how the logic-layer program (which is blUpdate-Transaction.php, by the way) and the accessor-layer program that ultimately changes the database know what row is to be operated on. The other hidden element is populated by a JavaScript function—more about that in a moment—and represents the modified amount of the transaction, as edited. These lines of code generate the hidden form elements:

```
echo "<input type='hidden' name='id' value='" . $id . "' size=15>";
echo "<input type='hidden' name='amount' value=0 size=15>";
```

There's something unusual about the ACTION attribute of the generated form. The whole opening FORM tag looks like this:

```
echo '<FORM name="transactionForm" action="http://' . $blHost .
'/acct/bl/blUpdateTransaction.php" onSubmit="return calculateAmount()">';
```

When a submit event occurs, in other words, when the Submit button is clicked, the form is to react to the return value of calculateAmount(), which is a JavaScript function. In other words, if calculateAmount() returns true, the form submission should proceed as normal. If the function returns false, submission should be aborted. What does calculateAmount() do, though? Here are its contents:

```
function calculateAmount()

{
transactionForm.amount.value = transactionForm.inflow.value -
transactionForm.outflow.value;
return true;
}
```

That function sets transactionForm.amount.value—the second hidden field—equal to the difference of the Inflow and Outflow boxes. That has to happen because the ACCT_register table, where this information is stored, has only one column for amount. Note also that this function also invariably returns true. It will never halt form submission. More importantly, it will always run before form submission and make sure the amount field is set properly. Figure 9.17 shows what editTransaction.php looks like.

9.4.5 Deleting Transactions

The transaction-deletion program, deleteTransaction.php, takes a transaction id number as an argument in an HTTP GET statement, like editTransaction.php. It also populates a form with the details of that transaction. Here is its code:

```
deleteTransaction.php
<html>

<head>
<title>Delete Transaction</title>
```

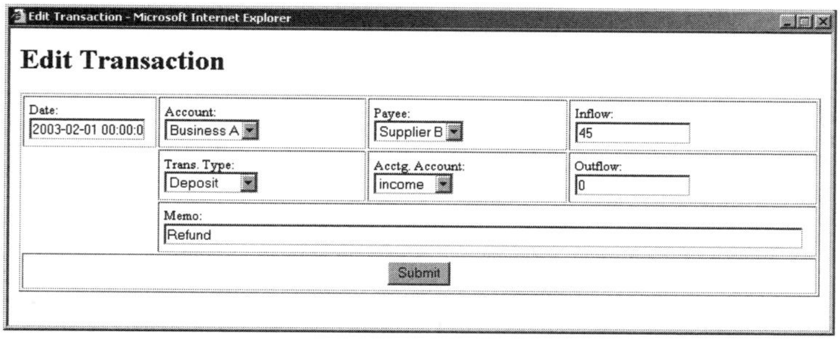

Figure 9.17: Edit transaction.

```
<SCRIPT LANGUAGE="JavaScript">

function submitForm(yesNo)

{

if (yesNo==1)
   {
   document.deleteForm.submit();
   }
if (yesNo==0)
   {
   self.close()
   }

}

</SCRIPT>

</head>

<body>

<H1>Delete Transaction</H1>

<P>

<?php

require_once('listboxes.php');
require_once('configuration.php');
```

```php
$parameters = array();

foreach ($_GET as $key => $value)

   {
   $parameters[$key] = $value;
   }

$soapclient = new soapclient('http://' . $accessorHost .
'/acct/accessor/getSpecifiedTransaction.php');

$result = $soapclient->call('getSpecifiedTransaction',$parameters);

$id = $result[0]['id'];
$date = $result[0]['date'];
$bank_account = $result[0]['bank_account'];
$number = $result[0]['number'];
$memo = $result[0]['memo'];
$account = $result[0]['account'];
$payee = $result[0]['payee'];
$amount = $result[0]['amount'];
$type = $result[0]['type'];

if($amount<0)
   {
   $inflow = 0;
   $outflow = abs($amount);
   }
      elseif($amount>0)
      {
      $outflow = 0;
      $inflow = abs($amount);
      }
         else
         {
         $inflow=0;
         $outflow=0;
         }


echo '<FORM name="deleteForm" METHOD="POST"
action="http://' . $blHost . '/acct/bl/blDeleteTransaction.php">';

echo '<input type="hidden" name="id" value="' . $id . '">';
```

```
echo '<TABLE border=1 cellpadding=5>';

echo "<tr>";
echo "<td colspan=2>";
echo '<B>Are you sure you want to delete this transaction?</B>';
echo "</td>";

echo "<td>";
echo '</tr>';

echo "<tr>";
echo "<td>";
echo '<input type="button" name="yesButton" value="Yes"
onClick="submitForm(1)">';
echo "</td>";

echo "<td>";
echo '<input type="button" name="noButton" value="No"
onClick="submitForm(0)">';
echo "</td>";
echo '</tr>';

echo '</TABLE>';

echo '</FORM>';


echo '<FORM name="transactionForm">';

echo "<input type='hidden' name='id' value='" . $id . "' size=15>";

echo "<input type='hidden' name='amount' value=0 size=15>";

echo "<TABLE border=1 cellpadding=5>";

echo "<tr>";

echo "<td>";
echo "Date: <input type='input' name='date' value='" . $date . "' size=15>";
echo "</td>";

echo "<td>";
echo "Account: <BR>";
menuBankAccounts("bank_account", $bank_account, 0);
```

```php
echo "</td>";

echo "<td>";
echo "Payee: <BR>";
menuPayees("payee", $payee);
echo "</td>";

echo "<td>";
echo "Inflow: <BR> <input type='input' name='inflow' value='" .
$inflow . "' size=15>\n";
echo "</td>";

echo "</tr>";

echo "<tr>";

echo "<td>";
echo "</td>";

echo "<td>";
echo "Trans. Type: <BR>";
menuTransTypes("type", $type);
echo "</td>";

echo "<td>";
echo "Acctg. Account: <BR>";
menuAccount("account", $account);
echo "</td>";

echo "<td>";
echo "Outflow: <BR> <input type='input' name='outflow' value='" .
$outflow . "' size=15>";
echo "</td>";

echo "</tr>";


echo "<tr>";

echo "<td>";
echo "</td>";

echo "<td colspan=5>";
```

```
echo "Memo: <input type='input' name='memo' value='" . $memo . "' size=100>";
echo "</td>";

echo "</tr>";

echo "</TABLE> \n";

echo "</FORM>";

?>

</body>

</html>
```

The Yes and No buttons are interesting. They're generated like this:

```
echo '<input type="button" name="yesButton" value="Yes"
onClick="submitForm(1)">';
echo '<input type="button" name="noButton" value="No"
onClick="submitForm(0)">';
```

Depending on which the user clicks, a different parameter gets sent to submitForm(). That JavaScript function looks like this:

```
function submitForm(yesNo)

{

if (yesNo==1)
    {
    document.deleteForm.submit();
    }
if (yesNo==0)
    {
    self.close()
    }

}
```

The function examines yesNo (the submitted parameter). If it's 1 (meaning the Yes button was clicked), form submission proceeds normally (blDeleteTransaction.php gets called). If it's 0, then the delete window just closes with no lasting effects. Figure 9.18 shows the Delete Transaction window.

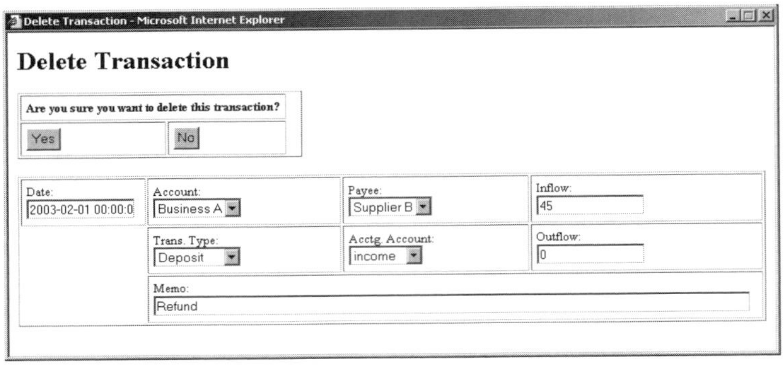

Figure 9.18: Delete transaction.

9.4.6 Adding Transactions

To allow the user to add new transactions to the bookkeeping database, Currawong Accounting provides enterTransaction.php on the presentation layer. This is essentially just a form, making heavy use of the list box-generating functions that appear in listbox.php, with which the user can specify the details of the transaction to be recorded. Here is a listing:

```
enterTransaction.php

<html>

<head>
<title>Enter Transaction</title>

<SCRIPT LANGUAGE="JavaScript">

function calculateAmount()

{

transactionForm.amount.value = transactionForm.inflow.value -
transactionForm.outflow.value;

return true;

}

</SCRIPT>
```

```php
</head>

<body>

<H1>Enter Transaction</H1>

<?php

require_once('listboxes.php');
require_once('configuration.php');

echo '<FORM name="transactionForm" method="POST" action="http://' . $blHost .
'/acct/bl/blEnterTransaction.php" onSubmit="return calculateAmount()">';

echo "<input type='hidden' name='amount' value=0 size=15>";

echo "<TABLE border=1 cellpadding=5>";

echo "<tr>";

echo "<td>";
echo "Date: <input type='input' name='date' value='yyyy-mm-dd' size=15>";
echo "</td>";

echo "<td>";
echo "Account: <BR>";
menuBankAccounts("bank_account",0,0);
echo "</td>";

echo "<td>";
echo "Payee: <BR>";
menuPayees("payee",0);
echo "</td>";

echo "<td>";
echo "Inflow: <BR> <input type='input' name='inflow'
value='0.00' size=15>\n";
echo "</td>";

echo "</tr>";

echo "<tr>";

echo "<td>";
```

```
echo "</td>";

echo "<td>";
echo "Trans. Type: <BR>";
menuTransTypes("type",0);
echo "</td>";

echo "<td>";
echo "Acctg. Account: <BR>";
menuAccount("account",0);
echo "</td>";

echo "<td>";
echo "Outflow: <BR> <input type='input' name='outflow' value='0.00' size=15>";
echo "</td>";

echo "</tr>";


echo "<tr>";

echo "<td>";
echo "</td>";

echo "<td colspan=5>";
echo "Memo: <input type='input' name='memo' value='Memo.' size=100>";
echo "</td>";

echo "</tr>";


echo "<tr>";

echo "<td colspan=6 align='center'>";
echo "<input type='submit' name='submitButton' value='Submit'>\n";
echo "</td>";

echo "</tr>";

echo "</TABLE>\n";

echo "</FORM>";

?>
```

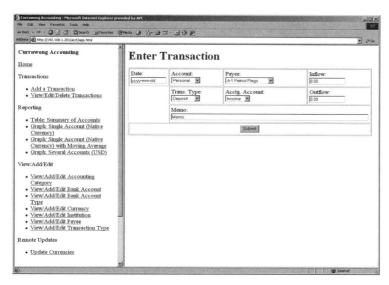

Figure 9.19: Currawong Accounting's "Add Transaction" form.

```
</body>
```

```
</html>
```

One unusual aspect of this program is the fact that calculateAmount(), a JavaScript function, gets called before the form actually gets submitted to the business-logic layer. Here is calculateAmount():

```
function calculateAmount()
{
transactionForm.amount.value = transactionForm.inflow.value -
transactionForm.outflow.value;
return true;
}
```

It sets a hidden field called amount equal to the difference between the Inflow and Outflow text fields. This is the same as is done in editTransaction.php, and it has to happen because there's only one amount field in the ACCT_register database.

Figure 9.19 shows how enterTransaction.php looks when rendered by a browser.

9.5 Questions and Exercises

1. In the transaction-entry form, there is nothing to catch errors in date format; the user has to enter dates in "YYYY-MM-DD" format. Can you write an efficient JavaScript

function to encourage the user to enter the date in the right format before the form is submitted?

2. In order to provide editing capability, Currawong Accounting relies on seven very similar programs. Can you design a single class that does the work of all seven, taking only parameters to distinguish its function in a particular case?

3. Consider the merits of a templating engine like Smarty. Under what circumstances would it be worthwhile putting a Smarty-based presentation layer on Currawong Accounting?

4. Most of the business elements represented by Currawong Accounting (such as currencies and transaction types) can't be deleted, on the logic that they might be used by a transaction. Can you modify the application to allow such deletions, complete with a check to see if the element to be deleted is used in a transaction?

The Elsewhere Layer

The elsewhere layer is the layer of a multi-tier application in which we recognize that our application is not merely a processing engine for figuring out what information the user wants, then accessing a body of data and manipulating some of its contents until the desired result is achieved. There is more to programming in an interconnected world than clients, servers, and processing logic.

Instead, we have available to us an entire global network packed with information, most of it free for the taking. We'd be foolish not to think about ways in which we could put this fantastic information resource to use in any application we're working on. The elsewhere layer is concerned with accessing and making use of remote information.

Currawong Accounting has an obvious need to make use of information available online. As a multicurrency bookkeeping application, it can make use of exchange rate information that's freely available on the Internet. It is, of course, possible for a human user to manually enter exchange-rate values, but an automated system for updating exchange rates, which is what we'll add to Currawong in this chapter, would eliminate a possible source of error and do away with a bit of tedium.

10.1 Means of Grabbing Online Information

Being able to send hypertext transport protocol (HTTP) requests out across the Internet and promptly receive a file in response is no small capability, but there are a couple of ways we can put it to use. Both work, but one is superior to the other. Remember, HTTP and simple object access protocol (SOAP) transactions are covered in greater depth (and in a way that's not specific to Currawong Accounting) in Chapters 3 and 4, respectively.

10.1.1 Screen Scrapes

An HTTP request (GET or POST, it doesn't matter) is essentially a file-open operation that returns a stream of characters. Most of the time, those characters compose a hypertext markup language (HTML) document.

It's possible to design a program that opens a given uniform resource locator (URL) and looks at the returned characters, line by line, until it finds a match for a particular string that is known to precede an interesting piece of data. For example, if we knew a given URL brought up an exchange-rate table whose HTML looked, in part, like this:

```
<TR>
<TD>
JPY
</TD>
<TD>
USD
</TD>
</TR>

<TR>
<TD>
0.0091
</TD>
<TD>
1.0
</TD>
</TR>
```

then we could devise a regular expression that matched the "JPY" in the first row of the table, then looked for the first cell in the next row of the table and assigned the value in that cell to a variable representing the exchange rate for the Japanese Yen.

The problem with this approach is twofold. First, it's tedious, having to look at that HTML and set up a regular expression that finds a match. Building a regular expression isn't hard, but it's still a messy way to do things.

Second, and more importantly, this approach is risky. If the maintainer of the site on which we were relying for our scraped data decided to change his or her formatting—something that happens all the time, without warning—we'd be stuffed. It is possible to build some flexibility into the regular expression used to pick the data out of the page, but not much.

Clearly, a better approach is needed. Web services offer the standardization we're after.

10.1.2 Web Services

As discussed in Chapter 4, Web services take the basic HTTP transaction, in which a transmitted request in the form of a text string yields a response in the form of a file or other stream of characters, and strip away the formatting that makes HTML screen scrapes so untrustworthy. To put it simply, Web services (specifically, the SOAP protocol) reply to an HTTP request not with an HTML document, but with an extensible markup language (XML) message.

That's a useful thing when it comes to solving the currency-update problem we're facing in Currawong Accounting. If we could find the right Web service, we could just send it a properly formatted request and expect the exchange rate we want to come back in an XML message. Whole libraries of Web services exist—again, plenty of them free for anyone to use—and we'll probably be able to find one that does what we want.

Isn't it true, though, that we're still susceptible to unexpected changes and outages? It is true, certainly when we're working with free services. In a production environment, we might use multiple free services in a redundant configuration, or use a commercial resource with some kind of contractual guarantee about availability.

10.2 Choosing a Web Service

As it happens, a Web service that does what we want exists on XMethods, a site dedicated to Web services experimentation. It's called Currency Exchange Rate, and was implemented in GLUE (a Java utility) by the XMethods staff. You can reach its description page (which has a long, truly ugly URL) via the XMethods home page: http://www.xmethods.net.

Its documentation indicates that the Currency Exchange Rate service takes two parameters: Two country names in string form. This is a bit inconvenient—it means we have to send strings like "great britain" and "singapore" instead of terse, standardized currency abbreviations like "GBP" and "SGD"—but it's a constraint we can deal with easily, because the names of countries appear in Currawong's currencies table. The returned value is a number of type float (a real number).

The best way to get a feel for what the Currency Exchange Rate service expects is to play with it under the SOAPscope. The SOAPscope is a handy online utility provided by a company called Mindreef. You use it to see what a specified Web service is expecting, then send its input values manually. You can then see the results and make sure they're what you want. Access the SOAPscope at http://www.mindreef.com or use the "Try It" link at the top of the Currency Exchange Rate documentation page on XMethods.

Figure 10.1 shows XMethods' Currency Exchange Rate program under analysis by the SOAPscope.

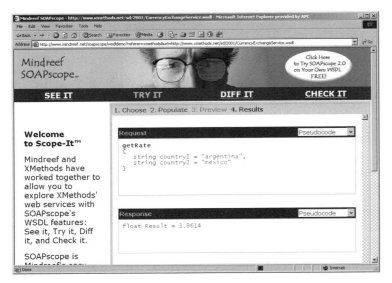

Figure 10.1: The Mindreef SOAPscope allows you to manually observe the behavior of a Web service.

10.3   Making Use of the Web Service

With a suitable Web service identified, we're ready to implement software that makes use of it. Essentially, we need to write a program that sends the right kind of messages to the XMethods method we want to use. In particular, we must be careful to send country names (not standardized currency abbreviations, which would make more sense) and expect float values in return.

10.3.1   Describing the Web Service

In order to make use of a Web service, we have to know where it is and what kind of messages it expects to receive and send. This kind of information is contained in a Web services description language (WSDL) document, which you can retrieve from the provider of the Web service you're going to use.

In the case of the Currency Exchange Service at XMethods, the relevant WSDL document is available here: http://www.xmethods.net/sd/CurrencyExchangeService.wsdl.

You can view it in a Web browser or download it for local examination. It also appears on this book's companion Web site, in the Elsewhere folder. Here's a listing:

```
currency.wsdl

<?xml version="1.0"?>
```

```
<definitions name="CurrencyExchangeService"
targetNamespace="http://www.xmethods.net/sd/CurrencyExchangeService.wsdl"
xmlns:tns="http://www.xmethods.net/sd/CurrencyExchangeService.wsdl"
xmlns:xsd="http://www.w3.org/2001/XMLSchema"
xmlns:soap="http://schemas.xmlsoap.org/wsdl/soap/"
xmlns="http://schemas.xmlsoap.org/wsdl/">
    <message name="getRateRequest">
        <part name="country1" type="xsd:string"/>
        <part name="country2" type="xsd:string"/>
    </message>
    <message name="getRateResponse">
        <part name="Result" type="xsd:float"/>
    </message>
    <portType name="CurrencyExchangePortType">
        <operation name="getRate">
            <input message="tns:getRateRequest"/>
            <output message="tns:getRateResponse"/>
        </operation>
    </portType>
    <binding name="CurrencyExchangeBinding"
type="tns:CurrencyExchangePortType">
        <soap:binding style="rpc"
transport="http://schemas.xmlsoap.org/soap/http"/>
        <operation name="getRate">
            <soap:operation soapAction=""/>
            <input>
                <soap:body use="encoded"
namespace="urn:xmethods-CurrencyExchange"
encodingStyle="http://schemas.xmlsoap.org/soap/encoding/"/>
            </input>
            <output>
                <soap:body use="encoded"
namespace="urn:xmethods-CurrencyExchange"
encodingStyle="http://schemas.xmlsoap.org/soap/encoding/"/>
            </output>
        </operation>
    </binding>
    <service name="CurrencyExchangeService">
        <documentation>Returns the exchange rate between the two
        currencies</documentation>
        <port name="CurrencyExchangePort"
binding="tns:CurrencyExchangeBinding">
            <soap:address
```

```
location="http://services.xmethods.net:80/soap"/>
    </port>
</service>
</definitions>
```

There are a number of interesting parts to that document. Let's begin with the definition of the service itself:

```
<service name="CurrencyExchangeService">
    <documentation>Returns the exchange rate between the two
    currencies</documentation>
    <port name="CurrencyExchangePort"
binding="tns:CurrencyExchangeBinding">
        <soap:address
location="http://services.xmethods.net:80/soap"/>
    </port>
</service>
```

That defines a service called CurrencyExchangeService, associated with a particular binding (tns:CurrencyExchangeBinding) and located at a specified URL (http://services. xmethods.net:80/soap). To determine what gets sent to that service, and what is expected back from it, we have to look at the definition of the binding, which is also part of this WSDL document. This is it:

```
<binding name="CurrencyExchangeBinding"
type="tns:CurrencyExchangePortType">
    <soap:binding style="rpc"
transport="http://schemas.xmlsoap.org/soap/http"/>
    <operation name="getRate">
        <soap:operation soapAction=""/>
        <input>
            <soap:body use="encoded"
namespace="urn:xmethods-CurrencyExchange"
encodingStyle="http://schemas.xmlsoap.org/soap/encoding/"/>
        </input>
        <output>
            <soap:body use="encoded"
namespace="urn:xmethods-CurrencyExchange"
encodingStyle="http://schemas.xmlsoap.org/soap/encoding/"/>
        </output>
    </operation>
</binding>
```

That binds the Web service to a particular protocol (HTTP in this case). It also specifies standard SOAP encoding for both the input and output messages. Most importantly, it defines the service being described as of the CurrencyExchangePortType. What's that? It's defined in this WSDL document, too:

```
<portType name="CurrencyExchangePortType">
<operation name="getRate">
   <input message="tns:getRateRequest"/>
   <output message="tns:getRateResponse"/>
</operation>
</portType>
```

That portType element defines an operation called getRate, which takes a getRateRequest message as input and replies with output in the form of a getRateResponse message. Those two messages have definitions in this document, too:

```
<message name="getRateRequest">
<part name="country1" type="xsd:string"/>
<part name="country2" type="xsd:string"/>
</message>
<message name="getRateResponse">
<part name="Result" type="xsd:float"/>
</message>
```

The getRateRequest message has two parameters, country1 and country2, both of type string. The getRateResponse message has a single element, Result, of type float.

So, by reading the descriptive WSDL document from bottom to top, we've figured out what needs to be sent to the Web service, and what can be expected back from it. We're ready to put it to work now.

10.3.2   Referring to the Web Service

You may recall from Chapter 6, in which we set up the database, that the ACCT_currencies table contains a column called xRate, which is meant to hold the ratio of the value of the listed currency to the U.S. dollar (meaning that the value of xRate for the Australian dollar, which is worth 72 U.S. cents at this writing, would be 0.72). We want to write a PHP program that makes use of the XMethods Currency Exchange service to populate the xRate column for all listed currencies automatically, in response to a call to a URL from the Currawong Accounting navigation bar.

The program that handles this work is updateCurrencies.php. It updates the currencies in the ACCT_currencies table (as revealed by the getCurrencies service on the local accessor layer, naturally) one at a time, showing its status progressively. Here's the full listing of the program:

updateCurrencies.php

```php
require_once('nusoap-0.6/nusoap.php');
require_once('configuration.php');

echo str_repeat(" ",256); // For the benefit of IE, which requires 256 bytes
before starting to render.

echo "<BR>Updating currency exchange rates.\n";
$country2 = "United States";
echo "<BR>Base country is $country2.\n";
echo "<BR>";
flush();

$parameters = array();
$soapclient = new soapclient('http://' . $accessorHost .
'/acct/accessor/getCurrencies.php');
$result = $soapclient->call('getCurrencies',$parameters);

foreach ($result as $key => $subarray)
    {
    $country1 = $subarray['country'];
    $name1 = $subarray['name'];

    print "<BR>Updating $country1 $name1.\n";
    flush();
    $parameters = array(
        'country1' => $country1,
        'country2' => $country2
    );

    $soapclient = new
soapclient('Currency.wsdl','wsdl');
    $xRate = $soapclient->call('getRate',$parameters);

    print "Exchange rate is $xRate.";
    flush();

    foreach ($subarray as $subkey => $subvalue)
        {

        $parameters2[$subkey] = $subvalue;

        }

    $parameters2['xRate'] = $xRate;

    $soapclient = new soapclient("http://" . $accessorHost .
```

```
                      "/acct/accessor/updateCurrency.php");
                      $result = $soapclient->call('updateCurrency',$parameters2);

                      print "<BR>Local database updated.\n";
                      print "<BR>\n";
                      }

                      print "<P>";

                      print "<a HREF='../welcome.html'>Return to welcome page.</A>";

                   flush();
```

Remember, the idea of this program is that it writes status messages to the screen one or two at a time, in a style not unlike a command line interface. That's why the flush() function appears so often in this program. The flush() function takes what's been written to the output buffer and asks the Web server to send it to the browser. In most cases, the browser will render whatever it gets, as it arrives, even if it's not a complete HTML document. The first set of status messages (plus an initialization of a variable) look like this:

```
                   echo str_repeat(" ",256); // For the benefit of IE, which
                   requires 256 bytes before starting to render.

                   echo "<BR>Updating currency exchange rates.\n";
                   $country2 = "United States";
                   echo "<BR>Base country is $country2.\n";
                   echo "<BR>";
                   flush();
```

Note the first line. That sends 256 blank spaces to the output buffer, because Microsoft Internet Explorer won't render anything unless it's received at least 256 bytes. Note also that this trick sometimes doesn't work when your Web server is hosted under Microsoft Windows, even if the server itself is the Apache HTTP Server.

With the initial status message written, the program makes a call to the accessor layer to get an array of currencies stored on the back-end database:

```
                   $parameters = array();
                   $soapclient = new soapclient('http://' . $accessorHost .
                   '/acct/accessor/getCurrencies.php');
                   $result = $soapclient->call('getCurrencies',$parameters);
```

It pops $result (the two-dimensional array containing currency information from the database) into a foreach loop, examining each returned row individually. It extracts the name of the country and the name of the currency from the current row and uses them to generate a status message:

```
                   $country1 = $subarray['country'];
```

264 Chapter 10: The Elsewhere Layer ■

```
$name1 = $subarray['name'];

print "<BR>Updating $country1 $name1.\n";
flush();
```

Then, it packs the $country1 value and the $country2 value (which is hard coded as "United States") into an array for transmission to the XMethods service:

```
$parameters = array(
    'country1' => $country1,
    'country2' => $country2
);
```

It calls the XMethods service and puts the result into $xRate:

```
$soapclient = new
soapclient('Currency.wsdl','wsdl');
$xRate = $soapclient->call('getRate',$parameters);
```

One note: It's important that both the Web service and any software that makes reference to it use precisely the same WSDL document to format their messages. For that reason, it makes sense to refer to a single WSDL document on the Internet, which should be maintained by the Web service provider. Here, however, I've chosen to cache the document locally, so as to save a bit of execution time.

After calling the XMethods service, it reloads the data that came back from the call to getCurrencies() into a new array:

```
foreach ($subarray as $subkey => $subvalue)
    {
    $parameters2[$subkey] = $subvalue;
    }
```

but replaces the xRate element with the value derived from the remote Web service call:

```
$parameters2['xRate'] = $xRate;
```

After that, it prints a status message and proceeds to the next currency. A link, rendered after the last currency has been updated, allows the user to go back to the welcome page if he or she wants.

Figure 10.2 shows updateCurrencies.php after it's updated all the currencies in the database. All status messages are shown.

10.4 Questions and Exercises

1. What are some of the terms you would put into a contract describing the provision of a Web service? In other words, how would you measure its usefulness and availability?

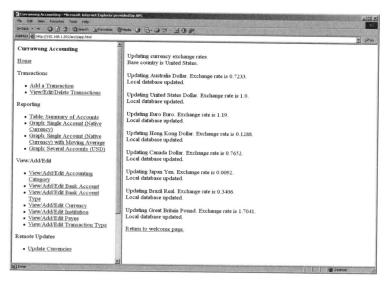

Figure 10.2: The user gets progressive status messages as Currawong Accounting uses a remote Web service to update its currency table.

2. Write a wrapper for the XMethods Currency Exchange service that accepts standard currency abbreviations (such as "USD" and "NZD") as parameters, but otherwise behaves the same.

3. How would you modify Currawong Accounting so that the base currency wasn't the U.S. dollar, but was in fact user-configurable?

4. Write a WSDL document (using a software tool, if you like) for some of the Currawong Accounting accessor-layer programs available as Web services.

Afterword

Much of the work in creating this book went into designing and implementing Currawong Accounting. It was admittedly designed to illustrate the principles of multi-tier software as much as it was meant to actually serve as a bookkeeping platform, but it's become a reasonably useful tool.

It requires a number of further improvements. These are left for the next edition, or as exercises for the ambitious reader.

- No way to distinguish between asset accounts (in which a positive balance is counted positively in net worth calculations) and liability accounts (in which a positive balance acts as a negative on the balance sheet).

- No record of historical exchange rates. It's unrealistic to show graphs of historical account balances in terms of present U.S. dollars. The historical values should use historical rates.

- Different base currency, preferably a changeable base currency. I hard coded the U.S. dollar as the base currency here, for no particular reason other than that's what *The Economist* (the British newsmagazine) uses as its standard global currency (I live in Australia, by the way). It would be better if one could see how the accounts had performed in terms of British pounds, European Euros, some other arbitrary currency.

- Object-orientation. Currawong Accounting isn't as object oriented as it could be, and with the release of PHP 5, the application is not as object oriented as it should be. In the accessor layer, for example, there should be a core class that knows how to connect to the database. Other classes should extend that class, implementing their own SQL code.

■ Modification of the application to use the SOAP and XML-RPC functions that are native to PHP 5, instead of the NuSOAP library. While NuSOAP still exists and is still supported, it makes more sense to use the native parts of the language. They are, after all, part of the PHP 5 distribution, and they appear to be the main way forward with respect to PHP and Web Services.

Index

The Morgan Kaufmann Practical Guides

Series Editor: Michael J. Donahoo

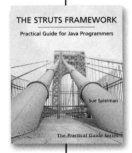

The Struts Framework: Practical Guide for Java Programmers
by Sue Spielman, Switchback Software LLC

Struts is well poised to become the framework for Web application development. Devoted to the latest version of the framework and vividly illustrated with real-world examples and sample code, this book is an essential resource for all programmers who want to be part of the next stage in the evolution of the Web.

Java Cryptography Extensions: Practical Guide for Programmers
by Jason Weiss, Sybase Inc.

The JCE is explored using numerous code examples and instructional detail, with clearly presented sections on each aspect of the Java library. An online open-source cryptography toolkit and the code for all of the examples further reinforces the concepts covered within the book. No other resource presents so concisely or effectively the exact material needed to begin utilizing the JCE.

TCP/IP Sockets in C: Practical Guide for Programmers
by Michael J. Donahoo, Baylor University and
Kenneth L. Calvert, University of Kentucky

This focused guide to TCP/IP Sockets is a quick and affordable way to gain the knowledge and skills you need to develop sophisticated and powerful networked-based programs using sockets. Written by two experienced networking instructors, this book provides a series of examples that demonstrate basic sockets techniques for clients and servers.